S0-BHS-704

GUY ON FIRE

GUY ON FIRE

130 RECIPES FOR ADVENTURES IN OUTDOOR COOKING

GUY FIERI

with Ann Volkwein

WM

WILLIAM MORROW

An Imprint of HarperCollinsPublishers

Photographs by John Lee.
Illustrations by Joe Leonard.

GUY ON FIRE. Copyright © 2014 by Guy Fieri. All rights reserved. Printed in the United States of America. No part of this book may be used or reproduced in any manner whatsoever without written permission except in the case of brief quotations embodied in critical articles and reviews. For information address HarperCollins Publishers, 10 East 53rd Street, New York, NY 10022.

HarperCollins books may be purchased for educational, business, or sales promotional use. For information please email the Special Markets Department at SPsales@harpercollins.com.

Designed by Kris Tobiassen / Matchbook Digital

Library of Congress Cataloging-in-Publication Data has been applied for.

ISBN 978-0-06-224471-0 (hardcover)

ISBN 978-0-06-235641-3 (Barnes & Noble signed edition)

ISBN 978-0-06-235642-0 (BAM signed edition)

ISBN 978-0-06-235787-8 (For sale in Canada only.)

14 15 16 17 18 ID/QG 10 9 8 7 6 5 4 3 2 1

To the two greatest outdoor cooks I ever knew.

My dad, *Jim*, and
my father-in-law, **Bob Brisson**

Thanks for teaching me that "out of the frying pan
and into the fire" is a good thing. *Guy!*

The next generation.

Burn, baby, burn!

Contents

What It's All About

Here we go . . . cookbook number five . . . something I'll tell you I never imagined happening for me. We've traveled the country together, back, forth, and back again with three installments of the *Diners, Drive-Ins and Dives* series. What a trip! And I feel like we've walked down memory lane together through *Guy Fieri Food*, which at the time, I figured, encompassed my entire life (in and out of the kitchen) in one big funky tattooed behemoth of a book. But here we are, back at it, and let me tell you, we're just getting started.

When it came time to start writing book number five, I really had to chew on it for bit. What do I write about? We've covered so much. But then, on second (or umpteenth) thought, it came to me: I just need to write what I know. I can write about my love of funky joints . . . check. I can write about my life story in the kitchen . . . check. And now, I can write about how I cook on an everyday basis with my family with my friends and with anyone who's lookin' to get down and dirty and make a great meal, anywhere, anytime.

Here in California, no doubt, we're blessed with great weather. So, since I first set off on my culinary path, I've always been about getting outside and cookin' it up in the great outdoors. Of course, I dig a great summer grill session in the sunshine. But I'm talking about much more than that, cooking as an adventure. From the simple backyard BBQ to tailgating to throwing a Dutch oven over the campfire, cooking outdoors is an art that's often either taken for granted or sometimes, very unfairly, overlooked as too difficult.

As humans, we love to be outside . . . we're meant to be that way. I mean, that's where we invented fire in the first place! As kids, we play outside. As adults, we vacation outside. We go to restaurants and ask to eat outside. So, let's take the mystery out of cooking outside. Hot, cold, windy, wet . . . I say bring it on. Got fire? We can do this.

Whether it's been as a kid packing into the Marble Mountains and wondering how on Earth my dad was able to bust out chicken and dumplings over a campfire or trying to figure out how to create the biggest, baddest tailgate party Raider Nation has ever seen, I've always been about making it happen outside. Having space. Doing the unexpected. And making it delicious.

You want to cook up a great summer grilling party? I've got you covered. Want to take the family camping but don't want to have to live on granola bars? Read on. Got a hankerin' for some real-deal BBQ? Check it out. Time to throw down the mother of all tailgate parties? Let's get 'er done!

Guy on Fire is about helping you master your own outdoor cooking adventures while you maximize your outdoor entertaining. Learn to be properly prepped and geared up, understand a few new (or super old school) cooking techniques, grab some key tricks of the trade, and then take a stab at some of my tried-and-true recipes that at first glance may not even seem like they are doable outdoors. But trust me, every dish in this book is something that I've busted out under the open sky, and I'm as excited about the stories that I've created making these dishes as I am about the food.

You don't have to live in the land of eternal sunshine to love cooking outside. Let me show you how to make awesome food happen anywhere, anytime, and all in the great outdoors. It's what I know. Now, let's get **FIRED UP**!

Love, Peace & Taco Grease,

Guy!

"Ryder, this is where it all starts."

Introducing the Outdoor Arsenal

Rustic cooking in your backyard, at a tailgate, in a rented cabin on a lake, or around a campfire doesn't have to mean dumbed-down or second-rate cuisine, and the first key to that is preparedness. Get the right arsenal together and you're on your way. Here I've compiled a rundown of some of the most useful equipment for outdoor culinary adventures.

Don't be afraid. While I've been known to haul all of the things on this list with me on monster camping trips, that's not necessary, and depending on whether you're cooking at a campground, in a trailer, or just in the backyard, what you need on hand will change. Use this list as a guide and to help you remember what to bring once you've planned your menus and studied your recipes.

A high level of confidence in your equipment will relieve you of a significant amount of stress while cooking or entertaining outdoors. You're entering an uncontrolled environment, and the elements can be against you. If you find yourself in a strong wind with dirt blowing around, struggling to work with a bunch of flimsy utensils and not enough heat on your fire, you may wish you just packed a sandwich. So, don't go out and buy the cheapest spatula or tongs specifically for camping or the occasional backyard grilling just because you think you're only going to use it twice a year. I can tell you from experience that it's always better to have one really good sharp chef's knife than two or three dull ones. You can build a set of quality equipment for the outdoors over time, but in the meantime go ahead and bring your trusted, familiar tools from home so you can prep the right way.

The flip side of this argument is that there's nothing more frustrating than losing your tools in the shuffle. Therefore, when we take stuff up to our cabin at the lake, we mark all those tools with zip ties around their handles so that they always make it back home instead of getting left in the cabin tool drawer.

Bottom line: Sturdy, reliable equipment sets you up for a positive culinary experience. Cheap does not always pay off.

THE EQUIPMENT RUNDOWN

Camping Stoves

The little camping stoves with the canister attached that looks like a spray paint can are nice for an omelet station at a buffet at the Ritz Carlton, but the type that I recommend are high BTU (British thermal units) camping stoves that typically have two or three burners and legs to stand on. These stoves are critical because they're sturdy and more windproof, their legs allow them to create their own platform, and they can handle more than one pot. Just remember, if you don't have a good burner, you don't have the option of going to the neighbors' house to use their stove.

Barbecues

GAS GRILLS

The best part of a gas grill is its reliability and consistency. There's a wide range of power, but the higher the BTUs, the better. Having a grill with more than one zone is also helpful. If your only choice is on or off, it's difficult to do more complex types of cooking that require different temperature zones. With three to five knobs, you have the ability to shut down some areas and use indirect heat.

CHARCOAL GRILLS

Probably the most underestimated piece of equipment is the charcoal barbecue. There's been a trend through the years toward easier and simpler grilling, but the benefits of a charcoal barbecue, in my opinion, surpass the advantages of a gas barbecue. I prefer using a charcoal barbecue because I believe the radiant heat allows for a better sear and infuses a deeper flavor into the food than a gas grill.

The majority of people don't use a charcoal barbecue because of fear and a lack of knowledge about how it can be used. Their first challenge is lighting the coals. The fact that we still sell lighter fluid today is barbaric to me because it has residual flavor and is unsafe. The chimney——or even a coffee can—is the best way to get your coals going. You can throw the chimney on top of a burner or in the campfire to start the process without using paper, or you can load it with paper and light it. But the point is that it will help you get reliable coals burning.

Be careful—as indestructible as they may look, charcoal grill lids can become dented. A tight-fitting lid on a charcoal barbecue is critical because there will be many times when you'll want to go low and slow and need to shut down that barbecue to lower the heat. For the same reason, your charcoal grill also needs to have an effective dampening system that's in good condition. The dampers, or vents, allow you to control the amount of oxygen feeding the flames.

The grates need to be cleaned after every use with a good grill brush. If anything is flaking or

Sauté Pan Grilling

You don't have to have both a camp stove and a grill in your setup. If you want to use your sauté pan directly on your barbecue, build a pile of hot coals in the middle of the grill that almost reaches the bottom of the grate and you've got an impromptu sauté station. An alternative is to take four or five sternos (the cans used to warm a chafing dish) and place them together in a platform made of bricks to make another impromptu stove.

rusting, it's time to buy new grates. The great thing is that replacement grates for the most common varieties of barbecues, like the Weber, are easily accessible at home improvement stores.

PORTABLE GRILLS/SMOKERS

There are inexpensive, portable grill and smoker combos, and if you've never experimented with a smoker, camping can actually be a great opportunity to give one a go. I think I'm like a lot of people in that food is of major importance when I'm camping. You may not experiment much with outdoor cooking at home, but when you're sitting around the fire or picnic table, you'll be much more inclined to decide it's the perfect time to start smoking some chicken (see recipe, page 124). Why? 'Cause you're camping, and most likely . . . you've got nothing else to do. This book is a testament to that fact because, across all the chapters, I created a big percentage of these recipes while camping.

Master Tool and Equipment List

I hope this will spark some ideas for the equipment you may want to have.

TOOLS FOR THE FIRE

Hatchet

Adjustable-height campfire grill grate or grill ring

Fire-starting "chimney"

Long lighters (a whole quiver of them for backup)

Smoke box

Fish-grilling basket

Cast-iron skillet

Cast-iron Dutch oven (see page 159)

Variety of durable pots and pans and lids, including sheet pans, roasting pans and wire rack

Barbecue gloves

Especially in competitions, rubber barbecue gloves are critical. Silicone oven mitts and hot pads are superior to cloth because they can be cleaned. But the use of gloves does not eliminate the requirement to wash your hands—they're not "magic gloves."

Barbecue fork

Tongs

Skewers (see page 220)

Basting brushes

Ladles

Long-handled spoons

TOOLS FOR FOOD PREP

Multiple plastic or synthetic cutting boards, preferably no wood, color coded for use with different foods

Measuring spoons and cups

Plastic bowls

Sharp knives

Zester

Box grater

Okay, why a box grater? Wouldn't it be easier just to buy shredded cheese? Well, here's the thing: You can do a lot with a box grater as a cutting tool while camping. For example, you can box-grate a carrot or onion on an unstable surface a whole lot easier than you can dice it with a knife.

Wine opener

Can opener

Colander

All-in-one salt and pepper grinder

Hand-press juicer

Meat tenderizer

Spray bottle for water

Squirt bottles for condiments, oils, and vinegars

Coffee maker and enamel kettle

First off, for safety I like to heat the water in an enameled coffee kettle with two handles. Nobody does instant coffee anymore, so I won't even address that, but premium ground coffee can be easily brewed in a French press (my favorite) or a cone drip. It's beneficial to have an air pot, which is like a big thermos, to pour the coffee into because you won't have a continual heat source to keep it warm. Another good tip for outdoor coffee prep is to prewarm your mugs or cups by filling them halfway with a little hot water from the pot first.

Good digital thermometer

Timers

Lights and headlamps

Bricks

Heavy-duty aluminum foil

Parchment paper

Immersion stick blender (if power is available)

Blender (if power is available)

SERVING AND STOWING EQUIPMENT

Plates, compostable/recyclable

If you're buying disposable plates, it's worth the extra bucks to buy good ones. It takes only one mishap of dropped food to make the purchase worth it. There are really solid compostable or recyclable plates on the market today, so no excuses.

Eating utensils

Nothing makes eating outdoors more enjoyable than proper metal utensils. You can eat off paper plates, but nobody likes a plastic fork—and no "sporks"' allowed. And finally, paper towels give more bang for the buck than paper napkins. (Always bring twice as many as you think you'll need.)

Drinkware

I'm not a big fan of mixing outdoors and glass: Broken glass is difficult to clean up, and people often go barefoot and wear flip-flops around a campsite. But most people don't like to drink wine out of a red Solo cup, so my recommendation is to get Govino Shatterproof cups. Another of my favorite all-purpose cups is the Tervis, which is like a thermos. You put something hot or cold in there and it keeps it hot or cold (and saves on ice). The Tervis also comes with a lid, which is nice when you're out there in the elements.

Coolers (see sidebar, below)

Coolers and Food Storage

The ideal is to have multiple coolers that serve different functions—for example, one for raw proteins, one for uncontaminated ice to use in drinks, and one for storing food and beverage containers.

PLEASE do not EVER use ice for iced beverages that any cans, bottles, or packages have ever had direct contact with. These items may have been kept in warehouses and on loading docks and could easily contaminate your ice. You should see what a freak I am about "clean" ice.

My preferred coolers are the industrial ones with the more durable metal latches. But in general, coolers should have secure-fitting lids and proper draining ability. You may not realize that coolers are labeled by how many days they will hold ice. So when shopping for a cooler you might notice $5 increments in price between types, but that extra $5 may mean the difference between keeping your ice solid for one day versus six. So read the small print—investing correctly in a good

cooler can be worth the money just in ice savings alone.

Bigger is not always better. Don't get coolers that are too big for your needs. Similar to the efficiency of a refrigerator, coolers are more effective when they're full and iced properly. And remember, large coolers are heavier and more difficult to move.

Frozen water bottles can be used in place of block ice or ice cubes if you prefer. Just fill your bottles three-quarters of the way with water and freeze them. If you fill the dead space in your coolers with frozen bottles, they will be more efficient, you don't have to drain them, and your items won't get wet from melting ice.

For the most economical and flexible way to store food in coolers, use quality, resealable gallon-size freezer bags.

If possible, store your coolers (cleaned thoroughly, of course) with the lid slightly open so that mold won't develop.

Ice packs or frozen water bottles

Resealable gallon-size freezer bags

Industrial-strength plastic bags

Collapsible tables

Most collapsible tables are at table height, not counter height, making them hard to use for food prep. But you can make most of these tables higher by attaching a 1½ by 12-inch piece of PVC pipe to each leg.

Collapsible trash barrel

Having a place to store your trash and keep your site clean and organized is critical. Too often the overloaded bag of trash that's connected to the picnic table or tied up to a tree attracts bees and animals, as well as generating unpleasant smells. Trash storage needs to be designated in a place well away from your work and living areas.

The way it always is . . . I'm cookin', they're eatin'.

THE RULES OF
THE BARBECUE

1. KEEP A CLEAN GRILL. That holds for both gas and charcoal. Remember, it makes all the difference in the world to your cooking process if you keep your gas grill free of grease and grit and clear those spider webs from the inside of the charcoal grill's flue. Designate a cleaning tub solely for grill cleaning and include an industrial-strength wire brush, steel wool soap pads, a sponge, a powder cleaner (such as Ajax), a degreaser of some kind, and disinfecting wipes. It doesn't hurt to have a couple paper clips on hand to clear out the flame openings—and at home, don't forget the stainless steel cleaner to keep the whole thing shining.

2. KEEP IT SAFE. Make sure that the grill is in sturdy condition. Nothing is worse than having a grill that wobbles because a leg has rusted away. We may all joke about the rickety old barbecue, but it's unsafe and nobody's laughing when the whole thing tips and your ribs end up in the dirt.

3. NEVER USE LIGHTER FLUID. Don't use any type of combustible liquid—gasoline, diesel fuel, lamp oil—none of it. As I've said, all of it has residual flavor and is unsafe.

4. WORK WITH ESTABLISHED COALS. Never put your food on coals that aren't burned through, because as they start to burn they will kick off a residue that's not pleasing to taste. You want your coals to form a white ash on the outside, not red flaming embers, so that you have consistent heat. Then, by piling the coals or lowering the grate up and down, you can get more or less intensity.

5. ESTABLISH A WORKSPACE. Define an area for food prep, just as you would at home. Restricting where you handle seafood and meats lessens the risk of cross-contamination.

6. SET UP A SANITARY BUCKET. If you don't have running water or a hand sink, one of the smartest things you can do is to set up a gallon bucket full of water with a tablespoon of bleach. That way you can clean your knife after cutting chicken and then move on to prep the vegetables for the salad.

7. ESTABLISH A DISHWASHING STATION. People often limit what they're going to cook outdoors based on their ability to clean the equipment, but the fact is that you can set up a system to clean and sanitize your pots, dishes, and utensils even without running water.

You'll need a three-bay setup of containers, tubs, or even five-gallon buckets from a home improvement store (I don't want you spending a million bucks to make this happen!).

- **The first bucket is the soap and water wash—fill it with warm water heated in a pot on the burner or grill.**

- **The second is a rinse bucket that holds warm, clean water.**

- **The third and final bucket is a sanitary rinse, which should hold 1 tablespoon of bleach for every gallon of water.**

Even if you're using a trailer, a wash station outside is a good idea, because you don't want to run out of water from washing the dishes.

WORKING WITH THE GRILL

Here are a few more practical grilling rules to get under your belt as you get to know your barbecue.

If you want to do just a quick sear, keep your coals hot and piled in the center. You can sear, then push the food off to the cooler sides. But if your intention is to sear and then go low and slow, start the coals in the middle and then, using a set of tongs or a spatula, stack your charcoal up on one side of the barbecue. This allows you to cook over cooler, indirect heat.

To smoke meat using a water pan smoker, drop soaked wood chips into the pan and place it on top of the coals. Then place the meat in the smoker above the water pan.

Another general grilling tip is to brine your meat. Brining pork and chicken is probably one of the most underestimated moisture and flavor enhancers that there is. There are a variety of dif-ferent styles of brine, but the basic recipe is equal parts of sweet and salty and whatever aromatics you choose. (Brining times vary according to your meat.) After brining, pat the meat dry and apply the rubs or seasonings you'd like. (Never put wet meat on the grill if you want a good sear.)

Be sure to oil the grill before putting your meat on it. That can be as simple as applying cooking oil to paper towels and wiping them on the grates.

Apply barbecue sauce only in the final minutes of cooking, as the sugars in the sauce will tend to burn and darken. For that matter, no marinades or oil-based products should be applied to meat or vegetables while they're cooking. When that oil hits the grates or the charcoal or the hot metal surface on a gas grill, it will create unsavory smoke—and a gray cloud of ash if you're working over charcoal.

There are a variety of ways to handle flare-ups:

- **One of the best ways is to use indirect cooking and drip pans. A flare-up is usually caused by one of two things—rendering fat or dripping marinade and sauces—and a drip pan can help eliminate both of those.**

- **Stop the supply of oxygen to the barbecue by closing a lid or vents.**

- **Simply remove what is flaring up, such as the meat or whatever is dripping.**

- **Use a spray bottle of water on gas grills. (If you try that method on a charcoal grill, the spray on the coals will create dust and ashes that will end up on your food.)**

Home, home on the range . . .

*Thanksgiving morning . . .
up early and lookin' rough!*

Types of Charcoal

There are many types of charcoal out there, but the most common are lump hardwood and pressed briquettes. My feeling is that the consistency of the burn is the most important factor. Some people love lump charcoal, which is made from pieces of wood. There's a purity to it that you can see. But lump charcoal is inconsistent in how it burns. Sometimes it burns hotter, sometimes colder, and sometimes it just burns out. It doesn't maintain itself. On the other hand, charcoal that's been engineered into briquettes—and I'm not talking about charcoal that's been infused with lighter fluid here—gives a more consistent heat and burn time. It lasts longer, too.

Types of Wood

Whether you're using a barbecue or gas grill, you have a great opportunity to perfume what you're cooking with wood. You can do that in a variety of ways, but the key is to know the types of woods you're working with. Always use hardwoods or fruitwoods, never soft, resinous, or sappy woods. Soak the wood chips or wood shavings in water so they will smolder when they hit the heat. This method of perfuming meats is not to be confused with using wood to smoke meat as you might in competition barbecue (see page 120). When you're doing low and slow barbecue, the meat only takes in the flavor of the wood smoke for the first few hours. After that it's not taking on much more flavor; you're just using the wood as the main fuel source to generate heat.

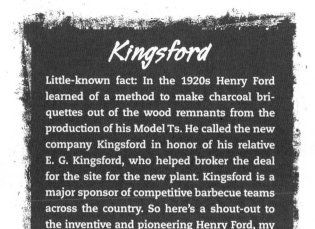

Kingsford

Little-known fact: In the 1920s Henry Ford learned of a method to make charcoal briquettes out of the wood remnants from the production of his Model Ts. He called the new company Kingsford in honor of his relative E. G. Kingsford, who helped broker the deal for the site for the new plant. Kingsford is a major sponsor of competitive barbecue teams across the country. So here's a shout-out to the inventive and pioneering Henry Ford, my Royal Barbecue Hall of Fame inductee brother.

Wood Type and Meat/Fish

Everybody who barbecues has a favorite wood to smoke with, and various regions are famous for specific types, such as mesquite in Texas. Here are some loose guidelines for what woods are generally used with which meats. Make them your own and experiment.

ALDER: Fish, pork, game birds and other poultry

APPLE: Poultry, pork

CHERRY: Poultry, pork, fish

PECAN: Poultry, pork, fish

OAK: Beef, wild game, fish

MAPLE: Pork, game birds and other poultry

MESQUITE: Beef, wild game

HICKORY: Pork, ham, and beef

Whether it's a graduation, a three-day weekend, a family reunion, or any celebration, having an eclectic repertoire of dishes for outdoor entertaining is key. Chicken wings are great, but not every time. When you have at your fingertips a range of recipes, then they're customizable to any outdoor event thrown at you.

Throughout the year, some of the biggest events going down in my backyard are birthdays. Cooking outdoors for a birthday in my family is just expected. Why? Yes, we live in sunny California and the majority of our birthdays are in the warmer months, plus there are usually just *so many* people coming. But there's more to it for me. First, I don't want to be stuck indoors cooking when all the action is outdoors, and second, I can't have everybody indoors getting in the way in the kitchen. So outdoors it is. Food and birthdays are just a Fieri thing, and it extends beyond my family. Some people may write you a song, some may paint you a picture, but me, I'll cook you a dinner.

It's gotten to the point where even close friends, not family members, will ask if they can have their birthday in my backyard because it's convenient. ("Hey, it's a big backyard and Guy's going to be cooking anyway!") From scavenger hunts to sleepovers to pool parties to mini golf excursions, the Fieri family has great birthdays. In fact, if it's your birthday month the celebration will last all month long, and you get to call the shots. Seriously! My mother and her best friend Fran started that tradition years ago. (She's crazy, who would do something like that? Next thing you know someone might start celebrating Festivus Maximus, where people from all over the country come to celebrate a week of festivities, ranging from road trips to house parties to restaurant takeovers. Who would have a party that involves some of the greatest *Diners, Drive-Ins and Dives* chefs from all over the country coming out to cook up some killer food for six or seven hundred of his closest friends? That's just pure craziness . . .) So here are some of my family's greatest hits for the Backyard Bash, with prep tips to maximize your time chillin' with the family.

Cookin' for the crew.

Crispy Zucchini Planks with Parmesan and Aioli

From cookouts to tailgates, if you're going to serve a vegetable with mass appeal for all ages, and it isn't a fried onion ring, it's gotta be crispy zucchini. Trust me—these will be a hot commodity at your next backyard party.

MAKES: 4 servings

TIME: 1 hour

YOU'LL NEED: Stovetop or propane burner, cast-iron or other heavy pot for deep frying, parchment paper

PREP-AHEAD TIPS:
Bread the zucchini planks, place them on a sheet pan, and refrigerate them so they can set up. Less moisture equals better frying, so leave them uncovered to dry out a bit. They'll actually fry up crispier and the coating will stick better when chilled. This can be done up to 8 hours in advance.

Make the aioli up to 2 days ahead of time and store in the refrigerator, covered.

Canola oil, for frying

2½ cups all-purpose flour

Kosher salt and freshly ground black pepper

2 large eggs

2 cups buttermilk

1 teaspoon dried oregano

1 teaspoon dried thyme

½ teaspoon granulated garlic

3 cups panko (Japanese breadcrumbs)

2 medium zucchini, thinly sliced lengthwise

Grated Parmesan cheese, for garnish

Chopped fresh flat-leaf parsley, for garnish

Lemon wedges, for garnish

Aiolis, for serving (recipes follow)

1. Pour a couple inches of oil into a large, heavy-gauge or cast-iron pot. Heat over medium heat until a deep-fry thermometer reads 350°F.

2. Place the flour in a shallow medium container. Season with salt and pepper. Whisk the eggs, buttermilk, oregano, thyme, and garlic in another shallow medium container. Put the panko crumbs in a third shallow container. Sprinkle with salt and pepper. Line a baking sheet with parchment paper.

3. Working in batches, dredge the zucchini strips in the flour, patting off the excess. Next, dip them in the buttermilk mixture. Moisten completely and allow the excess liquid to drip away. Dredge the zucchini in the panko crumbs and coat evenly. As you work, lay the zucchini strips on the lined baking sheet.

4. Once the oil is ready, fry the zucchini strips in batches until they are a crispy golden brown, 2 to 4 minutes. Transfer the fried zucchini to a paper towel–lined baking sheet to drain.

5. Serve the crispy zucchini on a platter, sprinkled with Parmesan and parsley. Serve with lemon wedges and your choice of aioli for dipping.

Hunter's buddies are as crazy as he is.

Aiolis

A lot of people, like my sister from another mista Rachael Ray, are not big fans of the food lube—and I've got to say, I'm not the biggest fan of mayonnaise out of the jar, either. But when you want flavor and a creamy texture, nothing can beat a well-made aioli, so here are a few for you to play with.

Roasted Garlic Aioli

Roasted garlic aioli is a staple. You should make a big batch and keep it in the refrigerator. It's great with French fries, of course, but you can also serve it with roasted root vegetables, smear it on a baguette to make garlic bread, or serve it with tempura green beans or steamed broccoli. You can even use it on grill meats like chicken breast, steaks, or pork chops.

MAKES: 1½ cups

TIME: 1 hour

YOU'LL NEED: Food processor or blender

PREP-AHEAD TIP: Roast the garlic up to 2 days ahead of time. Make the aioli and store in the refrigerator in an airtight container for up to 3 days.

2 or 3 garlic heads

Extra-virgin olive oil

Kosher salt and freshly ground black pepper

1½ cups mayonnaise

⅓ cup fresh lemon juice

2 tablespoons grated Parmesan cheese

1½ teaspoons Dijon mustard

⅛ teaspoon cayenne pepper

Dash of Worcestershire sauce

Chopped fresh parsley, for garnish

1. Preheat the oven to 425°F.

2. Cut the tops off the garlic heads to expose the cloves. Place them on a large piece of aluminum foil, drizzle lightly with olive oil, and sprinkle with salt and pepper. Wrap the foil into a tight pouch and roast for 35 to 45 minutes. Remove from the oven and set aside to cool. Squeeze the pulp from the skins.

3. In a food processor or blender, combine ⅓ cup of the roasted garlic, the mayonnaise, lemon juice, Parmesan, Dijon, cayenne, Worcestershire, and salt and pepper to taste. Pulse until well combined. Refrigerate to allow the flavors to meld together. Garnish with parsley.

Sriracha Aioli

This is a great dip, salad dressing, or sandwich spread. It's spicy, but not too hot!

1½ cups mayonnaise

2 tablespoons Sriracha

1 teaspoon smoked paprika

½ teaspoon toasted sesame oil

2 garlic cloves, minced

Juice of 1 lime

Kosher salt, to taste

MAKES: 1½ cups

TIME: 5 minutes

YOU'LL NEED: Food processor or blender

PREP-AHEAD TIP: Make the aioli and store in the refrigerator in an airtight container for up to 4 days.

In a food processor or blender, combine all the ingredients. Pulse until well blended. Refrigerate to allow the flavors to meld together.

Chipotle Aioli

This is awesome on any Mexican dishes where you'd like a little spicy creaminess as well as on grilled veggies that need some heat.

1½ cups mayonnaise

2 garlic cloves, minced

Grated zest of 1 lime

1 tablespoon minced chipotle in adobo sauce

¼ teaspoon agave syrup

½ teaspoon ground cumin

Kosher salt, to taste

2 tablespoons chopped fresh cilantro

MAKES: 1 cup

TIME: 5 minutes

YOU'LL NEED: Food processor or blender

PREP-AHEAD TIP: Make the aioli and store in the refrigerator in an airtight container for up to 4 days.

In a food processor or blender, combine the mayonnaise, garlic, lime zest, chipotle, agave, cumin, and salt. Pulse until well combined. Fold in the cilantro. Refrigerate to allow the flavors to meld together.

Homemade Hot Sauce

I am a hot sauce fan, big-time. Every fan's got their favorite bottle, but it's not something you typically find people making themselves. So, here's a chance, if you've got some free time, to create your dream super condiment—and make it as spicy as you want.

MAKES: About 1 cup

TIME: 35 minutes

YOU'LL NEED: Oven, food processor or blender, bottle for storing hot sauce

PREP-AHEAD TIP: Make big batches of this hot sauce, bottle it, and keep in the refrigerator. It'll keep for a month as long as you use sterilized, airtight bottles.

2 habanero chiles, stems removed, seeded, and cut in half

10 Fresno chiles, stems removed, cut in half lengthwise, seeded and ribbed

1 medium yellow onion, cut into quarters

2 Roma (plum) tomatoes, cut into quarters

3 garlic cloves

2 tablespoons canola oil

1 teaspoon kosher salt

½ teaspoon freshly ground black pepper

Juice of 1 lemon

1 teaspoon paprika

2½ tablespoons sugar

1 cup white vinegar

1. Preheat the oven to 400°F.

2. Toss the habaneros, Fresnos, onion, tomatoes, and garlic with the canola oil. Roast in a single layer until the vegetables are charred and tender, about 20 minutes. When cool enough to handle, dice all the vegetables into small pieces.

3. Put the vegetables in a food processor or blender along with the salt, pepper, lemon juice, paprika, and sugar. Puree until smooth. With the food processor still running, slowly pour in the vinegar in a thin stream until fully incorporated. Taste the sauce and add salt, pepper, and sugar as desired.

4. Strain the mixture through a fine sieve into a clean bowl, using a rubber spatula to push it through. Let the sieve sit over the bowl for up to 15 minutes to collect any drippings. Transfer the sauce to a sterilized bottle and refrigerate.

Pimento Cheese-Stuffed Jalapeños

An Arranged Marriage Appetizer

MAKES: 12 jalapeños

TIME: 45 minutes

YOU'LL NEED: Oven, stovetop, cast-iron skillet or griddle

PREP-AHEAD TIP: Make the pimento cheese mixture up to 2 days in advance. Stuff the jalapeños the day before so you are ready to cook the day of.

For the most part, pimento cheese stops at the border of the Mississippi River; for some reason you don't find it a lot west of there. Sure, you get a little in Texas and in the panhandle, but most people who aren't Southerners really don't appreciate the delicacy that is pimento cheese. And the jalapeño (and let's get the pronunciation right: *holla-pain-yo*) can be found in almost anything you can think of out West and less often in the East. So here's the meeting of two worlds, kinda like an arranged marriage. It's sweet and creamy meets hot and dreamy.

I can't believe I just said that—I'm not even drinking.

Rain or shine, the kids always want to get in the pool.

1. Preheat the oven to 350°F.

2. In a large saucepan over medium-high heat, crumble the chorizo into small pieces. Brown the meat for 8 to 10 minutes while continuing to break up the pieces with the back of a wooden spoon. Using a slotted spoon, transfer the chorizo to a paper towel–lined plate to drain. Pour the oil from the saucepan into a small bowl and reserve. When cool, chop the chorizo into small pieces and set aside.

3. In the same saucepan, using a teaspoon of the reserved chorizo oil plus the 1 teaspoon canola oil, sauté the corn kernels until slightly charred, about 10 minutes. Season with salt and pepper and set aside to cool.

4. In a cast-iron skillet or griddle, heat the 1 tablespoon canola oil over medium-high heat. Add the peppers, cut side down, and cook until the flesh is marked and slightly softened, 3 to 4 minutes.

5. Meanwhile, in a medium bowl, combine the cream cheese, mayonnaise, diced pimentos, Cheddar cheese, ½ cup of the pepper Jack cheese, garlic powder, smoked paprika, ½ teaspoon salt, and ½ teaspoon pepper. Add the corn and stir to combine.

6. Remove the peppers from the heat and spoon approximately 1 tablespoon of the cheese mixture into each pepper half. Sprinkle the remaining pepper Jack on top. Place the skillet in the oven and bake until the peppers are tender and the cheese has melted, about 12 minutes. For the last 30 to 60 seconds, broil on high to brown the tops.

7. Remove from the oven, drizzle approximately ½ teaspoon of the reserved chorizo oil over each pepper, and sprinkle liberally with finely chopped chorizo and a few sliced green onions.

1½ links chorizo sausage, casings removed

1 tablespoon plus 1 teaspoon canola oil

Kernels from 2 small ears of corn

Kosher salt and freshly ground black pepper

6 medium jalapeño peppers, halved lengthwise, seeds and ribs removed

2 ounces cream cheese, softened

1 tablespoon mayonnaise

One 4-ounce jar diced pimento peppers, drained

½ cup shredded sharp Cheddar cheese

¾ cup shredded pepper Jack cheese

¼ teaspoon garlic powder

¼ teaspoon smoked paprika

¼ cup thinly sliced scallions

Cast-Iron Beef Tenderloin with Blackberry Jalapeño Sauce

I am not a big fan of filet on the barbecue because it doesn't have a lot of fat or flavor. But for many folks, serving filet is a sign of going big and celebrating. So if we're going to barbecue filet, then we better bring the flavor. The best way to do that is with a killer Blackberry Jalapeño Sauce.

8 slices applewood smoked bacon

3-pound beef tenderloin, trimmed

Kosher salt and freshly ground black pepper

Canola oil, as needed

2 shallots, minced

3 garlic cloves, minced

1 jalapeño, seeded and minced

¾ cup port wine

1 pint blackberries, pureed in a food processor, plus a few blackberries for garnish

2 tablespoons blackberry preserves

2 tablespoons aged balsamic vinegar

¾ cup low-sodium beef broth

2 or 3 fresh thyme sprigs

1 tablespoon cold unsalted butter

MAKES: 8 servings

TIME: 45 minutes

YOU'LL NEED: Oven, grill or stovetop, large cast-iron skillet, twine, instant-read meat thermometer

PREP-AHEAD TIP: Cook the bacon and wrap the steaks up to 5 hours in advance. Refrigeration will help them "set up" and retain their shape when you sauté them.

1. Preheat the oven to 450°F.

2. In a large cast-iron skillet, parcook the bacon (in batches, if needed), about 2 minutes per side; the bacon should be pliable and not cooked through. With a slotted spoon, transfer to a paper towel–lined plate; leave any bacon fat in the pan to sear the steak.

3. Cut the tenderloin into 8 thick steaks (about 6 ounces each). Season the exterior of each steak with salt and pepper; wrap 2 bacon slices around each steak, securing with twine around the outside—this will not only hold the bacon in place but also help the steaks keep a nice round shape. Preheat the grill to high or turn a burner to high and, in the same cast-iron skillet, sear the steaks on one side for 5 to 6 minutes. Reduce the heat to medium, turn the steaks, and cook a further 8 to 10 minutes on the second side for a nice medium-rare. When a thermometer inserted into the thickest part of a steak registers 130°F to 135°F, it is medium-rare and done. Transfer to a plate and rest under foil for 15 minutes.

4. Wipe out the pan with paper towels to discard any burned or black residue. Coat with canola oil and add the shallots, garlic, and jalapeño to the skillet. Sauté 2 to 3 minutes. Off the heat, add the port and deglaze the pan by loosening any browned bits, then return the pan to the heat and simmer. Once the liquid has reduced to about 1 tablespoon, whisk in the blackberry puree, preserves, vinegar, broth, and thyme. Cook until reduced and thickened, 5 to 10 minutes, and season with salt and pepper to taste. Finish the sauce by stirring in the cold butter.

5. Remove the twine from the steaks and serve them topped with the sauce. Garnish with fresh blackberries.

Get to Know a Butcher

Butchers. I say it on my shows and in my demos: Your contacts should include a great fishmonger, a super mixologist, and a bail bondsman (ha ha . . . maybe not a bail bondsman), but a good butcher is the most important of all. Find a local butcher who works with organic, grass-fed, farm-to-table meat. We're supposed to eat less red meat, and less meat in general, so go for quality, not quantity. And it's worth the extra fifteen minutes to drive to the best butcher you can find because he (or she) will know what's fresh and what's best and can help you use the right product for the right dish. Butchers are also there to support you if your knife skills are not your strongest talent—they can butterfly your pork loin, French your lamb, and grind your meat. Not trying to get too preachy here, but it really is possible and it really is important.

California Brick Chicken with Apricot-Mint Chimichurri

This dish is about as old-school as it gets. In Italian this is called *pollo al mattone*, and to make it you start by removing the backbone and flattening the chicken. Then you brine it, dry it, season it, and cook it with the pressure of two hot bricks on top. Sounds caveman, I know, but wait till you try it. This version has my California spin on it with a dry rub that has a little heat, a little sweet, and a whole lotta flavor.

Two 4- to 5-pound whole free-range chickens

1 tablespoon chipotle chile powder

1 tablespoon ancho chile powder

2 tablespoons smoked paprika

2 teaspoons ground fennel seeds

2 teaspoons garlic powder

1 teaspoon onion powder

1 teaspoon dried oregano

1 teaspoon sugar

1 tablespoon kosher salt

1 teaspoon freshly ground black pepper

¼ cup extra-virgin olive oil

Salsa Verde (recipe follows)

MAKES: 4 to 6 servings

TIME: 30 minutes

YOU'LL NEED: Grill, 4 bricks wrapped in foil or a heavy cast-iron skillet, food processor or blender, instant-read meat thermometer

PREP-AHEAD TIP: Split, flatten, rub, and refrigerate the chickens a day or two in advance of the party (or pop them in a cooler if heading off on a different outdoor adventure). The longer they marinate in the dry rub, the better the flavor, and it makes for easy grilling when it's time for the backyard bash to start.

1. Remove the backbone from one of the chickens. Split the breast plate and press down on the chicken in all joints to flatten it. Tuck the wings under so that the chicken lies flat. This will help it cook evenly. Repeat with the second chicken.

2. In a small bowl, combine the chile powders, paprika, fennel, garlic powder, onion powder, oregano, sugar, salt, and pepper. Mix well, then rub the mixture all over the flattened chickens, making sure you get it into all the gaps in and around the joints. Marinate the chickens in the refrigerator for 1 hour uncovered. (Leaving the chicken uncovered helps the crust dry out and ensures you get a nice crispy skin when it cooks.)

3. Heat a grill to medium heat and rub down the grates with a lightly oiled paper towel to clean it and create a nonstick surface. Place the chickens skin side down on the grill. Watch for flare-ups when the

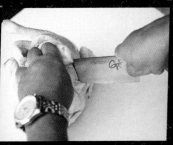

1. Removing the backbone.

2. Splitting the breast plate.

3. Press down on the joints to flatten the chicken.

4. Tuck the wings under so chickens lie flat and cook evenly.

5. I think they're challenging me to an arm wrestle.

6. Be generous with the dry rub, both sides.

7. Oil that grill first so the skin doesn't stick.

8. Place the foil-wrapped bricks on top of each chicken.

9. Remove the bricks and flip after 15 to 20 minutes.

10. The finished bird, let it rest 5 minutes.

11. Cut each chicken into 10 pieces.

12. Plating with apricot-mint chimichurri

Our buddy "Bucket"

chicken initially hits the grill, as the fat will render and drip down. If necessary, move the chicken to a new spot out of the flames. This will occur only in the initial drop. Place foil-wrapped bricks on top of the chickens to flatten them as they cook.

4. Cook for 15 minutes, then remove the bricks and flip the chicken. Cook for 18 to 20 minutes or until the internal temperature between the leg and thigh joint reaches 165°F on an instant-read thermometer.

5. Transfer the chickens to a cutting board and let rest for 5 minutes before slicing each one into 10 pieces. Serve with apricot-mint chimichurri.

Apricot-Mint Chimichurri

½ cup dried apricots

1 teaspoon honey

1¼ cups fresh mint leaves

¾ cup chopped fresh parsley

½ cup chopped fresh cilantro

⅔ cup red wine vinegar

4 garlic cloves, peeled

1 teaspoon kosher salt

½ teaspoon freshly ground pepper

1 teaspoon ground cumin

1 teaspoon lemon zest

Pinch of red pepper flakes

1 to 1¼ cups extra-virgin olive oil

MAKES: about 2 cups

PREP-AHEAD TIP: Make one day ahead and press plastic wrap on surface, to keep the color from turning, before storing in the refrigerator.

1. Place the apricots and honey in a glass bowl; cover with hot water and soak for 10 minutes.

2. Meanwhile, in salted, boiling water, blanch the mint, parsley, and cilantro for about 30 seconds. Shock immediately in ice water and spread on a paper towel–lined sheet to dry.

3. Remove the apricots from the hot water and roughly chop. In a food processor or blender, combine all ingredients except the olive oil and process until all ingredients are finely chopped. With the motor running, slowly incorporate the olive oil and pulse until just combined (the consistency should be like a thick sauce). Cover and store in the refrigerator to meld, about 10 minutes.

I'm a mean Apricot-Mint
Chimichurri machine.

Salt and Pepper Spareribs with Romesco Sauce

These ribs are simple and to the point, and nothing says a backyard barbecue like ribs. They're a tribute to my buddy Jayson, of Hundred Acre Winery in Napa, and the killer ribs he made for my fortieth birthday (get the full story below). I fortify them with a little old-school romesco sauce.

Salt and Pepper Ribs with Romesco plated up right proper.

1. **FOR THE RIBS:** Preheat the oven to 250°F. (Or see the Smoker Method, page 32!)

2. Mix together the salt, pepper, and paprika. Remove the thin membrane from the bone side of the ribs and discard. Lightly sprinkle the seasoning over both sides of the ribs, then place the racks rib side down on a baking sheet. Bake until the ribs have a nice crust (also known as bark) on the outside and the meat pulls away from the bone, 3½ to 4 hours.

3. **WHILE THE RIBS ARE BAKING, PREPARE THE ROMESCO SAUCE:** Set a large saucepan over medium heat and coat with a generous amount of olive oil. Add the bread cubes, season with some salt, and toast until golden, 6 to 7 minutes, tossing the bread cubes as they cook so they brown evenly all over. Remove from the pan and set aside. Add the almond slivers to the pan and toast until golden, stirring often, 3 to 4 minutes. Remove from the pan and set aside. Coat the pan with more olive oil, add the garlic, and sauté until fragrant, 1 minute. Add the drained red peppers and sauté for 2 to 3 minutes, then add the tomatoes. Season with more salt and the cayenne pepper. Bring to a boil, then reduce the heat and simmer until the liquid has slightly reduced, 8 to 10 minutes. Remove from the heat and set aside to cool.

4. Put the almonds and the tomato and pepper mixture in a food processor or blender. Pulse until well chopped, then add the bread cubes and continue to process. Add the sherry vinegar and, while the processor is running, drizzle in ½ cup olive oil. Continue to blend until the sauce has emulsified. Taste the sauce and season with salt if needed.

5. While the ribs are still hot, squeeze some fresh lime juice all over the racks. It will absorb into the meat and complement the rich, fatty spareribs perfectly. Cut the ribs at every second bone and serve with the romesco sauce on the side.

MAKES: 4 to 5 servings

TIME: 4 hours 20 minutes

YOU'LL NEED: Oven or smoker, food processor or blender, baking sheet

PREP-AHEAD TIP: Make the romesco up to 1 day ahead—just be sure to taste and reseason with vinegar or salt and pepper when you use it. The flavor can change over time.

Ribs

3 tablespoons kosher salt

2 tablespoons freshly ground black pepper

3 tablespoons smoked paprika

Two 3½-pound slabs pork spareribs

4 limes, halved

Romesco sauce

½ cup extra-virgin olive oil, plus more for the pan

1½ cups large-cubed sourdough bread, crusts removed

Kosher salt

½ cup blanched almond slivers

4 garlic cloves, bashed

One 12-ounce jar fire-roasted red peppers, drained

One 14½-ounce can diced fire-roasted tomatoes

⅛ teaspoon cayenne pepper

¼ cup sherry vinegar

Don't say my fingers are the size of the ribs.

Setting the Bar on Spareribs

My wild buddy Jayson Woodbridge from Hundred Acre Winery shows up to my fortieth birthday telling me he wants to cook. Now, I wasn't really sure what to expect, but what he did and the statement he made forever changed the way my friends have come to cook on my birthday.

Jayson rolled in towing a full-blown smoker—not a little backyard unit, but a smoker on a trailer. And then he proceeded to open up four—count 'em, four—huge cases of St. Louis–style ribs. Quickly and efficiently he seasoned all the ribs, as if he'd prepared them a thousand times before. But what was interesting was that he seasoned them only with kosher salt and freshly cracked black pepper. OMG. I thought, *You gotta be kidding me, there's no way this is gonna work.* Now, mind you, the entire time he was surrounded by all the barbecue bad-asses from Motley Que and a variety of Triple D chefs (all of whom will become the culinary maestros of my future birthday festivities).

So he seasoned the ribs and fired up the smoker, and we all waited with anticipation. The band was playin', the birthday party was in full-tilt boogie, and in came the ribs. The hungry crowd of about five hundred people rushed the rib table as Jayson liberally applied freshly squeezed lime juice. I stood back to watch this circus unfold, never anticipating the response. People about fell over—including one of my best bros, Sammy Hagar. I said, "All right, I gotta check this out." Let me just explain it to you this way: The beauty of these ribs is that you let the natural, delicious flavor of the pork stand on its own, simply seasoned with salt and pepper, roasted on the bone, basted in its own fat on the barbecue rotisserie, and accentuated with the citrus kiss of lime. This was as good as it gets. Jayson set the bar real high that year. And I thank him.

SMOKER METHOD

Dry rub and marinate the ribs as above but cook in a low smoker for 4 hours at 200°F to 225°F. Use a wood chip with subtle fruit notes, such as apple or cherry.

Grilled Lamb Chops with Olive-Orange Tapenade

Lamb chops are built-in finger food. That's what the corn dog wishes it could be. They grill up great, and the sweet, tender, juicy lamb is accentuated to the most delicious degree by the olive tapenade.

Fresh herbs do the talking in the marinade.

MAKES: 4 to 6 servings

TIME: 1 hour 30 minutes

YOU'LL NEED: Grill, food processor, large resealable plastic bag

PREP-AHEAD TIP: Make the tapenade ahead of time for sure as it'll keep in the fridge for up to 3 days. You can marinate the lamb chops for up to 4 hours ahead of time. And if you're cooking off-site, take them premarinated in an airtight container or bag straight to the grill.

lamb and marinade

Eight to twelve 2-inch-thick
T-bone lamb chops

2 fresh mint sprigs, torn or roughly
chopped

2 fresh parsley sprigs, torn or
roughly chopped

2 fresh rosemary sprigs, torn or
roughly chopped

2 fresh thyme sprigs, torn or
roughly chopped

1 bay leaf

Juice of 1 lemon

½ teaspoon kosher salt

4 grinds black pepper

½ cup extra-virgin olive oil, plus
extra for grilling

Olive-orange tapenade

2 cups pitted kalamata olives

3 tablespoons grated orange zest

3 tablespoons chopped fresh
parsley leaves

1 anchovy fillet, packed in oil

1 small Anaheim chile, seeded,
membrane removed, and finely
minced

3 to 4 tablespoons extra-virgin
olive oil

1 tablespoon fresh orange juice

Kosher salt and freshly cracked
black pepper

½ cup torn fresh mint leaves, for
garnish

1. FOR THE LAMB: With a sharp knife, clean the chops, trimming away the excess fat cap and any bone fragments. In a medium mixing bowl, combine the mint, parsley, rosemary, thyme, bay leaf, lemon juice, salt, pepper, and olive oil. Place the lamb chops in a large resealable plastic bag and pour the marinade over the top. Marinate at room temperature for up to an hour.

2. FOR THE TAPENADE: In a food processor, pulse together the olives, orange zest, parsley, anchovy, and chile until coarsely chopped. Drizzle in the olive oil and orange juice while continuing to pulse for about a minute, until the ingredients are incorporated and the tapenade is a coarse paste. Do not overprocess. Season with salt and pepper to taste and set aside.

3. TO GRILL: Preheat the grill to medium-high heat. Using tongs and a lightly oiled paper towel, wipe down the grill grates to clean them and create a nonstick surface. Remove the lamb from the marinade, wipe off the excess, and sprinkle with salt and pepper. Place the chops on the grill, fat side down. Grill for about 2 minutes, then rotate 45 degrees to form crosshatch marks. Continue grilling for another 2 minutes and flip. Grill for 2 to 3 minutes, then rotate the lamb chops 45 degrees to finish, another 2 to 3 minutes. The internal temperature should reach 135°F for medium-rare. Remove from the grill and allow to rest.

4. TO SERVE: Arrange the lamb chops on a serving dish, garnishing each with about 1 tablespoon tapenade and finishing with torn mint. Serve the remaining tapenade on the side.

Grilled Lamb Chops
with Olive-Orange
Tapenade at your
service, Flavortown
residents. Good one!
Ha ha.

Miso Side of Salmon with Pickled Carrots and Daikon

Salmon is the international ambassador of seafood. It takes on the flavors and styles of many cultures, and one of my hands-down favorites is this Asian interpretation.

Pickled carrots and daikon

1 cup rice wine vinegar

1 cup sugar

1 garlic clove, crushed

½ pound daikon root, peeled and julienned

½ pound carrots, peeled and julienned

½ cup fresh cilantro leaves

Miso salmon

2 tablespoons rice wine vinegar

2 tablespoons soy sauce

1 tablespoon brown sugar

2 garlic cloves, minced

1-inch piece fresh ginger root, minced

1 tablespoon toasted sesame oil

½ cup shiro miso paste

2 pounds whole side of salmon, skin on

1 bunch scallions

2 to 3 tablespoons olive oil

MAKES: 4 to 6 servings

TIME: 35 minutes, plus 24 hours for pickling

YOU'LL NEED: Oven or pizza oven, roasting pan

PREP-AHEAD TIP: Pickle the veggies up to 3 days ahead of time (the longer they pickle, the better!). They'll keep for up to 3 weeks, refrigerated. Make the marinade up to 1 day ahead, but don't use it on the fish until you're ready to cook.

1. FOR THE PICKLED VEGETABLES: In a small saucepan, combine 1 cup water, the rice wine vinegar, 1 cup water, sugar, and garlic. Bring to a boil to dissolve the sugar. Set aside to cool. Add the daikon and carrots and mix well. Cover and refrigerate for at least 24 hours to pickle—the longer the better.

2. FOR THE MISO MARINADE: Whisk together the rice wine vinegar, soy sauce, brown sugar, garlic, ginger, sesame oil, and miso paste. Place the salmon skin side down on a roasting pan and pour the marinade on top. Marinate for no more than 20 minutes. Meanwhile, heat the oven to 450°F (or get your pizza oven fired up!). Place a wire rack over a roasting tray in the oven to heat up—this will be used to cook the scallions. Bake the salmon for 20 to 25 minutes, until it flakes and the glaze on top of the salmon is golden and caramelized around the edges.

3. With 5 minutes of cook time remaining, toss the scallions with olive oil and remove the wire rack–lined roasting tray from oven. Place the scallions across the hot rack (they will sizzle and char from the preheated rack). Return to the oven and cook for 2 to 3 minutes, until cooked through. Remove and set aside.

4. Drain the pickled daikon and carrots and mix in the cilantro leaves.

5. Top the salmon with the pickled vegetable mixture and serve the grilled scallions on the side. Put this one in the middle of the table and enjoy family style.

This Miso Side of Salmon with Pickled Carrots and Daikon just answered your no-red-meat eater's prayers.

Lava Rock Shrimp with Honey-Lime Chipotle Sauce and Mango Jicama Salsa

We make this tried-and-true recipe from Tex Wasabi's with rock shrimp, but 21/25 shrimp cut in half work really well too. With its tangy, sweet sauce, this dish can be served as an appetizer or as an entrée with vegetables and rice. You can make the sauce ahead of time because it travels and holds well, and you can use it with chicken or pork if you prefer.

Honey-lime chipotle sauce

1 cup barbecue sauce, preferably Guy Fieri Bourbon Brown Sugar BBQ sauce

¼ cup honey

¼ cup fresh lime juice (about 3 limes)

¼ cup canola oil

2 teaspoons Dijon mustard

Pinch of dried red pepper flakes

Pinch of chili powder

Pinch of cayenne pepper

4 canned or jarred chipotles in adobo sauce

MAKES: 4 servings

TIME: 1 hour 5 minutes

YOU'LL NEED: Stovetop or propane burner, deep cast-iron pan, blender, saucepan

PREP-AHEAD TIP: Make the honey-lime chipotle sauce a day or two ahead of time. If you're transporting the dish, mix the flour dredge for the shrimp and put it in a gallon-size resealable bag. All you'll have to do to assemble is toss the shrimp right in the bag (no dishes, no cleanup!). Shallow-frying the shrimp in a cast-iron pan means you won't have to use or transport much oil. Mango jicama salsa is best made the morning of. Just store it in an airtight container in the fridge. To keep it bright and fresh, I like to gently press a piece of plastic wrap right on the surface of the salsa to eliminate air exposure.

1. FOR THE HONEY-LIME CHIPOTLE

SAUCE: In a food processor or blender, puree all the ingredients until combined. In a saucepan over medium heat, cook to reduce the sauce until slightly thickened, about 8 minutes. Set the sauce aside in the pan.

Helped Motley Que win the American Royal BBQ Competition

2. FOR THE SHRIMP: While the sauce is reducing, put the flour, salt, black pepper, cayenne, and chili powder in a medium bowl and stir to combine. Working in batches, add the shrimp to the flour mixture and toss gently to coat evenly.

3. Pour a couple inches of canola oil into a deep cast-iron pan and heat it to 350°F. Working in batches to avoid crowding, cook the shrimp until golden brown, turning as needed, 3 to 4 minutes. Remove from the oil and drain on a paper towel–lined plate. Keep warm.

4. Divide the rice noodles, if using, among 4 small bowls.

5. Add the shrimp to the reduced sauce and toss gently to coat evenly. Remove from the sauce with a slotted spoon or tongs and place in the prepared bowls. Garnish with Mango Jicama Salsa, chile threads and lotus chips, if using, and a few lime wheels. Serve immediately.

Mango Jicama Salsa

Toss all the ingredients gently in a bowl and refrigerate for 20 to 30 minutes before serving.

Rock shrimp

1½ cups all-purpose flour

1½ teaspoons kosher salt

1½ teaspoons freshly cracked black pepper

¼ teaspoon cayenne pepper, or to taste

½ teaspoon chili powder

1½ pounds peeled rock shrimp (about 3 cups)

Canola oil, for frying

2 cups cooked rice noodles (3 ounces uncooked), optional

½ cup Mango Jicama Salsa (recipe follows)

2 pinches of chile threads, optional, for garnish

Lotus chips, optional, for garnish

1 lime, thinly sliced into wheels, for garnish

MAKES: 1¾ cups

1 cup peeled, ⅛-inch-diced jicama

1 cup ⅛-inch-diced ripe mango

¼ cup ⅛-inch-diced red onion

2 teaspoons minced jalapeño pepper

1 tablespoon chopped fresh cilantro

1 tablespoon sweet chili sauce

¼ teaspoon sea salt

Smoky Bean Chili

One of my favorite things about chili is that it's a great way to handle leftovers. The beans are hearty, the seasoning is rich, and the leftover proteins and vegetables just blend right in. So use this recipe as a guide, but feel free to throw in what you have on hand!

2 cups dried pinto beans, soaked in water overnight

2 tablespoons canola oil

8 ounces thick-cut applewood smoked bacon, chopped

1 pound andouille sausage, cut into ¼-inch rounds

2 medium yellow onions, chopped

2 jalapeños, seeds and ribs removed, finely chopped

3 garlic cloves, minced

1 smoked ham hock, about 12 ounces

1 tablespoon tomato paste

2 tablespoons chili powder

2 teaspoons paprika

¼ teaspoon cayenne pepper

1 tablespoon ground cumin

3 tablespoons minced chipotle chiles in adobo sauce

One 28-ounce can crushed fire-roasted tomatoes, with juice (such as Muir Glen)

1 bay leaf

1 quart low-sodium chicken broth

Kosher salt and freshly ground black pepper, as needed

Juice of 1 lime plus 1 lime, cut into wedges, for garnish

¼ cup chopped fresh cilantro

Crème fraîche

2 ripe avocados, sliced

MAKES: 6 to 8 servings

TIME: 2 hours 30 minutes

YOU'LL NEED: Stovetop or propane burner, Dutch oven

PREP-AHEAD TIP: The chili can be made 1 to 2 days in advance and reheated. It'll keep in the fridge, covered, for a few days.

1. Rinse the beans under cold running water and discard any stones or debris.

2. In a large Dutch oven, heat the canola oil over medium-high heat. Add the bacon and andouille sausage and cook for 5 minutes, until both are golden and brown around the edges. Add the onions and jalapeños and sauté for 5 minutes, or until the onion is translucent. Stir in the garlic and cook for 1 minute. Add the ham hock and turn to coat with the oil and aromatics. Cook until the hock is browned on all sides.

3. Stir in the tomato paste, chili powder, paprika, cayenne, cumin, chipotle chiles, tomatoes (with their juices), and bay leaf. Add the pinto beans and stir well. Add the chicken stock and enough cold water to cover the beans by about 2 inches. Bring to a boil, then reduce the heat to a simmer and cook over low heat for 2 hours.

4. Remove the ham hock and pull off and discard the tough outer skin. Remove the tender meat from the bone and return it to the chili.

5. Taste and season with salt and pepper if required. Finish the chili with the lime juice and fold in the cilantro.

6. Serve with a dollop of crème fraîche, a few slices of avocado, and a lime wedge.

Guy's Straight-Up Burgers with a Pig Patty and Donkey Sauce

If I wanted to have a pool party in the rain, all I would need to do is tell our friends and family that I was making my burgers straight up with a pig patty and they would show up, swimsuits and all. P.S.: These burgers were first invented for Guy's Burger Joints, on Carnival Cruise Lines. We quit counting after the first million burgers were served, and that's on four ships.

MAKES: 4 servings

TIME: 2 hours 50 minutes

YOU'LL NEED: Grill, cast-iron skillet with a domed lid, heavy metal spatula or press to flatten burgers, brick covered in aluminum foil, parchment paper

PREP-AHEAD TIP: An obvious prep-ahead tip here is to boil the bacon in advance. In fact, you could even boil it 2 to 3 days before you're making your burgers, form the patties, and store them in the fridge. Prepped ahead and cooled, you'll find they actually set up better when you go to cook 'em. Make the Mornay and donkey sauces in advance as well—they'll hold in the refrigerator for a few days. And why not make extra, since both sauces go great with many things beyond burgers? Same thing goes for roasted garlic butter. Make a big batch ahead of time and you can use it for just about anything, from baked potatoes to sautéed veggies, garlic bread to steaks, chicken . . .

The masterpiece, final construction of Guy's Straight-Up Burger with a Pig Patty.

1. Start by making the "pig patties." Set a medium pot of cold water over high heat and add the bacon. Bring to a medium boil and cook until the bacon is very tender and almost falling apart, 1½ to 2 hours. Drain and set aside to cool. It's important to cool the bacon at this stage. If you work with hot bacon it's much harder to portion and form into patties, and it'll turn mushy instead of crisp when when you press it.

2. Preheat the grill to high heat. Set a large flat cast-iron skillet on the grill. Divide the bacon into 4 even portions, form each portion into a burger-size round, and place on the skillet. Press down with the foil-covered brick to squash each round together and into a flat patty. Cook until golden and crispy, 4 to 5 minutes, then flip and cook 3 to 4 minutes more. Remove and keep warm.

3. Divide the ground beef into four ½-pound portions and form each one into a tight ball. Sprinkle the balls all over with salt and pepper. Place the balls on the skillet (which still has some of the bacon fat in it) and flatten with a strong, flat metal spatula to approximately ⅓-inch thickness.

4. Cook, continuing to press down with the spatula, until the burgers develop a crust on the first side, 1½ minutes. Flip and cook to develop a crust on the second side, 1 minute. Top each burger with 1 tablespoon of Mornay sauce (if using) and then top each burger with 2 slices of cheese. Place a dome lid over the pan. Pour the chicken broth mixture into the pan so the liquid runs under the dome and creates steam to cook the burgers and melt the cheese. When the burgers reach the desired point of doneness and the cheese is completely melted, remove the dome lid and set the burgers aside.

5. Brush the cut sides of the buns lightly with the garlic butter. Toast the buns on the grill until golden and crisp, 3 to 4 seconds. Flip and toast the outsides so they are also lightly toasted, 3 to 4 seconds.

12 ounces thinly sliced applewood smoked bacon

2 pounds ground beef (80/20 blend)

Kosher salt and freshly ground black pepper

¼ cup Mornay Sauce, optional (recipe follows)

8 slices yellow American or Cheddar cheese

¼ cup low-sodium chicken broth mixed with 2 tablespoons water

Garlic Butter (page 46)

4 soft brioche hamburger buns, cut in half

Donkey Sauce (recipe follows)

1 kosher dill pickle, thinly sliced

½ Vidalia onion, very thinly sliced

1 heirloom tomato, thinly sliced

¼ head iceberg lettuce, thinly sliced

6. TO ASSEMBLE: Smear the Donkey Sauce on the cut side of both bun halves. Layer the base with pickle slices and the hamburger patty. Add a bacon pig patty. Top with the onion, tomato, and lettuce, then the top bun half. Wrap in parchment paper and serve immediately.

Boil that bacon until it's almost falling apart.

To achieve greatness, flatten those patties!

Those buns get the necessary garlic butter treatment.

The Cheese Sauce (Mornay Sauce)

MAKES: 1½ cups

2 tablespoons unsalted butter

3 tablespoons all-purpose flour

1 cup whole milk, warmed

1 teaspoon kosher salt

Pinch of grated nutmeg

3 ounces grated yellow American cheese

1. In a medium saucepan, melt the butter over medium heat. Sprinkle with the flour and stir with a whisk. Cook over low heat until the butter and flour combine into a mixture like wet sand. Stir for 1 to 2 minutes more to cook the flour (but without adding color).

2. Pour in the milk slowly as you whisk to combine. Continue stirring until the mixture thickens up, 3 to 4 minutes. Add the salt, nutmeg, and cheese and stir until the cheese has melted and the mixture is smooth. Set aside and keep warm until ready to use or, if making ahead, store covered in the refrigerator for a few days.

Donkey Sauce

Combine all the ingredients in a bowl and stir until smooth. The sauce will keep in the fridge for up to 6 days.

MAKES: 1¼ cups

1 cup mayonnaise

¼ cup roasted garlic
(see page 46)

1 teaspoon yellow mustard

4 dashes Worcestershire sauce

¼ teaspoon kosher salt

4 pinches of freshly ground black pepper

The mise en place for the Donkey Sauce.

Black and Blue Burger with Bacon and Avocado

Blackening spice and blue cheese along with a juicy burger . . . once you try this you'll ask yourself, "Why haven't I always been doing it this way?" By the way—please don't be scared of blackening spice. It isn't necessarily hot. You'll have leftover roasted garlic, which can be used in marinades, in mayonnaise, in vinaigrettes or anywhere you'd use garlic.

Garlic butter

1 garlic head

Extra-virgin olive oil

Kosher salt and freshly cracked black pepper

2 tablespoons unsalted butter, softened

Burgers

2 pounds ground beef (80/20 blend)

4 ounces blue cheese, crumbled

8 slices applewood smoked bacon

3 to 4 tablespoons blackening spice

4 soft brioche hamburger buns, cut in half

¼ cup Donkey Sauce (see page 45)

1 kosher dill pickle, thinly sliced

½ Vidalia onion, very thinly sliced

1 heirloom tomato, thinly sliced

1 ripe avocado, sliced

¼ head iceberg lettuce, thinly sliced

MAKES: 4 servings

TIME: 1 hour 45 minutes

YOU'LL NEED: Flat-top grill (or griddle pan on a grill) and oven, food processor

PREP-AHEAD TIP: Make the roasted garlic butter up to 4 days ahead and refrigerate. Up to 1 day ahead, form the blue cheese–stuffed burger patties, place a piece of wax paper between each, and store in an airtight container in the refrigerator until you're ready to cook.

1. Preheat the oven to 375°F.

2. FOR THE GARLIC BUTTER: Cut off the top third of the garlic head to expose the cloves. Place the garlic on a piece of foil. Drizzle with some olive oil and sprinkle with salt and pepper. Wrap the garlic in the foil and bake for about 1 hour 15 minutes. Remove from the oven and set aside to cool. Squeeze the cloves from their husks. Mince 1 teaspoon of the roasted garlic and melt with the butter in a small saucepan. Season with salt. Gently warm until the garlic becomes fragrant. Pour the mixture into a small bowl and refrigerate to firm up the butter.

3. FOR THE BURGERS: Divide the ground beef into 8 equal portions (4 ounces each) and form into thin patties. On 4 of the patties, sprinkle 1 ounce of crumbled blue cheese in the center; add a second patty on top. Crimp the edges of the 2 patties together tightly, sealing in the cheese and forming one burger. Place in the fridge to firm up for about 30 minutes.

4. TO COOK THE BURGERS: On a hot griddle, cook the bacon until crisp, then drain on a paper towel–lined plate. Discard all but a little of the bacon fat. Sprinkle the burger patties all over with blackening spice. Place the patties on the hot griddle in the bacon fat and cook for 3 to 4 minutes per side for medium-rare. Set aside on a plate to rest.

5. Brush the cut sides of the buns lightly with the garlic butter. Toast the buns on the griddle until golden and crisp, 15 to 20 seconds. Flip to lightly toast the outside of the buns, another 15 seconds. Spread a little donkey sauce on the burger halves. Layer the base with pickle slices and a hamburger patty. Top with the bacon (2 slices per burger), onion, tomato, avocado, and lettuce, then add the top bun half.

Philly Cheese Steak Egg Rolls

This recipe might get me arrested the next time I visit the City of Brotherly Love. But nonetheless it'll get me huge high fives and "attaboys" from the rest of the country, because it just doesn't get any more funky than a Philly cheese steak shoved in an egg roll.

Canola oil, for frying

2 large eggs

2 tablespoons milk

2 tablespoons extra-virgin olive oil

1 small red onion, thinly sliced

1 small red bell pepper, thinly sliced

1 small green bell pepper, thinly sliced

1 pound precooked roast beef,* thinly sliced

16 ounces pepper Jack cheese, shredded

8 ounces sharp Cheddar cheese, shredded

8 egg roll wrappers

* You can use leftover roast beef from another meal; simply refrigerate and then thinly slice. Refrigerating helps firm up the beef and makes it easier to slice thinly. You can also use roast beef from the deli, in a pinch.

MAKES: 8 egg rolls

TIME: 40 minutes

YOU'LL NEED: Stovetop or propane burner, medium saucepan, medium sauté pan

PREP-AHEAD TIP: Make the rolls up to 4 hours ahead of time and wrap each one in a small sheet of parchment (so they don't stick together). Place them in an airtight container and refrigerate until you're ready to fry and serve!

1. Fill a medium saucepan with enough oil that the egg rolls will not rest on the bottom of pan. Preheat the oil to 350°F over medium-high heat.

2. In a small bowl, beat the eggs and milk together with a fork to make an egg wash.

3. In medium sauté pan over medium heat, combine the olive oil, onion, and peppers. Sweat the vegetables until slightly softened, about 2 minutes. Add the roast beef and sauté until the onion is translucent, about 5 minutes more. Remove from heat, strain any excess moisture, and set aside to cool. Add the cheeses and mix thoroughly.

4. Divide the cooled mixture into 8 equal parts. Place part of the mixture in the center of each egg roll skin. Fold in the corners and roll, sealing the edges with egg wash. Submerge the egg rolls in oil and fry, working in batches to avoid overcrowding and making sure the rolls do not touch the sides or the bottom of the pan, until golden brown, 6 to 7 minutes. Transfer the egg rolls to paper towels to blot the excess oil. Cut the egg rolls on the bias, place on a serving platter, and serve hot.

Turkey and Blistered Green Chile Burger Melt

If it's bikini season, everybody feels a little bit better if they're eating a turkey burger. (For the full lowdown on how ground turkey entered the Fieri family repertoire, see the Turkey Takeover story on page 51.)

MAKES: 4 servings

TIME: 40 minutes

YOU'LL NEED: Grill, cast-iron pan

PREP-AHEAD TIP: Up to 1 day ahead: Blister the chiles and make the garlic butter, then refrigerate. Up to 6 hours in advance: Form the burgers, separate them with a sheet of wax paper between each burger, and store in the refrigerator until ready to cook.

Turkey and Blistered Green Chile Burger Melt ready for takeoff.

Garlic butter

4 garlic cloves

1 stick (½ cup) unsalted butter

Blistered chile

1 large poblano pepper

Extra-virgin olive oil

Sautéed onions and peppers

Extra-virgin olive oil

1 medium red onion, thinly sliced

½ large red bell pepper, seeds and membrane removed, julienned

½ large yellow bell pepper, seeds and membrane removed, julienned

¼ teaspoon paprika

Kosher salt and freshly cracked black pepper

Turkey burgers

1 pound ground turkey

2 teaspoons Dijon mustard, plus more for serving

2 teaspoons Worcestershire sauce

½ teaspoon ground cumin

Pinch of white pepper

Kosher salt

Extra-virgin olive oil

4 slices Monterey Jack cheese

4 soft brioche hamburger buns

1. Preheat the oven to 350°F. Preheat the grill to medium-high heat.

2. FOR THE GARLIC BUTTER: Place the garlic in a small sauté pan and set it over medium heat. Add the butter and warm through. Cook the garlic until fragrant, 4 to 5 minutes. Pour the garlic butter into a small bowl and refrigerate until firm.

3. FOR THE BLISTERED CHILE: Toss the poblano with olive oil to coat. Place the pepper under the broiler or char on the grill over a direct flame until the skin blisters. Set aside to cool, then remove the seeds and stem and roughly chop the pepper. Reserve.

4. FOR THE ONIONS AND PEPPERS: Set a large sauté pan over high heat. Add a drizzle of olive oil and sauté the onion and bell peppers until wilted, 5 to 6 minutes. Season with the paprika, salt, and pepper.

5. FOR THE TURKEY BURGERS: In a large mixing bowl, combine the turkey, mustard, Worcestershire, cumin, white pepper, and chopped poblano. Sprinkle with kosher salt. Mix gently until well combined. Form into four 4-ounce patties. Wipe down the grill with oil-blotted towels, then place the burgers on the hot grill and cook for 3 to 4 minutes. Flip the burgers, top with a slice of cheese, and cook until the burgers are cooked through and the cheese has melted, 3 to 4 minutes. Set aside to rest.

6. Smear the buns with the garlic butter. Grill the buns until golden and crispy, 20 to 30 seconds on each side.

7. To build the burgers, place 1 turkey burger on the bottom half of a bun. Top with a good heaping of onions and peppers. Finish with the top half of the bun and skewer to hold the whole thing together. Serve with extra mustard on the side.

The Fieri Family Turkey Takeover

Almost every food demand or expectation in our house comes from me. Then in second place comes Hunter, because of his desire to learn to cook and his culinary expectations. Next comes Ryder with his sometimes picky eight-year-old attitude, and last is Lori, because she's so damn easygoin' and doesn't want to argue with the three of us. But she made one monumental and I gotta say life-changing culinary decision: *Let's put ground turkey in the chili.*

Now, this happened five or six years ago, and I will tell you honestly it was met with some resistance, mainly from me. Well, actually, only from me because we didn't tell the kids that we had substituted ground turkey in our family's long-standing, much-anticipated ground beef chili. Because Lori had done the shopping, she had purchased the ground turkey. All my *mise en place* of peppers and onions, beans and tomatoes had been done. There was no turning back. So I had to use the turkey, while declaring loudly that I was most likely not going to be participating in our family's enjoyment of the dish, as there's no way that the ground turkey would ever measure up. With great fear that the turkey was going to be a sorry substitute flavor-wise, I fortified the dish with copious amounts of roasted peppers, extra garlic, and additional seasonings. The chili cooked low and slow until it was time for dinner.

The kids arrived at the table, the chili was placed in front of them, and I began to mull over my "I told you so" speech. It went something like this: "If it ain't broke, don't fix it— we're never again adding ground turkey to our family's favorite chili."

You can probably imagine what happened. Ryder, Mr. Finicky, dug right in, and Hunter piped in with, "Wow, Dad, this might be the best chili you ever made." Neither of them knew what I was stewing on, no pun intended, and *I* even liked the chili. And that, ladies and gentlemen, began the slow integration of ground turkey into our family's repertoire. From tacos, to sloppy Joes, to burgers, to my show *Guy's Big Bite*, to this cookbook: Ground turkey is here to stay. Thank you, Lori, for sticking to your guns.

Seared Tuna Burgers with Sesame and Spicy Mayo

If I see seared tuna on a menu—unless it's at a truck stop, ha—I'll order it. I'm always looking for ways to work with seared ahi, and this one's a slam dunk, including one of my favorite flavors: Sriracha hot sauce.

1 tablespoon toasted sesame oil

1 tablespoon low-sodium soy sauce

¼ teaspoon dried red pepper flakes

1 large egg, lightly beaten

1 pound sushi-grade tuna, finely diced

¼ cup finely diced red bell pepper

2 scallions, finely sliced

Kosher salt and freshly ground black pepper

½ cup panko (Japanese breadcrumbs)

Vegetable oil, for cooking

4 seeded hamburger buns, split

Spicy Sriracha Mayo (recipe follows)

4 medium butter lettuce leaves

1 beefsteak or heirloom tomato, sliced

MAKES: 4 servings

TIME: 1 hour 5 minutes

YOU'LL NEED: Grill, large cast-iron pan

PREP-AHEAD TIP: Make a batch of Spicy Sriracha Mayo, minus the grilled scallion, and keep it in the refrigerator, covered, for up to 4 days. Grill the scallions when you make the burgers and stir into the prepped mayo.

1. Combine the sesame oil, soy sauce, red pepper flakes, and egg in a large mixing bowl. Mix well, then fold in the tuna, bell pepper, and scallions. Mix well to coat the tuna evenly. Sprinkle with salt and pepper and fold in the panko to lightly bind the mixture. Divide it evenly into 4 patties, set them on a platter, and refrigerate so they firm up and hold their shape when cooked, 15 to 20 minutes.

2. Preheat your grill to high. Heat a large cast-iron pan over high heat. Coat the pan with a little vegetable oil and cook the tuna patties for 3 minutes per side (when done, the patties will be browned on the outside and medium-rare in the center).

3. Grill the hamburger buns over high heat until grill-marked and crispy.

4. Serve the tuna burgers on the buns slathered with the Sriracha mayo and topped with lettuce leaves and tomato slices.

Spicy Sriracha Mayo

MAKES: About 2 cups

Combine the mayonnaise, sour cream, Sriracha, lemon juice, honey, and scallions in a large mixing bowl. Stir well to combine, season with salt and pepper, and refrigerate until ready to serve.

1 cup mayonnaise

½ cup sour cream

1½ tablespoons Sriracha

1 teaspoon fresh lemon juice

1 teaspoon honey

4 grilled scallions, chopped

Kosher salt and freshly ground black pepper

You, too, can deliver the (three-handed!) joy of Seared Tuna Burgers with Sesame and Spicy Mayo.

"Danger Dogs"— Bacon-Wrapped Hot Dogs with Spicy Fruit Relish

Bacon-wrapped hot dogs with spicy relish—or as my buddy Reid calls them, "Tijuana Danger Dogs." For some reason, they just taste incredible at 2 a.m. on the streets of Tijuana. Here's my rendition.

MAKES: 4 servings

TIME: 30 minutes

YOU'LL NEED: Grill, toothpicks

PREP-AHEAD TIP: The night before, parcook the bacon and prep and wrap the dogs, so all you have to do is throw them on the grill the next day.

Hot dogs

4 slices applewood smoked bacon

4 large hot dogs

8 round pickled jalapeño slices, drained

Canola oil, for the grill

4 seeded hot dog buns

Ketchup, optional, for serving

Mustard, optional, for serving

Spicy fruit relish

1 cup Fruit Salsa (page 306)

½ cup pickle relish

1 medium red chile (Fresno or Cayenne), finely diced

1. Preheat the grill to medium and parcook the bacon on the grill for 1 or 2 minutes to render some of the fat, but don't let it get crispy. Set aside on paper towels.

2. FOR THE SPICY FRUIT RELISH: In a small bowl, combine the fruit salsa, pickle relish, and red chile.

3. FOR THE DOGS: Using a sharp knife, make a lengthwise cut down the center of each dog. Cut open the jalapeño slices and unravel them into long, thin strips. Place 2 strips of pickled jalapeño into each hot dog, spacing them out so they fill the length of the dog. Wrap each dog tightly with a strip of bacon and secure with toothpicks at each end to hold in place.

4. Coat the grill surface with canola oil to ensure the hot dogs don't stick; grill until the bacon is cooked through and crisp and the dogs are charred, rotating several times to cook the bacon evenly—8 to 10 minutes total.

5. During the last minutes of grilling, split each bun and grill for 1 to 2 minutes per side. Remove the toothpicks and nestle the hot dogs into the toasted buns. Top with spicy fruit relish and serve with ketchup and mustard, if desired.

Danger Dogs dressed to kill.

Soft-Shell Crab Sandwiches with Homemade Slaw and Tartar Sauce

If you have yet to enjoy soft-shell crab, this may be the recipe that breaks you out. Don't worry, the crabs can be cleaned for you. And these babies cook up nice and crispy and crunchy. Look for them at your fishmonger between April and September.

Tartar sauce

1 large egg yolk

Pinch of kosher salt

1 tablespoon Dijon mustard

¼ teaspoon sugar

1 cup canola oil

1 tablespoon fresh lemon juice

1 tablespoon sour cream

¼ teaspoon freshly ground black pepper

1 small shallot, finely minced

2 tablespoons finely chopped dill pickles

2 tablespoons finely chopped rinsed capers

2 teaspoons finely chopped fresh dill

MAKES: 4 sandwiches

TIME: 25 minutes

YOU'LL NEED: Stovetop or propane burner, large cast-iron pan, whisk, bamboo skewers

PREP-AHEAD TIP: Make the tartar sauce up to 1 day ahead and keep covered in the refrigerator.

1. FOR THE TARTAR SAUCE: In a small bowl, combine the egg yolk, salt, mustard, and sugar. Whisk together, then add the canola oil in a slow, steady stream until it begins to emulsify. Once thickened and creamy, add the lemon juice and sour cream. Season with pepper and fold in the shallot, pickles, capers, and dill. Cover and refrigerate until ready to use.

2. FOR THE SLAW: In another bowl, combine all the slaw ingredients. Mix well, then cover and refrigerate until ready to use.

3. FOR THE CRABS: In a shallow dish, combine the flour, cornmeal, ½ teaspoon salt, ¼ teaspoon pepper, and Old Bay seasoning. In another shallow dish, combine the beaten eggs and Tabasco. Dip each crab into the egg wash and then the flour mixture, shaking off the excess as necessary.

4. Heat the oil in a large cast-iron pan over medium-high heat. Add the crabs, top side down, and cook until crisp and browned, 3 to 4 minutes. Flip and cook the other side until just cooked through, about 3 minutes more. Transfer to a paper towel–lined plate to drain. Season with salt.

5. TO ASSEMBLE: Spread tartar sauce on each side of the toasted roll. On the bottom half, layer a leaf of Bibb lettuce, a crab, a heaping tablespoon of slaw, and a slice of tomato. Close the sandwich, secure with bamboo skewers, and serve!

Slaw

¼ cup red wine vinegar

2 tablespoons honey

½ red onion, thinly sliced

2½ cups thinly sliced green cabbage

1½ cups grated carrot

1½ teaspoons celery salt

Freshly ground black pepper

Soft-shell crabs

½ cup all-purpose flour

½ cup fine yellow cornmeal

Kosher salt and freshly ground black pepper

1 tablespoon Old Bay seasoning

2 large eggs, lighten beaten

¼ teaspoon Tabasco

4 large soft-shell crabs, cleaned

2 tablespoons canola oil

4 potato rolls, toasted and brushed with melted butter

2 large Bibb lettuce leaves

1 red heirloom tomato, thinly sliced

Did Hunter land the flip?

Grilled Baby Artichokes

It's funny what kids like and don't like. I never would have guessed in a million years that Ryder, at the age of three, would like grilled artichokes. Now I just hope he learns to love and adapt to the rest of the vegetable family.

MAKES: 4 servings

TIME: 30 minutes

YOU'LL NEED: Grill, large pot

PREP-AHEAD TIP: You can blanch the artichokes the morning of, but I wouldn't do it any earlier than that or they might turn brown (artichoke hearts are pretty delicate). Store them in the refrigerator under a wet paper towel in an airtight container or in a resealable plastic bag until ready to grill.

8 baby artichokes, about 2 pounds

2 lemons, halved, plus ½ lemon for serving

2 teaspoons kosher salt

¼ teaspoon freshly ground black pepper

3 tablespoons extra-virgin olive oil

2 garlic cloves, minced

¼ cup grated Parmesan cheese

2 tablespoons chopped fresh parsley, for garnish

1. FOR THE ARTICHOKES: Bring a large pot of water to a boil. Prepare an ice bath large enough to hold the artichokes. Squeeze the juice from the 2 lemons into the water, then throw the halves into the water as well. (This is called acidulated water; it will help prevent the artichokes from turning brown as they cook.) Remove the tough outer leaves of the artichokes and trim the stems. Use a vegetable peeler to remove the tough outer green layer from the stem. Add the artichokes to the boiling water and blanch them for 8 to 10 minutes, or until tender (you can test doneness by inserting the tip of a paring knife into the stem of an artichoke; it should go through with little resistance when tender). Drain the artichokes, then immediately shock them in the ice bath. Transfer to a paper towel–lined plate to cool.

2. Heat the grill to medium-high.

3. Cut the artichokes in half lengthwise and toss them with the salt, pepper, olive oil, and garlic. Over a medium-high flame, grill the artichokes, starting cut side down, for 2 to 3 minutes per side, until well browned and slightly charred.

4. To serve, sprinkle with cheese, garnish with parsley, and finish with an extra squeeze of lemon juice.

Ahi Poke and Toasted Seaweed Salad

If you want the real ahi poke and seaweed salad—and I mean the real deal, off the hook, legit, poke experience—you gotta hang out and cook with my buddy Reno or visit his restaurant, Fresh Catch, in Hawaii. This is one of my faves.

MAKES: 2 to 4 servings

TIME: 10 minutes

YOU'LL NEED: Sharp knife or mandoline

PREP-AHEAD TIP: Chop everything *except* the tuna ahead of time, so when it comes time to serve you can simply dice the tuna and fold it together with everything else. It's also a good idea to place the tuna in the freezer for about 10 minutes before slicing so it firms up and is easier to dice finely.

1 pound fresh ahi (yellowfin tuna)

1 teaspoon finely chopped macadamia nuts

1 teaspoon toasted sesame oil

1 teaspoon soy sauce

¼ teaspoon dried red pepper flakes, optional

Kosher salt

¼ cup shaved Maui onion

2 tablespoons finely sliced scallions

Freshly cracked black pepper

⅛ cup finely julienned, toasted dried seaweed

Cut the ahi into ¾-inch cubes and put in a large mixing bowl. Add the nuts, sesame oil, soy sauce, red pepper flakes, and salt to taste. Lightly toss together. Add the Maui onion and scallions; lightly toss to combine. Season with additional salt, if needed, and black pepper to taste. Garnish with seaweed. Serve immediately.

This is taking farm-to-table to a whole new level!

Presenting the best dish for octo-novices: Octopus and White Bean Salad.

Charred Octopus and White Bean Salad

Fifty percent of the people who buy this cookbook are going to turn up their noses at charred octopus and white bean salad . . . and to be honest, ten years ago I woulda been one of them. But it's all worth it for the few who try it, and I rock their kitchen.

MAKES: 4 to 6 servings

TIME: 40 minutes

YOU'LL NEED: Grill, stand mixer with a hook attachment, skewers

PREP-AHEAD TIP: Up to 6 hours in advance, tenderize the octopus and poach it so all you need to do is skewer and grill it when you're ready to eat. Vinaigrettes are also great to make up to a couple days ahead; just refrigerate them in an airtight container until ready to serve.

1. FOR THE OCTOPUS: Place the cleaned octopus and salt in a stand mixer with the hook attachment. "Mix" the octopus on the lowest speed until the tentacles curl and can be separated, 15 to 20 minutes; this tenderizes the meat. Remove the octopus from the mixer, rinse under cold running water in a colander, drain, and pat dry. Cover and refrigerate until ready for use.

2. FOR THE VINAIGRETTE: Whisk together the vinegar, garlic, preserved lemons, and Meyer lemon zest and juice in a medium glass bowl. Slowly whisk in the oil until completely incorporated and smooth. Add the basil and gently whisk. Season with salt and pepper to taste. Cover and refrigerate until ready for use.

3. Preheat the grill to high heat. Using tongs and an oil-blotted paper towel, wipe down the grill grates to clean and create a nonstick surface. Separate each of the legs from the head of the octopus. Thread each leg lengthwise onto a skewer; this will prevent it from curling

Octopus

One 3- to 4-pound octopus, cleaned*

¼ cup flaky sea salt

White balsamic–basil vinaigrette

1 tablespoon white balsamic vinegar

¼ teaspoon finely minced garlic

2 tablespoons chopped Simple Preserved Lemons (recipe follows), plus more for garnish

Juice and grated zest of 1 Meyer lemon (about 3 tablespoons)

¼ cup extra-virgin olive oil, plus extra for garnish

3 fresh basil leaves, finely julienned

Kosher salt and freshly cracked black pepper

* To clean fresh octopus, turn the head inside out and remove the ink sac, innards, and mouthparts. Rinse gently, pat dry, and re-invert.

White bean salad

Olive oil, for the grill

Kosher salt and freshly cracked black pepper

4 lightly packed cups baby arugula

1½ cups canned white beans, drained and rinsed

2 tablespoons finely sliced Fresno chile

2 radishes, finely sliced on a mandoline or with a sharp knife

½ red onion, finely sliced

Flaky sea salt, for garnish

up on the grill and make it easier to turn and cook evenly. Drizzle the octopus with a few tablespoons of olive oil and sprinkle with kosher salt and pepper.

4. Place the octopus on the hot grill and sear. Allow it to char around the edges, then turn, 3 to 4 minutes per side. The octopus is done when just cooked through yet nicely charred around the edges. Do not overcook or it will be tough. Remove and let rest for 1 to 2 minutes. Cut the octopus tentacles and head into bite-size pieces, then toss with about 3 tablespoons of the vinaigrette. Set aside.

5. Toss the arugula, white beans, chile, radishes, and red onion with the remaining vinaigrette. Add the warm octopus and carefully toss to combine. Season with flaky sea salt and pepper. Serve immediately, garnishing with more preserved lemon, if desired, and a drizzle of extra-virgin olive oil.

Octopus Prep

So I'm in Hawaii at my buddy Reno's after shooting Fresh Catch on Triple D—and Reno is telling me how he tenderizes his octopus. I go to his house, and there I find a giant food-safe metal cement mixer where he puts the fresh octopus to tumble-tenderize it. I will tell you, had I not eaten this type of octopus before and realized how phenomenal it is I might've been a little wigged out, but the octopus was the bomb dot com. (And by the way, no cement was harmed in this mixer.) As in the recipe, an easy at-home version uses the stand mixer with a dough hook!

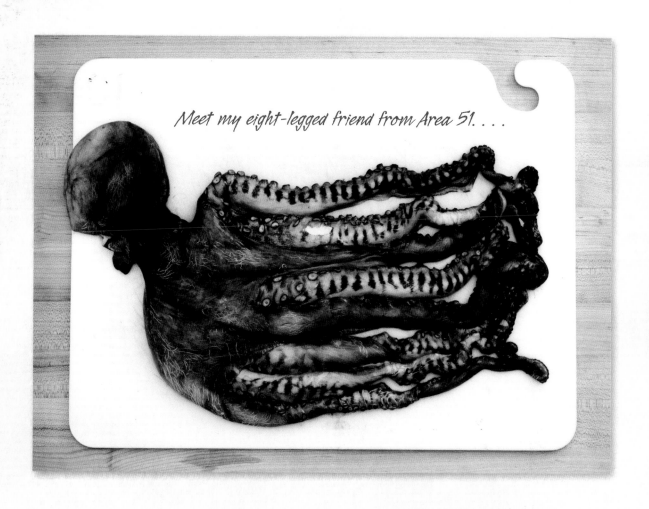

Meet my eight-legged friend from Area 51. . . .

Simple Preserved Lemons

Quarter the lemons and rub them with the salt. Combine in a Mason or canning jar and press the lemons to release their juice. Top with water or lemon juice to cover. Seal and age for 2 weeks in the refrigerator before using. They will keep up to a year if stored correctly, in a sealed container in the refrigerator.

MAKES: 1 pint

4 Meyer lemons

⅓ cup salt

Water or freshly squeezed lemon juice, to cover

Salted Bourbon Caramel Milkshake

Not many things will get my kids out of the pool like a salted caramel milkshake, and not many things will increase your odds of being pushed into the pool like drinking a salted Jack Daniel's caramel milkshake with me and my buddies.

MAKES: 2 servings

TIME: 20 minutes

YOU'LL NEED: Blender, medium saucepan

PREP-AHEAD TIP: Make the salted caramel up to a week ahead of time. In fact, make a big batch of it and keep it in your refrigerator. It goes great with just about any dessert: apples, ice cream, chocolate cake, bananas . . . you name it.

4 ounces (½ cup) bourbon, optional

1 cup sugar

¾ cup heavy cream

2 tablespoons unsalted butter

1 teaspoon flaky sea salt, plus extra for topping

½ teaspoon vanilla extract

1 cup vanilla bean ice cream

½ cup whole milk

1 cup whipped cream

1. Pour ⅓ cup water and the bourbon into a medium saucepan and set over high heat. Carefully pour the sugar directly into the center so none of it splashes up the sides of the pot. Bring to a boil and cook until the sugar starts to turn brown. Do not stir the pot. If you need to, gently swirl the pot to help melt all the sugar.

2. Once the sugar turns a rich, deep brown, remove the pan from the heat and carefully pour in the cream, taking care as it will splatter a little. Add the butter, salt, and vanilla. Swirl the pot until the butter dissolves completely and evenly into the caramel sauce—this makes it shiny and rich.

3. Drizzle a little of the caramel sauce into 2 tall milkshake glasses. Combine the ice cream, milk, and the remaining caramel sauce in a blender, reserving a little of the caramel for the topping. Blend until smooth and pour into the glasses. Top each with a little whipped cream, a pinch of sea salt, and a drizzle of the reserved salted caramel sauce.

Salted Bourbon
Caramel Milkshake . . .
or call it the JD shake
on the down low . . .

Blueberry Peach Crisp

I can't say that blueberries are my favorite berries raw. But when you cook them with sweet peaches in a crisp with a little crunch on top and they create that beautiful purplish blue, I'm down with them.

Filling

6 cups sliced peaches (about 5 peaches)

¾ cup blueberries

¼ cup dark rum

¼ cup sugar

2 tablespoons cornstarch

1 teaspoon ground cinnamon

¼ teaspoon grated lemon zest

1 teaspoon fresh lemon juice

½ teaspoon vanilla extract

Topping

1 cup all-purpose flour

1 cup rolled oats

½ cup sugar

½ teaspoon kosher salt

1½ sticks (¾ cup) cold unsalted butter, cut into small cubes

2 tablespoons heavy cream

Powdered sugar, for garnish

MAKES: 4 to 6 servings

TIME: 1 hour

YOU'LL NEED: Oven, 10-inch cast-iron skillet

PREP-AHEAD TIP: The day before, make the filling and refrigerate it in an airtight container until ready to bake. The lemon juice will keep the peaches from turning. Combine the dry filling ingredients and keep in an airtight container until ready to assemble and bake.

1. Preheat the oven to 375°F.

2. FOR THE FILLING: In a large bowl, combine the peaches, blueberries, dark rum, sugar, cornstarch, cinnamon, lemon zest and juice, and vanilla extract. Mix well to coat the peaches and blueberries evenly. Set aside.

3. FOR THE TOPPING: In a large mixing bowl, combine the flour, oats, sugar, and salt. Add the cold butter cubes and cut the butter into the flour (either with a pastry blender or your hands). Mix until the texture is coarse and clumps in your hand when you squeeze a handful. Add the heavy cream and mix until the dough just comes together a bit more.

4. Pour the filling into a 10-inch cast-iron skillet and spread out evenly. Sprinkle evenly with the topping mixture, then place in the center of the oven and cook until the topping is browned and the fruit is bubbling around the edges, 35 to 40 minutes. Dust with powdered sugar when done.

Rock and Roll Mai Tai

It's sad when I see some of the original super party drinks like the Mai Tai being generically overproduced. So, for the true fans of the Mai Tai, here's a wild one with fresh, bright flavors and colors. This is the way it's supposed to be done.

MAKES: 1 serving

TIME: 5 minutes

YOU'LL NEED: Cocktail shaker

PREP-AHEAD TIP: You can make this in batches up to 4 hours ahead of time.

In a cocktail shaker, muddle the blackberries, then add the guava nectar, pineapple juice, white rum, ginger liqueur, lime juice, and bitters. Add ice, shake, and serve with a cherry on top.

4 fresh blackberries

¼ cup guava nectar

¼ cup pineapple juice

2 ounces (¼ cup) white rum, such as Sammy's Beach Bar Rum

1 tablespoon ginger liqueur, such as Canton's, or ginger syrup

1 tablespoon fresh lime juice

3 dashes Angostura bitters

Ice

Cherry, for garnish

Ryder's puppy . . . yes, puppy . . . six-month-old Roxy.

The Big Island Punch

I know you're going to read this recipe and go . . . "Elderflower, seriously?" And I hate to send you to the store to buy a bunch of ingredients you're going to use only one time. But trust me, with this one, once you make it one time you'll be going back to the store for another bottle of elderflower liqueur. It's worth it.

MAKES: 1 serving

TIME: 5 minutes

YOU'LL NEED: Cocktail shaker

PREP-AHEAD TIP: Make a big batch of punch through the mango juice up to 6 hours ahead of time, pour it into a big pitcher, and refrigerate. Stir it up with a wooden spoon or bar stirrer before pouring and top with spiced rum and grenadine when ready to serve.

2 ounces (¼ cup) white rum

½ ounce (1 tablespoon) elderflower liqueur, such as St. Germain

¼ cup pineapple juice

2 tablespoons fresh lime juice

2 tablespoons mango juice or nectar

Ice

2 ounces spiced rum, for pouring a "float" on top of poured drink

1½ teaspoons grenadine

Lime wheel, for garnish

Orange wheel, for garnish

Pineapple wedge (unpeeled), for garnish

1. TO BUILD THE PUNCH: In a shaker, combine the spirits and juices. Shake well, then pour over ice in a tall island-style glass. Place a spoon rounded side up in the glass, with the tip of the spoon touching the top of the punch. "Float" the spiced rum and grenadine on top by pouring them over the spoon.

2. Garnish with the lime and orange wheels and the pineapple wedge.

Big Island Punch behind Raspberry Picante Paloma Pitcher

Raspberry Picante Paloma Pitchers

Oh yeah!! This is one they won't forget. I can hear it now—"Yeah! The drink had raspberries *and* jalapeños, and it was so the bomb!"

MAKES: 2 quarts (6 to 8 servings)

TIME: 15 minutes

YOU'LL NEED: A couple of big pitchers

PREP-AHEAD TIP: Make the base recipe (minus the club soda) in big batches, up to a day ahead, and hold it in the fridge, so when the party is on all you need to do is pour (rather than stand behind the bar making drinks all night). Just top off each glass with club soda as you're serving so the drinks stay nice and effervescent.

1. FOR THE COCKTAILS: In a glass pitcher, muddle the raspberries and jalapeño, then fill halfway with ice. Add the tequila, grapefruit juice, lime juice, and agave. Take a second pitcher (the same size) and pour one into the other repeatedly to mix the drink together. Top it off with club soda or lemon-lime soda.

2. FOR THE GRAPEFRUIT SALT: Crush the salt and grapefruit zest together with a mortar and pestle, then spread on a plate. Run a lime wedge around the rim of each glass, then dip the glasses in the grapefruit salt. Fill with the cocktails.

Cocktails

12 fresh raspberries

4 thin slices jalapeño pepper

12 ounces (1½ cups) tequila (preferably 100 percent blue agave tequila blanco)

1½ cups fresh ruby red grapefruit juice

¼ cup plus 2 tablespoons fresh lime juice

¼ cup plus 2 tablespoons agave syrup

1¼ cups club soda or lemon-lime soda

Grapefruit salt

¼ cup kosher salt

Grated zest of 1 grapefruit

Lime wedges, for the glasses

I've been invited to more than my fair share of sporting events, concerts, and large gatherings that involve tailgating, and while the draw may sometimes be my sparkling personality, I think it's because my menus are off the hook. A true tailgate is a competitive environment and everybody's doing the craziest things. Now, it's great to have all the amenities, like the flat screen and the big RV, and I've even seen people pull up with couches and recliners. But the heart and soul of any tailgate is the menu. A tiny little barbecue with a couple hot dogs and a six-pack does not cut it. You might have the cheap seats on the inside, but on the outside you're front row.

In great tailgating, planning, prep, timing, and execution are key. If you plan on stopping by the store to get all your goods on the way to the game, you'll miss good tailgating time and you'll definitely forget something. Prepare your tailgating adventure like you're getting ready for Thanksgiving. Remember, you'll have a very limited work surface, large crowds around you, and usually not a lot of storage space. Somehow you have to get it all there, set it all up, make great food, and then break it down and clean it up in time to make it to the game. Who forgot the spatula? Who didn't bring the ice? Where's the hot sauce? Once there, people will beg, borrow, and steal to be a champion of the culinary gridiron. My tailgating success led to a television show, *Tailgate Warriors*, and that's what being a tailgate warrior is all about: how to get it done through prep and planning. Tailgating is an attitude, and my tailgating philosophy is very simple: Go Big or Go Home.

Essentials for Tailgating

Aside from the prep setup for your recipes, you'll need these basics:

A spice box that holds staples like paprika, onion powder, granulated garlic, cayenne, red pepper flakes, Italian seasoning, and salt and pepper. (Me, I take the whole spice cabinet out of the house. Then I know they're not old and I have what I need.)

Pantry standbys such as Worcestershire sauce, soy sauce, red wine vinegar, and olive oil come in handy. (I like to take my standard squeeze bottle collection.)

Tongs

Spatula

Cutting board (a couple of them)

Knives

Citrus press

Charcoal chimney

Cloth and paper towels

Aluminum foil

Paper plates and bowls

Trash bags

Sanitizing wipes

Fold-out tables: At least one for prep, and don't forget the bar table, too.

2 ice chests: One for food and drink storage, one for drink ice.

Tunes: Set your playlist.

And never forget this important rule: Work clean and look good. If your tailgate area looks like a yard sale, your food is going to taste like it.

The barbecue trailer in full smokin' Kulinary Gangsta glory.

Bacon-Wrapped Scallops Glazed with Maple Butter

At Flavortown Stadium, we've been cooking scallops at tailgating events for decades. They're tender, they cook fast, they're great finger food, they play well with other flavors, they don't hog the cooktop, and they make you look really cool. I mean, come on—it's a scallop, at a tailgate! Save the extra maple butter for other seafood, grilled corn, or fried chicken and waffles.

MAKES: 4 servings

TIME: 20 minutes

YOU'LL NEED: Propane burner or grill, large cast-iron skillet, toothpicks

PREP-AHEAD TIP: Make the maple butter up to 2 days in advance. Parcook the bacon the night before, but don't wrap the scallops in bacon until the morning of the tailgate.

1 stick (½ cup) unsalted butter, softened

2 tablespoons pure maple syrup

1 tablespoon seeded, minced Fresno chile

1 tablespoon minced fresh parsley

1 tablespoon minced garlic

Kosher salt, to taste

12 slices applewood smoked bacon

12 large sea scallops, cleaned

Freshly ground black pepper

1 to 2 tablespoons olive oil

Lemon juice, to finish

1. In a small bowl, combine the butter, maple syrup, chile, parsley, garlic, and salt. Set aside.

2. Arrange the bacon in a large skillet and cook over medium-high heat until lightly browned and pliable, 3 to 4 minutes (it will finish cooking later). Transfer to a paper towel–lined plate. Wipe out the skillet.

3. Lightly season the scallops with salt and pepper. Wrap each scallop in a piece of bacon, securing with a toothpick. Heat the olive oil in the skillet over medium-high heat and sear the scallops until they're golden brown and the bacon is crisp on the bottom, 3 to 4 minutes. Turn them over, spoon 2 tablespoons of maple butter into the skillet, and baste the scallops as they finish cooking, another 2 to 3 minutes.

4. Finish with a squeeze of fresh lemon juice. Serve the scallops basted with pan sauce.

Grilled Chicken Wings Two Ways

This is the quintessential tailgate food, and "it ain't no thing but a chicken wing." If you want to have a Wing Warrior Weekend, here are some great recipes for you.

YOU'LL NEED: Grill, spice grinder

PREP-AHEAD TIP: Brine the wings the night before, then drain and pat dry. Make the rubs anytime in advance. If you're taking the wings to the tailgate, toss them in the rub and transport in a resealable bag or airtight container on ice so all you have to do is throw them on the grill on-site. (Alternatively, to really save time, you can brine, rub, and bake them at home, then reheat them on the grill at the tailgate.) The Cilantro-Avocado Crema can be made the night before—just press a piece of plastic wrap directly onto the surface of the sauce so no air hits it and it doesn't oxidize. Store in the fridge in an airtight container.

Hunter is now officially taller than me! Damn!

Jerk Chicken Wings

If you're tailgating in the sun, these jerk wings will remind you of Jamaica. If you're tailgating in the snow, these jerk wings will take you to Jamaica. Yah mon.

MAKES: 4 servings

TIME: 5 hours 30 minutes

1. To make the brine, combine 8 cups water, the sugar, salt, and garlic in a large bowl or container. Submerge the wings in the brine and refrigerate for up to 4 hours.

2. Meanwhile, combine all the jerk spice rub ingredients except the sugar in a dry pan and toast lightly for 30 to 40 seconds over high heat until aromatic and warmed. Place in a clean spice grinder and grind until powdered. Mix the sugar into the dry rub. Transfer to a large bowl.

3. Drain the wings and pat dry. Toss them in the spice mixture and place in the refrigerator to marinate for at least 1 hour uncovered.

4. Preheat a grill to medium heat. Grill the wings until golden, 15 to 20 minutes, turning halfway. Create grill marks on the lime wedges and scallions on the hot grill to garnish the platter of wings.

Brine

¼ cup light brown sugar

¼ cup kosher salt

4 garlic cloves, smashed

5 pounds chicken wings, cut at the joint and tips discarded

Jerk spice rub

2 teaspoons granulated garlic

1 teaspoon ground ginger

1 tablespoon dried thyme

1 teaspoon rubbed sage

½ teaspoon cayenne pepper

2 teaspoons ground allspice

¼ teaspoon grated nutmeg

1½ teaspoons freshly cracked black pepper

1 teaspoon kosher salt

1 dried Scotch bonnet pepper, seeded

1 teaspoon light brown sugar

Lime wedges, for garnish

Scallions, for garnish

Mexican Chicken Wings

If you're in a tailgate chicken wing competition and you've seen everybody bring their best "Buffalo," don't worry; your team may not win inside the stadium but you're definitely going to dominate the culinary gridiron with these Mexican chicken wings.

Brine

¼ cup brown sugar

¼ cup kosher salt

4 garlic cloves, smashed

5 pounds chicken wings, cut at the joint and tips discarded

Mexican spice rub

2 tablespoons ground cumin

2 tablespoons smoked paprika

2 tablespoons ancho chile powder

2 tablespoons chipotle chile powder

1 tablespoon light brown sugar

2 teaspoons dried oregano

2 tablespoons granulated garlic

1 teaspoon ground cinnamon

2 teaspoons kosher salt

Chipotle-Lime Butter (recipe follows)

Cilantro-Avocado Crema (recipe follows)

Shaved radishes, for garnish

MAKES: 4 servings

TIME: 20 minutes

1. To make the brine, combine 8 cups water, the sugar, salt, and garlic in a large bowl or container. Submerge the wings in the brine and refrigerate for up to 4 hours.

2. Combine the spice rub ingredients in a large bowl. Drain the wings, pat dry, and toss in the rub mixture to coat the wings evenly.

3. Preheat a grill to medium-high heat. Grill the wings until golden, 15 to 20 minutes, turning halfway. Immediately toss the wings with Chipotle-Lime Butter until well coated. Serve with Cilantro-Avocado Crema as a dipping sauce and garnish with shaved radishes.

Chipotle-Lime Butter

MAKES: About ¾ cup

TIME: 5 minutes

Combine the butter, pepper, and lime zest and juice in a small bowl. Season with salt and mix together.

1½ sticks (¾ cup) unsalted butter, room temperature

1 chipotle pepper in adobo sauce, finely minced

2 limes, zested on a Microplane grater

1 tablespoon lime juice

½ teaspoon kosher salt

Cilantro-Avocado Crema

MAKES: About 3½ cups

TIME: 5 minutes

Puree all the ingredients in a food processor until smooth. Taste for seasoning. Store in the refrigerator, or in a sealed container in a cooler, until ready to use.

3 cups low-fat sour cream

1 cup chopped fresh cilantro

1 jalapeño pepper, seeded and minced

1 ripe avocado, cut into chunks

Juice of 2 limes

Kosher salt and freshly ground black pepper, to taste

Bee Sting Wings

I love chicken wings. No one said it better than Chris Farley in *Tommy Boy*: "Me lovey wingy." They're one of my quintessential foods, and have been since I was about nine years old. My first time, I was all over the buffet with the teriyaki wings at my Aunt Patty's wedding. I sat there and ate all of them, thinking they were the greatest thing in the world. Regardless of my newfound passion, when I was growing up the rule in my family was that if we cooked chicken, my mom got the wings. And today . . . my mom still gets the wings.

It's just always been a thing. In fact, I used to have a fryer set up outside my house solely for making wings for Monday Night Football. That's right, I'd brought a fryer from the restaurant home just to make wings for the game. That's how much of a Wing Warrior I was. It became a ritual, and people would show up with different things to cook, knowing the fryer would be there. So one day I asked my buddy to fire up the fryer. He did and came back, saying, "Hey, you've got to come see this, there's a bee in your fryer."

I said, "How can that be?" (No pun intended.) So I went out there and scooped out the bee, no big deal.

He came back about five minutes later and said, "Dude, you've got to come out here, there's more bees in it."

I was thinking, how could there be more bees in it? So I went and scooped out a few more. Finally, by the time the fryer really got cookin', about three hundred bees came to the surface of the oil. Clearly, someone had left the lid off and the bees had smelled the meat and dive-bombed into the frying oil.

So, we scooped them all out and stood there drinking a couple of beers.

Then everybody started showing up and my buddy and I looked at each other and realized we were thinking the same thing: Theoretically the oil has been so hot that it's cooked out all the bees. But is there a chance that there could be some poison in that oil, and one of our friends might get sick from a tainted wing?

We had to pour out all the oil. I think that was the only time we didn't have wings for Monday Night Football.

This is me with my sister, Morgan, at the party where I discovered chicken wings.

Andouille-Stuffed Pork Loin with Creole Mustard

If you want to add great flavor to a pork loin, brine it. If you want to add super flavor to your pork loin, stuff it with your favorite Cajun-country sausage. This recipe is worth all the effort.

MAKES: 6 to 8 servings

TIME: 3 hours

YOU'LL NEED: Grill with lid, large freezer bag, honing steel, instant-read meat thermometer

PREP-AHEAD TIP: Prepare and brine the pork loin the morning of. Drain it, pat it dry, and stuff with andouille before you transport it to your tailgate, so all you have to do on-site is unwrap it and grill it.

1. To prepare the brine, bring 6 cups water, the salt, sugar, peppercorns, garlic, thyme, bay leaves, and onion to a simmer in a medium pot over medium heat. Stir until the sugar and salt have completely dissolved. Remove from the heat and add the ice cubes to cool.

2. Place the pork loin in large freezer bag (or large plastic container with a lid). Pour the brine into the freezer bag, submerging the roast completely, seal, and set aside for 2 hours.

3. Preheat the grill and set up two zones—one hot for searing and another medium for cooking through.

4. Using the tip of a paring knife, pierce the casing of the sausage all over (this will ensure the flavor of the sausage goes into the pork as it cooks). Remove the pork from the brine and pat it dry with paper towels. Using a clean honing steel, poke a hole into the center of the loin lengthwise and work it all the way through so it creates a cavity. Insert the sausage into the cavity so that it sits neatly within the roast. Season the roast with salt, pepper, granulated garlic, paprika, and cumin.

Brine

½ cup kosher salt

½ cup sugar

12 black peppercorns

6 garlic coves, roughly chopped

6 fresh thyme sprigs

2 bay leaves

1 small yellow onion, peeled and sliced into rings

4 cups ice cubes

Pork

One 3-pound boneless pork loin roast with a nice fat cap layer on top

1 large (about 4-ounce) andouille sausage link

Kosher salt and freshly ground black pepper

1 tablespoon granulated garlic

1 tablespoon paprika

1 teaspoon ground cumin

1 to 2 tablespoons canola oil

Creole mustard (e.g., Zatarain's)

"Andouille"-like pork loin?
Yes, we do!

5. Wipe down the grates of the grill with oil-blotted towels. Place the roast on the hot part of the grill and sear fat side down, 3 to 4 minutes, and then on each of the three other sides. Transfer the roast to the cooler part of the grill (indirect heat) and cook until the internal temperature hits 165°F on an instant-read thermometer, 45 to 55 minutes. Set the roast on a platter and tent with foil. Allow it to rest for 15 minutes before carving into thick slices. Served drizzled with juices from the platter and the Creole mustard.

TRADITIONAL OVEN COOKING METHOD

Pan-roast the pork by searing the roast on all four sides in a hot cast-iron pan over high heat, 3 to 4 minutes per side. Transfer the pan to a preheated 350°F oven and roast for 20 to 25 minutes, until cooked through to a temperature of 165°F in the center. Rest the roast in the pan, then slice and serve with the pan juices and mustard.

St. Louis Ribs with Tequila BBQ Sauce

There are many great debates—Republican or Democrat, light beer or dark, imports or domestics—but the one to top them all in my book is *baby backs versus spareribs.* Me, I want 'em big-boned and meaty—give me the spareribs, St. Louis–style.

MAKES: 4 servings

TIME: 4 hours plus marinating time

YOU'LL NEED: Grill, blender, medium saucepan, heavy-duty foil, roasting pan

PREP-AHEAD TIP: Make the rub and marinate the ribs well in advance. You can actually prep the ribs and wrap them in foil pouches so all you have to do is throw them on the grill at the tailgate. Make the tequila BBQ sauce a day in advance and reheat it in a small pot on the grill so it's ready to baste the ribs in the final grilling stages.

1. Combine the dry rub ingredients in a small bowl and mix.

2. Rinse the ribs in cool water and pat dry with paper towels. Remove the thin membrane from the bone side of the ribs and trim off any excess fat. Coat both sides of the meat with a thin layer of mustard and a heavy coating of the dry rub. Refrigerate overnight.

3. To make the tequila BBQ sauce, place the dried chile in a bowl with ¼ cup hot water to rehydrate. In a medium saucepan, combine the tomato paste, brown sugar, tequila, lime juice, garlic, and molasses.

On Ribs: Baby Back vs. St. Louis

What's the difference? Baby back ribs are the ones that sit right on top of the back of the pig. The theory is that the smaller and younger the pig, the more tender the rib. Once the baby back ribs are defined and cut, the remaining rib is known as the sparerib. (St. Louis ribs are spareribs that are cut down to a more useful size.) People attribute the tenderness and fattiness of the baby back to the fact that the top of the pig's ribcage has less physical and muscular responsibility. But others, like me, argue that the sparerib/St. Louis rib is more flavorful *because* of its more muscular and meaty attributes. Spareribs take a bit longer to cook, are less fatty, and are typically a little less expensive.

Stir well and bring to a gentle simmer over low heat. Add the chile and soaking water, season with salt and pepper, and simmer until the flavors meld, 2 to 3 minutes. Process with a blender until smooth and set aside.

4. Set out a few large sheets of foil (one for each slab). Place 1 rack on each sheet meat side down and fold the foil over to form a sealed pouch around the rack. Place pouches on roasting pans and grill over indirect heat for 2 hours. After 2 hours, open up the foil and peel it back so the ribs are exposed. Carefully turn the meat over so the meat side is on top, and cook for 1½ more hours with the open foil. When done, the ribs will be tender and the meat will have shrunk back from the bones.

5. For the last 10 minutes, remove the ribs from the foil and place directly on the hot side of the grill. Brush with the BBQ sauce and allow the heat to caramelize the sauce and crisp the exterior. Flip, brush the other side, and cook for a final 5 minutes. Serve with additional BBQ sauce.

TIP: A rib stand is a good investment and a great way to cook ribs in a smoker. If you lay them flat you can cook only two racks at a time, but if you get a stand you can fit four or five racks in the smoker at once.

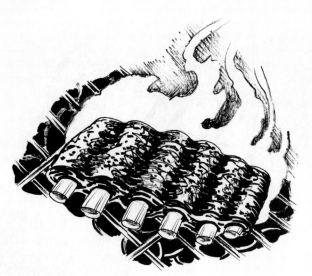

Dry rub

1 tablespoon freshly ground black pepper

2 tablespoons kosher salt

2 tablespoons ground cumin

¼ cup paprika

3 tablespoons granulated garlic

2 tablespoons onion powder

¼ cup light brown sugar

3 tablespoons ancho chile powder

Spareribs

Two 3-pound slabs St. Louis rib racks

⅓ cup yellow mustard

Tequila BBQ sauce

1 California or New Mexico dried chile

One 6-ounce can tomato paste

1 cup light brown sugar

½ cup white tequila

¼ cup fresh lime juice

2 garlic cloves, minced

1 tablespoon dark molasses

Kosher salt and freshly ground black pepper

Korean Glazed Sticky Short Ribs

Short ribs are kinda like egg rolls—when they're good, they're really good, but when they're bad, they're still kind of good. I mean come on, you'll see a frozen egg roll at a buffet and still pick it up and try it, even though you know it's going to be mushy and flavorless. You just risk it, am I right? That's exactly what you do.

So Korean short ribs are the same for me. Even when they're not cooked enough, even when the connective tissue isn't broken down, I still love 'em. There's something about eating them on the bone, all the flavor . . . but you don't need to settle.

MAKES: 4 to 6 servings

TIME: 3 hours (plus overnight marinade)

YOU'LL NEED: Propane burner; heavy pot or Dutch oven

PREP-AHEAD TIP: This is a good one for very little fuss and cleanup at a tailgate. Marinate the ribs overnight. You can even cook the ribs the day before as they become even more tender and flavorful when reheated the next day.

1. To make the marinade, mix all the ingredients in a medium bowl. Pour the mixture over the short ribs, stir to coat, and marinate in the refrigerator overnight.

2. Remove the short ribs from the marinade, pat dry, and season with salt and pepper (be sure to reserve the marinade). In a large Dutch oven over high heat, brown the short ribs on both sides in canola oil. Remove the meat and set aside on a platter. Discard all but 2 tablespoons of the fat drippings from the pot.

The Secret of the Silverskin

The membrane that rides on the inside of the ribs, known as silverskin, was once responsible for shielding all the vital organs from the rib cage. Some argue that if you leave the silverskin on it will help the meat retain flavor and moisture. Others, like me, argue that if you don't remove it, the silverskin will inhibit the penetration of the marinade and dry rub. You be the judge?

Marinade

1 cup light brown sugar

1 cup soy sauce

1 small yellow onion, grated

6 garlic cloves, minced

1-inch piece fresh ginger root, grated

1 tablespoon toasted sesame oil

2 tablespoons mirin

¼ cup gochujang (Korean hot pepper paste)

1 teaspoon dried red pepper flakes

Peel of 1 orange, sliced into thin strips

Short ribs

5 pounds beef short ribs

3 tablespoons canola oil

2 carrots, cut into 2-inch chunks

1 large yellow onion, cut into 2-inch chunks

Kosher salt and freshly ground black pepper

2 bay leaves

½ cup fresh orange juice

4 to 5 cups beef broth, as needed

Toasted sesame seeds, for garnish

Chopped scallions, for garnish

Steamed white rice, for serving

3. Add the carrots and onion and cook until tender and browned, 8 to 10 minutes; season with salt and pepper. Return the short ribs to the pot, plus the bay leaves, orange juice, and enough beef broth to just cover the meat. Bring to a boil, reduce to a simmer, cover, and cook for 2 to 2½ hours, until the meat is tender and just about falling off the bone. While the short ribs are cooking, bring the marinade to a boil in a small saucepan. Reduce to a simmer and cook for 20 minutes, or until it's reduced by about three quarters and is nice and rich.

4. Remove the short ribs from the Dutch oven, turn the heat to high, and reduce the braising liquid for 20 minutes. Strain the liquid to remove the vegetables, add the reduced marinade, and reduce over high heat for 7 to 8 minutes, until the sauce is dark and syrupy. Reduce heat to medium-high. Return the short ribs to the pot and spoon the sauce over the meat, making sure all sides are glazed and well coated. Be sure to keep your eye on the sauce as you glaze the meat—it can burn quickly at this stage!

5. Garnish with sesame seeds and chopped scallions; serve over white rice with extra sauce.

Crispy Asian-Style Fried Chicken

Parbake these wings and drumsticks at home and quick-fry them when you're ready. It doesn't get any easier than that. The key is to render the fat and then crisp the skin. Don't fall into the belief that it all has to happen in the fryer. You can get crispy wings and drumsticks; just don't crowd them on the sheet when you parbake them, so they have a chance to expel their moisture in the cooking process.

MAKES: 2 to 4 servings

TIME: 50 minutes

YOU'LL NEED: Propane burner, heavy pot for deep-frying, baking sheet, medium sauté pan

PREP-AHEAD TIP: Parcook the chicken a day ahead and refrigerate it so all you need to do on-site is fry the chicken. Make the glaze up to 2 days ahead of time and transport it in an airtight container. You will need to reheat the glaze for tossing with the chicken at the tailgate.

My buddy Paul is a wing-eatin' machine.

1. Preheat the oven to 350°F.

2. Season the chicken with salt and pepper. Place it on a baking sheet and parcook it in the oven for 30 minutes to render some of the fat.

3. In a large sauté pan over medium heat, combine the 2 tablespoons canola oil and the ginger. Cook for 2 minutes. Add the sherry, vinegar, sesame oil, honey, soy sauce, and chili garlic sauce and cook for 2 minutes more. Remove from the heat.

4. In a large pot or heavy cast-iron pan, heat 3 inches of canola oil to 350°F. Place the drumsticks in the oil and cook for about 10 minutes, or until crispy and golden brown. Next, fry the wings, 5 to 6 minutes. Remove each batch from the oil and drain on paper towels.

5. Add the crispy wings and drumsticks to the sauce and toss to coat evenly. Garnish with chopped scallions and sesame seeds.

---

1 pound chicken wings

1 pound chicken drumsticks

Kosher salt and freshly ground black pepper

2 tablespoons canola oil, plus more for frying

3 tablespoons grated fresh ginger

¼ cup sherry

¼ cup white vinegar

2 tablespoons toasted sesame oil

¼ cup honey

½ cup soy sauce

¼ cup chili garlic sauce

Chopped scallions, for garnish

Sesame seeds, for garnish

Apricot Glazed Chicken Thighs with Pickled Red Onions

I used to hate chicken thighs, but now I gotta say that besides the wings they're probably my favorite. No . . . I'll say they're definitely my favorite, but it took a long time for me to get there. The chicken thigh is to the chicken as the rib is to the pig as the porterhouse steak is to the cow. In my opinion, they're the prize of the poultry, and one of the most resilient pieces of meat to use when tailgating. They've got tons of flavor and they don't dry out.

To read a rant about how much I hated chicken thighs as a kid, see page 185 of *Guy Fieri Food*.

MAKES: 4 to 6 servings

TIME: 2 hours 15 minutes

YOU'LL NEED: Grill, large freezer bag, instant-read thermometer

PREP-AHEAD TIP: Brine the chicken the night before or morning of. Drain and transport to the tailgate in an iced cooler, ready to simply season and grill. Make the glaze 1 day ahead and refrigerate in an airtight container. Take the container to the tailgate and simply pop off the lid and glaze your chicken. Pickle the onions up to a week in advance.

1. To make the brine, combine 3 cups water, the apple cider, onion, rosemary, thyme, salt, sugar, garlic, bay leaf, and peppercorns in a medium saucepan. Bring to a simmer to dissolve the sugar and salt. Remove from the heat and add the ice. When cool, place in a freezer bag and add the chicken to the brine, submerging it completely. Refrigerate for 2 hours.

2. To make the pickled onions, bring the vinegar, sugar, and salt to a boil in a small saucepan. Remove from the heat and pour over the sliced onion. Let the mixture sit at room temperature for 1 hour, then refrigerate.

3. To make the glaze, whisk all the ingredients in a small saucepan over medium heat. Bring to a boil, reduce the heat to medium-low, and simmer until slightly thickened, 3 to 5 minutes. Remove from heat and let cool to room temperature.

4. Heat a grill to medium and wipe down the grates with oil-blotted paper towels to clean them and create a nonstick surface.

5. Remove the chicken from the brine and pat it dry with paper towels. Season with salt and pepper. Place the thighs on the grill skin side down and cook for 8 to 10 minutes, until browned. Flip the thighs, brush the cooked side with glaze, and cook for 8 to 10 minutes more. When the chicken is just about done, turn and brush both sides again with any remaining glaze to caramelize the skin. The chicken is done when it has reached an internal temperature of 165°F. Serve with pickled red onions on top.

Brine

1 cup apple cider

1 medium yellow onion, sliced

2 fresh rosemary sprigs

2 fresh thyme sprigs

⅓ cup kosher salt

¼ cup light brown sugar

4 garlic cloves, smashed

1 bay leaf

1 teaspoon black peppercorns

2 cups ice

10 bone-in, skin-on chicken thighs

Pickled red onion

½ cup red wine vinegar

2 tablespoons sugar

1 teaspoon kosher salt

1 red onion, thinly sliced

Glaze

¾ cup apricot preserves

3 tablespoons apple cider vinegar

½ teaspoon dried red pepper flakes

1 tablespoon stone-ground mustard

Kosher salt and freshly ground black pepper, to taste

Brazilian Bacon-Wrapped Chicken Thighs with Peri Peri Sauce

I know I had you at Brazilian, but it doesn't end there. Juicy chicken thighs . . . wrapped in bacon . . . in a peri peri hot sauce that will deplete the drink cooler. And did I mention Brazilian?

MAKES: 6 servings

TIME: 2 hours 30 minutes

YOU'LL NEED: Grill, food processor or blender, toothpicks

PREP-AHEAD TIP: Brine and wrap the chicken thighs the night before. Transport in an airtight container in an iced cooler to the tailgate. Make the peri peri a day in advance, which allows the flavors to meld together nicely.

1. To make the brine, in a large container, combine 2 quarts water, the salt, sugar, garlic, orange, and thyme. Submerge the chicken thighs in the brine and refrigerate for 2 hours.

2. In a medium skillet over medium heat, cook the bacon for 3 to 5 minutes, until barely colored and still pliable. Set aside.

3. Meanwhile, make the peri peri sauce: Roast the chiles and red pepper at 400°F for 20 minutes (or over an open flame if camping). Once cool enough to handle, chop finely. Meanwhile, sweat the onions and garlic in canola oil for 5 to 8 minutes, until softened.

4. Put the chopped peppers, onion, garlic, salt, paprika, red pepper flakes, and tomato paste in a food processor and pulse until combined. Add the vinegar and lime juice and pulse again to incorporate. With the food processor running, stream the olive oil in slowly to achieve a smooth puree (similar to the texture of ketchup). Fold in the chopped cilantro.

5. Preheat a grill to medium heat and wipe the grates with an oiled paper towel. Remove the chicken from the brine, pat dry, and season lightly with salt and pepper. Wrap each thigh in 2 pieces of bacon, securing with a toothpick. Grill the chicken, turning once, for 10 to 15 minutes per side, basting with the sauce for the final 5 to 8 minutes. Remove the toothpicks and serve with extra peri peri sauce.

Brine

2 tablespoons kosher salt

¼ cup sugar

2 garlic cloves, smashed

Peel of 1 orange

3 fresh thyme sprigs

Chicken

6 bone-in, skin-on chicken thighs, trimmed of any excess fat

12 slices thick-cut applewood smoked bacon

Kosher salt and freshly ground black pepper

Peri peri sauce

6 red cayenne chiles, seeds removed, cut in half lengthwise

1 red bell pepper, cut into big chunks

¼ cup diced yellow onion

4 garlic cloves, minced

1 teaspoon canola oil

2 teaspoons kosher salt

¼ teaspoon smoked paprika

¼ teaspoon dried red pepper flakes

2 teaspoons tomato paste

½ cup white vinegar

Juice of 1 lime

½ cup extra-virgin olive oil

2 tablespoons finely chopped fresh cilantro

Spicy Cracked Chile Crab

Every year when crab season opens, in the beginning of November in Northern California, my boys at Santa Rosa's G&G market (www.gandgmarket.com) always have a great price on the fresh crab—and the key is that they'll clean it for you. So when the crab comes out we go nuts at my house. We're talkin' paper on the table, hot towels with hot water and lemon, all the utensils. We throw down. We do crab feeds. Everyone likes their crab a different way. I like mine hot, cioppino style, Lori likes hers hot with a garlic lemon butter, and Dad enjoys it any way, but always likes it cold. When I've got the crabs (ha ha ha) the recipes start flyin', and this is one of my favorites. It works great at a tailgate with a cold beer.

How to Clean Your Crab

1. Pry open the top shell of the body.

3. Pull off the gills and pull out the entrails.

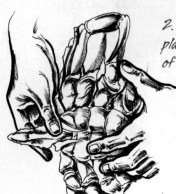

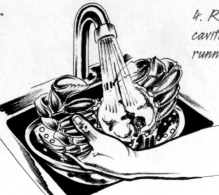

2. Pull off the smaller plate on the underside of the crab.

4. Rinse out the cavity under cold running water.

The highest crab mountain in Flavortown.

Crabs and poaching liquid

1 cup California dry white wine

1 bay leaf

1 bunch fresh cilantro stems (use the leaves for garnish)

2 garlic cloves, smashed

½ cup kosher salt

1 teaspoon black peppercorns

1 lemon, sliced thinly

2 live Dungeness crabs, about 3½ pounds total

Marinade

2 tablespoons ketchup

½ teaspoon fish sauce

1½ teaspoons dark brown sugar

1 tablespoon sambal chile sauce

1 tablespoon oyster sauce

1 tablespoon soy sauce

Wok

1 tablespoon peanut oil

1 tablespoon toasted sesame oil

3 garlic cloves, minced

1 shallot, diced

2-inch piece fresh ginger root, grated

2 Fresno chiles, thinly sliced

1 tablespoon fermented black bean paste, optional

Chopped scallions, for garnish

Chopped fresh cilantro, for garnish

Lemon wedges, for garnish

MAKES: 2 to 4 servings

TIME: 25 minutes

YOU'LL NEED: Grill or propane burner, heavy wok or large cast-iron pan, large pot

PREP-AHEAD TIP: Poach the crab before you head out to the game. Chill it down, clean and cut it up, crack it, and place the pieces in an airtight plastic container in an iced cooler. Make the marinade and pop it in a jar so all you have to do is add it to the wok with the crab when you're at the tailgate.

1. To make the crabs, combine 6 cups water, the wine, bay leaf, cilantro, garlic, salt, peppercorns, and lemon in a large pot and bring to a boil. Submerge the live crabs in the water and poach lightly until they turn red, about 5 minutes. Drain and set aside to cool; when they're cool enough to handle, pull off and discard the top hard shell. Cut off the "apron," scrape out the gills, and discard the innards from the body. Cut the body in half, from head to tail, then portion each half into 3 pieces, cutting between every second leg, so that you have 6 pieces total. Lightly crack the legs and claws with a hammer or the heel of knife.

2. If using a grill, preheat to high.

3. In a small bowl, combine the marinade ingredients and stir well. In a large wok or cast-iron sauté pan over high heat, combine the oils, garlic, shallot, ginger, chiles, and black bean paste; stir-fry for 2 to 3 minutes, until fragrant, then add the crab legs and sauté for 5 to 7 minutes. Add the marinade mixture to the wok, toss to coat, and cook for 4 to 5 minutes more, to thicken the sauce and coat the crab legs.

4. To plate, pile the crab legs high on a large platter. Spoon any excess sauce over the crab and garnish with scallions, cilantro, and lemon wedges.

Tri-Tip Dip Sandwich with Horseradish Cream Sauce

This is without question one of my favorite sandwiches. I'm a French dip fanatic. The only thing I don't like about the French dip is it's typically made with the leftover prime rib from the night before. Sometimes it's old, dried, and worn out. So the way to make the perfect dip is to cook the meat specifically for the sandwich. West of the Mississippi it's easy to find the tri-tip. It's got great flavor and the right amount of fat, and when it's sliced super-thin on the bias it makes magic. The other key is toasty bread and a lot of jus. Jus means the juice (broth in this case) and au means "with" so *au jus* means "with juice." So it's funny when you see on a menu that a sandwich is served "with au jus" because it translates to *with with juice* . . .

Thinly slicing the meat is paramount.

MAKES: 6 sandwiches

TIME: 35 minutes

YOU'LL NEED: Grill, propane burner

PREP-AHEAD TIP: Chill the cooked tri-tip so it's easier to slice nice and thin. Make the jus ahead of time, and when you reheat it you can fortify it with any off-cuts from the beef. Garlic butter and horseradish mayo can be made a day or two in advance. Simply store them in the fridge or cooler in an airtight container.

The Tri-Tip Dip Sandwich with Horseradish Cream Sauce served up...

1. To make the jus, set a medium saucepan over medium heat. Sauté the shallots and garlic in the olive oil and butter until caramelized lightly, 7 to 8 minutes. Add the flour and mix together to form a loose paste. Deglaze with the brandy and whisk in the demi-glace, Worcestershire sauce, and beef stock. Bring to a boil, then reduce the heat and simmer for 25 minutes, or until the aroma and flavor of the jus is rich and deep. Remove from the heat. Strain the broth to remove the garlic and shallots and return the liquid to the pot. Add the butter and swirl to melt and distribute it through the sauce—this adds a nice shine and richness. Season with salt and pepper to taste. Keep warm.

2. To prepare the horseradish mayo, combine all the ingredients in a medium bowl. Refrigerate.

3. Prepare a hot grill. Combine the soft butter with the minced garlic. Brush the cut sides of the ciabatta rolls with the butter and toast them on the grill on both sides until crispy. Smear with horseradish mayo.

4. To assemble each sandwich, dip the slices of tri-tip into the jus to rewarm for 30 to 45 seconds. Pile the meat onto the bottoms of the ciabatta rolls, top with cheese if you like, close the sandwich, cut in half, and serve with extra jus on the side for dipping.

Jus

½ cup chopped shallots

2 garlic cloves, minced

1 tablespoon extra-virgin olive oil

1 tablespoon unsalted butter

1 tablespoon all-purpose flour

¼ cup brandy

¼ cup demi-glace

1 tablespoon Worcestershire sauce

3 cups low-sodium beef stock

1 tablespoon cold unsalted butter, cut into cubes

Kosher salt and freshly ground black pepper

Horseradish mayo

½ cup sour cream

½ cup mayonnaise

1 teaspoon fresh lemon juice

½ cup prepared hot horseradish

1 teaspoon minced garlic

½ teaspoon kosher salt

Sandwich

1 stick (½ cup) unsalted butter, at room temperature

2 garlic cloves, minced

6 ciabatta rolls, sliced

2 to 3 pounds thinly sliced Santa Maria Tri-Tip (see page 294)

6 slices pepper Jack cheese, optional

Grilled Sausage Kebabs Three Ways

Kebabs at a tailgate are like peanuts at a ballgame.

Chicken-apple kebabs

**2 links chicken sausage,
cut into 1-inch pieces**

**2 Fuji apples, cored and
cut into 1-inch pieces**

8 cipollini onions, peeled

Italian pork kebabs

**2 links Italian pork sausage,
cut into 1-inch pieces**

8 cherry tomatoes

4 pickled sweet cherry peppers

**1 small zucchini, cut into
1-inch pieces**

Andouille and pepper kebabs

**2 links andouille sausage,
cut into 1-inch pieces**

**1 small sweet onion, cut into
1-inch chunks**

**1 red bell pepper, seeded
and cut into 1-inch chunks**

**1 yellow pepper, seeded and
cut into 1-inch chunks**

Olive oil, as needed

**Kosher salt and freshly ground
black pepper**

Sourdough rolls

Spicy Ketchup (recipe follows)

**Funky Hot Mustard
(recipe follows)**

MAKES: 12 kebabs

TIME: 45 minutes

YOU'LL NEED: Grill, heavy skewers (either thick bamboo or metal skewers)

PREP-AHEAD TIP: Make the condiments up to 3 days in advance and store in the refrigerator, then simply take in an iced cooler to the tailgate. Thread the kebabs the night before or morning of and transport in an airtight container in the cooler.

1. Soak twelve 8-inch skewers in water for 30 minutes. Preheat a grill or grill pan to high heat. Make 4 skewers from each kebab mixture, alternating the ingredients and colors on each kebab. Brush each kebab lightly with olive oil and season with salt and pepper. Grill the kebabs for 3 to 4 minutes on each side, until well charred and cooked through on the last turn, 12 to 15 minutes total.

2. Serve with crusty sourdough rolls, Spicy Ketchup, and Funky Hot Mustard.

Spicy Ketchup

MAKES: 1 cup

TIME: 5 minutes

1 cup ketchup

1 tablespoon minced chipotle in adobo sauce

1 teaspoon honey

½ teaspoon kosher salt

¼ teaspoon garlic powder

¼ teaspoon onion powder

Mix all the ingredients in a small bowl until well combined. Refrigerate until ready to use.

Funky Hot Mustard

MAKES: 1 cup

TIME: 5 minutes

1 cup yellow mustard

1 tablespoon hot sauce

Pinch of cayenne pepper

2 teaspoons light brown sugar

1 teaspoon apple cider vinegar

½ teaspoon kosher salt

Mix all the ingredients in a small bowl until well combined. Refrigerate until ready to use.

Grilled Lamb Sandwiches with Harissa Mayo and Quick-Pickled Cucumbers

You can call it a quest, a PR campaign, or a chef's soapbox message, but whatever you want to call it, I tell you that lamb needs more respect. I don't know where the problem comes from. Does it stem from wartime days, when people were eating mutton and hiding its musky flavor with mint jelly? Or the fact that people tend to overcook it to the point that it's just a sad, gray slab? I don't know, but lamb needs more love, and this grilled lamb sandwich should do the trick. You can ask your local butcher to butterfly it for you.

MAKES: 6 to 8 servings

TIME: 3 hours

YOU'LL NEED: Grill, large resealable bag, bamboo skewers or toothpicks

PREP-AHEAD TIP: Marinate the lamb in a large resealable bag the night before and transport to the tailgate to grill on-site. Harissa mayo and pickled cucumbers can be done a day ahead; just keep them refrigerated or on ice in an airtight container. Another good tip is to put the harissa mayo in a squeeze bottle so it's easy to put on the sandwiches. It makes cleanup a breeze . . .

1. To make the yogurt marinade, finely mince the capers, oregano, and garlic together. Put in a small bowl along with the yogurt, olive oil, lemon zest, and salt and pepper to taste, stirring until well combined. Place the lamb in a large resealable bag and pour in the marinade. Mix it around to coat the lamb completely. Squeeze out any air, reseal the bag, and refrigerate for at least 2 to 3 hours or up to 24 hours.

Guido Had a Little Lamb

When I was a kid one of the local ranchers gave me a lamb. He'd never docked its tail, so I had this little lamb with a long tail, and it followed me around like a dog. It would come up to the back door of the house and just wander around, going everywhere with me. My dad finally asked me what I was doing with the lamb, because our whole intention was to raise the lamb for sale. It was how I was making my money. Man . . . I'll tell you what, taking your dog to the vet and putting it down is horrible, but it's even worse when you think about taking your pet to the market for someone else to eat. That was the last lamb I raised.

1½ teaspoons button capers packed in salt, rinsed

1 tablespoon fresh oregano leaves

4 garlic cloves

2 cups plain yogurt

2 tablespoons extra-virgin olive oil, plus more for grilling

½ teaspoon grated lemon zest

Sea salt and freshly cracked black pepper

One 4-pound leg of lamb, butterflied

2 sourdough baguettes

Harissa Mayo (recipe follows)

Quick-Pickled Cucumbers (recipe follows)

2. Preheat the grill to medium-high heat.

3. Remove the marinated lamb from the bag and wipe off any excess with paper towels. Press the lamb flat, drizzle with a little olive oil, and sprinkle well with salt and pepper on both sides; this will help form a nice crust. Grill for about 15 minutes, then flip and cook until the lamb is cooked through and has some nice color, another 12 to 15 minutes on the second side. Remove from the grill, tent with foil, and let rest for 10 to 12 minutes, then carve the lamb across the grain into thin slices.

4. Split the baguettes lengthwise so you have long halves. Place on the grill to warm the bread through and get slightly crisp, about 2 minutes per side.

5. To assemble the sandwiches, smear the warm bread with the mayo and stack with slices of lamb and pickled cucumbers. Secure the top of the baguette with bamboo skewers or toothpicks. Slice the sandwich into quarters and serve.

Harissa Mayo

1 cup mayonnaise

½ cup sour cream

3 tablespoons harissa paste

1 teaspoon red wine vinegar

½ teaspoon ground cumin

Kosher salt and freshly cracked black pepper

MAKES: About 1¾ cups

TIME: 5 minutes

Mix the mayonnaise, sour cream, harissa, vinegar, and cumin in a medium bowl and whisk to combine. Season with salt and pepper. Refrigerate until ready to use.

Quick-Pickled Cucumbers

1 hothouse cucumber, thinly sliced

½ Fresno chile, halved lengthwise, seeded if desired, and thinly sliced

1 cup white vinegar

¾ cup sugar

1 teaspoon kosher salt

MAKES: About 2 cups

TIME: 25 minutes

Put the cucumber and chile slices in a medium bowl and toss to combine. In a medium saucepan over low heat, combine the vinegar, sugar, and salt with ½ cup water. Heat gently, stirring, just until the sugar and salt dissolve. Pour the liquid over the cucumbers and chiles. Set aside to cool and marinate at least 15 minutes, then refrigerate until ready to use.

Lamb and Feta Sliders with Mint Tzatziki

I think I've made my point about lamb, but let me add another verse to the lamb appreciation theme. This ground lamb with mint tzatziki and thinly sliced cucumbers is a hit at all my Johnny Garlic's restaurants.

MAKES: 16 sliders

TIME: 25 minutes

YOU'LL NEED: Grill, bamboo skewers

PREP-AHEAD TIP: Make the lamb burgers the night before and place a piece of parchment between each to keep them from sticking. Wrap tightly in plastic wrap and store in the fridge. Mint tzatziki can be made the night before or morning of, but don't make it too far in advance as you want the mint to stay bright, fresh, and fragrant.

Lamb sliders getting branded on the grill.

1½ pounds ground lamb

2 garlic cloves, minced

¼ cup finely diced red onion

½ cup crumbled feta cheese

Kosher salt and freshly ground black pepper

1 tablespoon balsamic vinegar

1 tablespoon pomegranate molasses

1 tablespoon soy sauce

1 tablespoon canola oil

½ hothouse cucumber, peeled and sliced paper thin

16 small Hawaiian sweet rolls or potato dinner rolls

Mint Tzatziki (recipe follows)

1. Preheat a grill to indirect heat, low setting, approximately 325°F.

2. In a medium bowl, combine the lamb, garlic, red onion, and feta. Sprinkle with salt and pepper and mix well with your hands. Form the mixture into 16 small patties (about 2½ inches across and 1¼ inches thick). Use your index finger to press a shallow dimple into the center of each patty. Cover and refrigerate until ready to grill.

3. In a small bowl, combine the vinegar, pomegranate molasses, and soy sauce.

4. Oil a paper towel with the canola oil and wipe down the grill grates several times to create a nonstick surface. Immediately place the patties on the grill (dimple side down) and cook for 8 minutes. Turn over, baste with the balsamic mixture, and cook for 4 to 6 minutes more. Remove from the grill and place each on a roll; add a teaspoon of mint yogurt, top with 2 slices of cucumber, and secure the top half of the roll with a bamboo skewer.

Mint Tzatziki

1 cup plain Greek yogurt

1 garlic clove, minced

¼ teaspoon mustard powder

2 tablespoons finely chopped fresh mint

Kosher salt and freshly ground black pepper

MAKES: 1 cup

TIME: 5 minutes

Combine the ingredients in a bowl and mix well. Refrigerate for 30 minutes before using.

Lamb and Feta Sliders with Mint Tzatziki, bite-size lamby delights for the asphalt tailgate gridiron.

Grilled Tequila Lime Fish Tacos with Cilantro-Lime Crema

When I'm down in Mexico with my family one of my favorite things to do is to walk to the end of the village where the fishing boats come in and buy what's fresh. I build my menu from there. Fresh fish and a hot grill make for killer fish tacos.

Fresh slaw

½ cup red wine vinegar

2 tablespoons sugar

1 tablespoon kosher salt

2 cups finely shredded red cabbage

1 cup chopped fresh cilantro

Fish and marinade

3 tablespoons tequila

1 tablespoon ground cumin

2 teaspoons minced garlic

Juice of 1 lime

1 teaspoon diced jalapeño

2 teaspoons paprika

1 teaspoon kosher salt

¼ teaspoon freshly ground black pepper

Four 6- to 8-ounce boneless, skinless mahi mahi fillets (or other firm white fish), cut into 1-inch cubes

1 to 2 tablespoons canola oil

MAKES: 4 servings

TIME: 45 minutes

YOU'LL NEED: Grill, skewers

PREP-AHEAD TIP: Make the fish marinade in a large resealable plastic bag. Thread the fish skewers and wrap them. Keep them separate until you get to the tailgate. Once there, pop the fish in the bags and gently shake around to marinate the fish on-site while you set up. (You don't want to marinate the fish too far ahead of time, as it'll turn into ceviche.) The Cilantro-Lime Crema can be made the night before and kept cold. Load it into a squeeze bottle to make it easier to work with at the tailgate.

1. TO MAKE THE SLAW: In a large mixing bowl, combine the vinegar, sugar, and salt and mix together well. Add the cabbage and stir to combine well. Marinate for 15 minutes, then fold in the cilantro and set aside until ready to use.

2. TO MAKE THE MARINADE: In a large mixing bowl, combine the tequila, cumin, garlic, lime juice, jalapeño, paprika, and salt and pepper. Add the fish to the marinade. Set aside to marinate for no more than 4 or 5 minutes.

3. TO COOK THE FISH: Heat a grill to high and coat with a little oil. Thread 4 or 5 pieces of fish on each skewer. Place the skewers on the grill and cook until the fish is white and cooked through, about 1 minute on each side and about 4 minutes total. Set the skewers of fish aside on a platter.

4. Warm the tortillas in batches on the grill for about 2 minutes on each side. Remove the tortillas and keep them warm by wrapping them in a kitchen towel.

5. TO BUILD THE TACOS: Double up 2 tortillas and drizzle with a little Cilantro-Lime Crema. Top with some of the cabbage mixture (let it drip to drain some of the liquid) and place a skewer of fish on top. Slide out the skewer so the fish stays on the taco in a line. Finish with more crema. Garnish with some crumbled Cotija and hot sauce and serve with a wedge of lime on the side. Repeat to make the rest of the tacos.

Tacos

Sixteen 6- to 7-inch soft flour tortillas (see page 111)

1 cup Cilantro-Lime Crema (recipe follows)

2 cups crumbled Cotija cheese

Hot sauce, for garnish, if desired*

Lime wedges, for garnish

*My favorite hot sauces for tacos are Tapatio, Cholula, and Valentina.

Cilantro-Lime Crema

MAKES: About 2 cups

TIME: 1 hour

In a small bowl, combine the sour cream, milk, cilantro, garlic, cumin, and lime juice and chill for 1 hour. Season with salt and pepper. Keep chilled until use.

1½ cups sour cream

¼ cup milk

2 tablespoons finely chopped fresh cilantro

1 garlic clove, minced

½ teaspoon ground cumin

Juice of 2 limes

Kosher salt and freshly cracked black pepper

Fresh Corn and Flour Tortillas

A lot of kids like to be involved in the cooking process. Making corn and flour tortillas with a tortilla press and cooking them off on the plancha (a cast-iron griddle) is a great way to make everyone feel involved. Just like pizza dough, you can buy pretty good tortillas from the store, but nothing tastes better than the ones you make at home yourself.

Corn Tortillas

MAKES: Eighteen 6-inch tortillas

TIME: 1 hour

YOU'LL NEED: Propane burner or grill set to high, tortilla press (optional; if you have one it makes it easier—and you'll look like a pro) or rolling pin, cast-iron skillet, wax paper

PREP-AHEAD TIP: Make the tortillas and store them in an airtight container or bag.

2 cups masa harina (yellow corn flour)
½ teaspoon kosher salt
1½ cups lukewarm water
Canola oil, as needed

1. Whisk the masa and salt in a medium bowl. Stir in the water and knead until a smooth, pliable dough forms. Add more water by the teaspoon if the mixture looks too crumbly, or add more masa if it feels too wet. Cover with plastic wrap and let rest for 30 minutes.

2. Measure a heaping tablespoon of dough and form it into a ball. Using a tortilla press lined in plastic wrap or wax paper and a rolling pin, flatten the dough into a 6-inch tortilla. Repeat to make the rest of the tortillas. You can stack them, separated by wax paper.

3. Heat a large cast-iron skillet over high heat and lightly brush the surface with oil. Cook each tortilla until it's slightly charred in spots and the edges curl in, 30 to 60 seconds per side. Keep the tortillas wrapped in a kitchen towel to stay warm.

Flour Tortillas

1. In the bowl of a food processor fitted with the chopping blade, add the flours and salt and pulse 2 or 3 times to combine. Add the cold lard and butter and pulse until the mixture has a cornmeal-like texture. Add the warm water and pulse until a dough ball forms.

2. Turn the dough out onto a well-floured board and knead until the dough is elastic and smooth and no longer sticky, 3 to 4 minutes. Form into a small loaf shape, about 4 by 6 inches. Wrap tightly in plastic wrap and let rest at room temperature for 1 hour.

3. Cut the dough into 8 equal pieces. Working with one piece at a time, roll into a ball about the size of a golf ball and dust lightly with flour. Repeat with the remaining dough.

4. Place a ball in a well-floured tortilla press, press down, and remove (or use a rolling pin). You should have a 6-inch disc at this point. Place the disc on a floured board and roll out to 8 to 9 inches in diameter, until almost paper thin, lightly dusting with flour and turning as needed. Repeat to make the rest of the tortillas. You can stack them, separated by wax paper.

5. Heat a cast-iron skillet or griddle over medium heat. Cook the tortillas one at time for 30 to 45 seconds per side, or just until the bubbles puff up, then turn and repeat. Keep the cooked tortillas in a folded kitchen towel, to keep them warm and pliable.

MAKES: Eight 8- or 9-inch tortillas

TIME: 90 minutes

YOU'LL NEED: Propane burner or grill set to medium, food processor, tortilla press (optional; if you have one it makes it easier—and you'll look like a pro), cast-iron skillet, rolling pin, wax paper

PREP-AHEAD TIP: Make the tortillas and store them in an airtight container or bag.

1½ cups all-purpose flour, plus more for kneading

½ cup whole wheat flour

2 teaspoons kosher salt

¼ cup cold lard

1 tablespoon cold unsalted butter

⅔ cup warm water (about 100°F)

Competition Barbecue by the Motley Que Crew

Our winning chicken at the Houston Livestock Rodeo.

I met these characters down in Houston, Texas, in a barbecue class being run by barbecue champions James and Lola Rice at Klose Pits. We've been barbecuing and competing together for ten years now, and in that time we've won two of the most prestigious awards in barbecue: the 2011 American Royal Open Grand Champions and the Houston Livestock Rodeo Grand Champions. The other original members are Matt "Mustard" Sprouls, who worked for AT&T and now works for Jimmy Johns (whom he happened to meet at the American Royal); Robert "Taz" Riley, truck driver; Mike "Mikey Z" Zemenick, pharmacist; and Ron "UnYawn" Walker, engineer.

American Royal: Invitational and Open

The American Royal is actually two separate contests. The Invitational contest is by invitation only. To be invited you must be a Grand Champion, having won a qualifying contest or one of the *big* contests such as the Jack Daniel's, Memphis in May, or Houston Livestock and Rodeo, which we've been lucky enough to win in recent years. It usually has over 150 teams.

The Invitational is cooked Friday night and turned in and judged on Saturday. Also on Friday is turn-in for the side categories: beans, sausage, potato, vegetable, and dessert. All the corporate parties are on Friday night, and I bet there are fifty different bands playing.

The second contest at the American Royal is the Open contest. It's one of the largest BBQ contests in the world, at just over five hundred teams. Teams will start cooking their meat on Saturday night for turn-in on Sunday. Turn-in times are: Chicken: 12:00; Ribs: 12:30; Pork: 1:00; Brisket: 1:30. (And ya can't be late.)

Taking out the competition: Mikey Z, Mustard, and Unyawn

Holdin' BBQ court!

Motley Que Crew BBQ Timeline

Here's a to-the-hour rundown of what goes down during a barbecue competition, from setup to cookin' and smokin' and finally delivering (the "turn-in") to the judges. Much like a successful tailgate, competition barbecue is all about exceptional prep and planning.

DAY	TIME	MISC.	CHICKEN	RIBS	BUTT	BRISKET
Friday	9:00 AM 12:00 PM	Check in Set up site Get meat inspected				
	3:00 PM				Prepare pork injection	Prepare beef injection
	4:00 PM	Set up all cookers with gurus Lump and smoke wood	Trim chicken	Trim ribs and pull membrane	Trim, prepare, & inject	Trim, prepare, & inject
	5:00 PM	Cooks' meeting Time the walk to turn in				
	6:00 PM	Start dinner				
	9:00 PM				Remove butts from cooler Season	Remove briskets from cooler Season
	10:00 PM	Light cooker	Lightly season chicken Put on rack (open) in cooler		Set guru to 250°	Set guru to 250°
	11:00 PM	Wash, prepare lettuce and parsley			Put butts on cooker Fat side up 3rd shelf Set meat probe to 165°	Put briskets on cooker Fat side up Top 2 shelves Set meat probe to 165°
Saturday	12:00 AM	Pre-make boxes with lettuce and parsley				
	2:00 AM				Check water & fuel	
	3:00 AM				At 165° internal, wrap, add marinade, set probe in money muscle @ 197°	At 165° internal, wrap, add beef broth, set probe in flat muscle @ 197°
	5:00 AM			Stabilize cooker @ 275°		
	6:00 AM			Apply rub		

DAY	TIME	MISC.	CHICKEN	RIBS	BUTT	BRISKET
Saturday	7:00 AM			Remove ribs from cooler Reseason Put ribs on cooker @ 275° (3 hrs.)		
	8:00 AM	Set up Cajun grill with lump, cherry wood & chips			Use Thermopen to check internal temp. when guru reaches meat set point	Use Thermopen to check internal temp. when guru reaches meat set point
	9:00 AM 9:30 AM	Prepare chicken in pan Light lump on Cajun grill, stabilize	Stabilize cooker @ 275° Reseason chicken	Baste Ribs		
	10:00 AM		Put chicken on cooker Cook uncovered 45 minutes	Check for tenderness Cook for 45 min. to 1 hr. more at 275° if needed		
	10:30 AM 10:45 AM	Prepare BBQ sauce for chicken Prepare glaze for ribs	Reseason (if needed) Cover pan w/ foil Cook 45 minutes	Prepare foil for ribs Set guru down to 250°		
	11:00 AM	Keep BBQ sauce/ glaze warm		Wrap ribs and put back on cooker for 30 min. @ 250°	Pull butts @ 195° to 200° Open foil, let cool 5 min. Put in cambro	Pull briskets @ 197° to 200° Open foil, let cool 5 min. Put in cambro
	11:30 AM	Keep BBQ sauce/ glaze warm	Dunk in sauce, put on rack Set sauce on cooker w/smoke 5 min. Make box & run	Apply glaze Loosly wrap and let rest 30 min.		
	12:00 PM	Keep BBQ sauce/ glaze warm	CHICKEN TURN-IN	Slice ribs, make box & run		
	12:30 PM	Keep BBQ sauce/ glaze warm		RIB TURN-IN	Slice & pull butts Make & run box	Remove briskets from cambro Glaze & put on Cajun grill Set glaze w/smoke 10 min.
	1:00 PM	Keep BBQ sauce/ glaze warm			BUTT TURN-IN	Slice briskets Make & run box
	1:30 PM	Keep BBQ sauce/ glaze warm				BRISKET TURN-IN

Motley Que & A

What's your favorite style of barbecue?

UNYAWN: Backyard style. I like any type of meat simply seasoned with garlic pepper and grilled with *no* sauce.

RILEY: Favorite style is a tough one! Good BBQ is good BBQ, wherever it's from. I'd have to say, though, mine would have to be a Carolina-style pulled pork sandwich. A real close second would be a Texas-style brisket.

MUSTARD: I enjoy all styles, but Carolina is where it all started for me. A good vinegar bite stirs my soul. I love the complete spectrum of Carolina barbecue.

MIKEY Z: I like Memphis style, a little spicy and lightly sauced. However, the BBQ in front of me will always do. I love BBQ!

GUIDO: Without question it would have to be Argentinean. . . . Nooo, I love Argentinean barbecue, but my boys at Motley Que would kill me if I said that. So, I would have to say mine is Carolina style. Pork is probably my favorite protein, and I like the vinegar flavor with a sweet and salty complexity. I'm not a heavy sauce guy; I like sauce but not a ton of it.

What's your favorite BBQ competition moment?

UNYAWN: Well, I have a few. First, as a whole team, winning the American Royal will be hard to top. Second, cooking at the Jack Daniel's Invitational, and last, the people we have met over the years have been unbelievable.

RILEY: My favorite moment would have to be winning the Houston Livestock and Rodeo contest. The American Royal was really exciting, but Houston was a completely new style of contest for us and we won it with the chicken category. We had to cook whole chickens, and that was something we'd never done before. The recipe was made up as we went along!

MUSTARD: I have a few: At the 2012 Houston Livestock and Rodeo, we rolled in cooking on borrowed smokers, using an untested chicken recipe, changing the recipe for the second turn-in . . . and it wins Overall Grand Champion. When we won the American Royal it felt like the world stopped for a few hours. Bucket list moment. Watching Guid teach Johnny Trigg how to roll sushi at the American Royal.

MIKEY Z: My favorite moment was putting the crown and robe on after winning the American Royal. It's kind of like putting on the green jacket after winning the Masters.

GUIDO: (Aside from winning, DUH! Plus the boys already mentioned that . . .) When Motley Que was in its second or third season and things were really rollin', I was bringing out all my posse from California. We had all the Motley Que guys and probably six of my buddies: Uncle Milt, Possum, Spaniard, Kleetus, and all these dudes were coming out. We were a new team that was becoming pretty well known (trust me, because of my and everyone's antics) competing with all these badass veteran barbecue dudes from all over the country. We rented a 20 by 40 pop-up tent. But this isn't just any pop-up tent; this is a pop-up tent that we got a deal on for $1,200. We were excited; this was going to be great. But when they came and set the tent up, the top of it was pink and black. It's like a circus tent with multiple colors to it. Oh, my god, if we weren't already the biggest circus in the world in a barbecue competition, we now had this tent. Oh, it was horrible. You have to sleep in your tent because you're cooking your barbecue through the night, so we go to Cabela's and we buy cots. We're ready to compete, sleeping on our cots in our sleeping bags. Probably about ten people are in the tent. Eight of them are over two hundred pounds and at least two of them are over three hundred pounds. And let the snoring begin. With the depth in tone of snoring you would have thought the tent was the stable for all the animals that were going to be butchered for the barbecue. We weren't more than five feet away from our port-o-potty; then there was our hand-wash sink and cooking area, and it's all squeezed up against somebody else's tent and trailer. We were the only ones with the regular catering tent with the barrels securing it, and we turned that thing into our living environment.

So, there we were, asleep in the tent at the parking lot at the American Royal center, and it started to rain. Now the fact that it's raining is not that big of a deal. But all of a sudden one of the guys woke up and started screaming, "Pick up your gear!" And then came a flash flood. We happened to be in the low zone of the parking lot, and in came the water. I'm talking about three inches—and it carried stuff with it. We're talking cups, lids, rubber gloves, caps, flip-flops. Our tent had sides to the ground, but when the water pressure built up it just pushes them out of the way. So the water was flowing through the tent, and we were all on our cots with our bags on top of us, all of our cooking equipment was just soaked, and we had to compete the next morning. That was my most memorable experience.

What music do you like to listen to while you cook?

UNYAWN: While we listen to all types of old-school rock and blues, two of my favorite bands that we always roll with are Tab Benoit and JJ Grey and Mofro.

(GUIDO: What?)

Ramblings from Riley on the Royal

The American Royal starts for me when I get the application ready for turn-in, in late June or early July. This is when I start asking around to see who's planning on attending that year. We rent a 20 by 30 or 20 by 40 tent to sleep in, so space is limited. Some folks stay in motels, but most want to rough it. It's like an over-forty (sometimes fifty) camping trip! And it truly is camping: cots, sleeping bags, and no A/C or heat. The weather in Kansas City in October is anything but predictable, so you can expect all four seasons in the four days you're there.

The American Royal is always held the first weekend in October, Thursday through Sunday. I usually arrive Wednesday to drop off my 6 by 10 trailer. It's loaded with cots, sleeping bags, coolers, tables, chairs, cookers, and just about everything we need aside from food and alcohol. It's also the time to make sure that the tent rental folks have everything set up as requested. We rent one for sleeping and a 15 by 20 or 20 by 20 for a cooking/prep area. Both depend on the number of people coming. We also rent several tables and some chairs.

Thursday is arrival day! I pick up the boys (UnYawn and Guido) at the airport. Mikey, Mustard, and Riley usually drive in. They also come loaded down with cots, cookers, and so on. Then it's off to Grinders to have a few beers and pizza with our good friend Stretch. The rest of the day is pretty much getting camp set up.

The biggest expense and probably the hardest thing to manage is food! Once we're on site we're limited to one vehicle in and out, and only for a few hours each day. So I usually plan on buying food for one day at a time. On Friday nights it's customary for us to have a big pot of gumbo or jambalaya. Friday night is party night, and if there's good weather you can expect 75,000 folks having a good time. So when I say big pot, I mean enough for a hundred! Not to mention the soft-shell crabs and fried shrimps. Breakfast is usually brisket hash, corned beef hash, or some kinda chorizo and egg scramble. Lunch can be sausage sandwiches, Baltimore bad boys, beef sammies or fried bologna sammies—the list goes on. Saturday evening, since we're competing that night, is a little simpler, usually fajitas, pork carnitas, beef noodles, or smoked chicken tacos. Now keep in mind, not only are we cooking enough food to feed twenty-five to a hundred people every time we cook, but our neighbors are doing the same, and everyone wants to share. We really do eat and drink for four days straight!

RILEY: Music is a little of everything but heavy on the blues.

MUSTARD: JJ Grey and Mofro, and it gets very eclectic from there.

MIKEY Z: We seem to always be listening to the blues, especially Stevie Ray Vaughan, Tab Benoit, JJ Grey, and John Lee Hooker.

GUIDO: When cooking competition barbecue I'm a big classic rock guy, blasting a lot of Lynyrd Skynyrd and AC/DC out there—all old-school hard rock.

Do you have any prep rituals?

UNYAWN: "UnYawns"—slang for a shot of Gentlemen Jack, preferably at 9:22 a.m. on contest day, or any day.*

RILEY: Most teams do a shot at 09:22 on "turn-in" mornings.

MUSTARD: I have an annual anxiety attack two weeks before the Royal; it's all good after that.

MIKEY Z: I like to dress up for the battle: MQC tattoo, team-issued shirt and shorts, orange Harley-Davidson visor, and orange bandana. Gets me in the zone.

GUIDO: Jack Daniel's.

What are you responsible for bringing to the competition?

UNYAWN: Due to the fact that I'm the resident Cajun, I'm responsible for bringing fresh shrimp, soft-shell crabs, andouille for the gumbo, and all the fixings for the jambalaya.

RILEY: Logistically for us, it all falls on the shoulders of the closest team member to the contest, usually Mikey, UnYawn, or myself. We're probably the only team in the USA or maybe even the world that has five members living in five different states.

MUSTARD: I usually end up with a list of the oddball one-off items for the meals—anything from a log of mortadella to one duck. (I threw the duck in for you, Mikey.)

MIKEY Z: I usually drive to the events and bring whatever is needed, but always cigars.

GUIDO: We have great parties, very memorable moments and a lot of friends in barbecue, and one of the things I'm responsible for is bringing the energy and making sure we keep it fun (or keep it weird). And a lot of times I am the resident cook, making the dishes we eat between competitions.

HOW TO BUILD A FIRE PIT

A fire pit at its most basic level is a pit built out of cinder blocks arranged to contain a large amount of hot coals (and hardwoods for smoke, of course). The cinder blocks are stacked on the ground in rows and at the second layer you leave an opening through which you can fill the pit with hot coals. A few layers up (about row four) in the cinder block walls you lay rods that run across the top of the pit. On top of these rods you can place an entire piece of expanded sheet metal or cattle fence. This will act as the grill on which you place you meats to be cooked over the fire pit.

When it comes to fire pits, there are a few principles to follow:

- Heat your coals in a separate pit and then use a shovel to place the smoldering coals into the pit.

- Once the coals are in the pit, place hardwoods such as apple or peach or pecan that will add a smoky flavor to your meats.

- Give yourself plenty of time—fire pits take a lot of coals, and it'll take 4 to 6 hours to build up enough coals to fill your fire pit and get them to just the right temperature.

---

* The 9:22 shot is a tradition across barbecue competitions, time chosen because no one is doing anything at 9:22—everybody's timing their cooking on the quarter or half hour.

Motley Que Championship Pork Butt

Now, when you're cooking barbecue for competition, you cook off a few extra butts just to make sure you get enough of the exact pieces you want. But when you're cooking with the boys of Motley Que, you cook off more than a few extra so that you have enough to enjoy the next day.

You'll see we use Royal Oak lump charcoal and split logs of wild Ozark cherry in our competition recipes because it burns consistently and, well, we just like it. Substitute a charcoal that you have faith in and a fruit-wood you prefer, as desired. And for the rubs and sauces listed, they're what we prefer and recommend, but for sauce you could substitute Blues Hog thinned out with a little apple juice (6 to 1 ratio); any rub you prefer may be substituted with success. We like Parkay margarine but any margarine will do. The solids in butter can burn.

MAKES: 2 pork butts

TIME: About 48 hours

YOU'LL NEED: Fire pit for smoking, Royal Oak lump charcoal, small split log of wild Ozark cherry wood, heavy-duty aluminum foil, plastic wrap, injector (meat syringe), large basting brush or BBQ mop, instant-read meat thermometer, insulated grilling gloves

PREP-AHEAD TIP: Make the pork marinade that gets injected into the meat one day ahead of time. Inject the meat and keep chilled in the bag the night before cooking.

1. Begin by trimming the pork butt of any bone fragments or veins that might be showing. You can trim some of the fat if you like, but remember, the fat is where the flavor is.

2. Fill the meat syringe (injector) with the Motley Que Pork Marinade. Now the fun part, injecting! I suggest you wear an apron for this. You can also cover the meat with plastic wrap to prevent any squirting. We usually use a 2-ounce kitchen injector and inject in a grid pattern, about every inch or two. Get as much injection into the meat as it will hold. After injecting you can apply a light coat of mustard, then a generous amount of rub on the meat. Double-wrap the meat in plastic, then refrigerate the meat for at least 8 hours or overnight. (Repeat with the second butt if you're making one.)

3. About 30 minutes to 1 hour before you're ready to cook your pork butt, remove it from the refrigerator and let sit at room temperature. Start a fire pit and get it to an approximate temperature of 240°F. Place the log of Ozark cherry wood on the pit.

4. Unwrap the pork butts and put them on the pit to cook. Cook for about 9 hours, or until the internal temperature of your pork butt reaches about 170°F. At this point, set each butt on a double layer of heavy-duty foil large enough to wrap the meat. Add about a cup of Guy's Carolina #6 BBQ Sauce to each butt. Wrap tightly and continue to cook until the internal meat temperature is 195°F to 200°F, about 1 more hour.

5. Remove the meat and open the foil slightly to let the meat cool a bit before handling. A good pair of insulated gloves will also come in pretty handy right now! Save the juice in the foil—you can add it back into the meat if it turns out a little dry.

6. You can use your favorite sauce if you like, but I think you'll find it's very good just the way it is.

7. Now you're ready to eat, or compete!

Two 8- to 10-pound bone-in pork butts

Motley Que Pork Marinade (recipe follows)

Yellow mustard, as needed

Smokin' Guns Hot BBQ Rub, as needed

2 cups Guy Fieri Carolina #6 BBQ Sauce

Motley Que Pork Marinade

MAKES: Enough for 1 or 2 butts

In a large saucepan over medium heat, combine all the ingredients with 2 cups spring water. Heat the mixture until the butter is melted. Let the mixture stand for 15 to 20 minutes, then load it into the meat injector.

½ cup sugar

⅓ cup kosher salt

1 cup white vinegar

1 tablespoon UnYawn (onion) powder

1 tablespoon garlic powder

1 teaspoon cayenne pepper

1 teaspoon Worcestershire powder

1½ quarts unsweetened apple juice

½ cup Butcher BBQ Pork Rub

2 sticks (1 cup) unsalted butter

←——We are not in this picture. We are over there.

Motley Que 2011 American Royal Ribs

We treat our ribs like a hen does an egg: Keep them at just the right temperature, handle with tender loving care, never let them leave our sight, and when they come out of their shell (Styrofoam container) everybody at the barnyard is impressed.

My lucky red shoes . . . (not really).

1. Apply a light coating of the Smokin' Guns rub to the ribs, followed by a heavy coat of Cimarron Doc's rub. Ensure that both rubs coat the ribs evenly all over on both sides. Leave to marinate for 2 to 3 hours, uncovered. Meanwhile, after 2 hours of marination, start a fire pit and get the temperature to 275°F. Place the Ozark cherry log onto the pit.

2. Place the ribs in the pit bone side down and smoke for 1½ hours. Flip, rotate, and paint the bone side with a heavy coating of Parkay squeeze margarine. Cook for another 1½ hours, but check regularly for doneness—the ribs should be toothpick-tender.

3. When done, place each of the racks meat side down on a large sheet of foil. Season both sides with sifted brown sugar and a tight spiral of honey. Turn the ribs meat side down and add 2 tablespoons apple juice to each rack. Wrap the foil tightly to create a sealed pouch around the ribs. Place the ribs back on the pit and cook for 30 minutes more.

4. In a saucepan over medium heat, stir together the Kansas City BBQ Sauce with the honey.

5. Remove the ribs from the pit, open the top of the foil, and carefully turn them so the meat side is up. Glaze the ribs with finishing sauce. Loosely re-cover the ribs with foil and hold warm until ready to serve.

MAKES: About 6 servings

TIME: 6 to 7 hours

YOU'LL NEED: Fire pit, Royal Oak lump charcoal, small split log of wild Ozark cherry wood, heavy-duty aluminum foil

PREP-AHEAD TIP: Make the finishing sauce up to a week ahead of time.

4 ounces Smokin' Guns Hot BBQ Rub

3 racks St. Louis–style pork ribs

8 ounces Cimarron Doc's Sweet Rib Rub

1 squeeze bottle (12 ounces) Parkay margarine

2 cups light brown sugar, sifted

1 cup orange blossom honey

6 tablespoons unsweetened apple juice

Finishing sauce

¾ cup Guy Fieri Kansas City BBQ Sauce

¼ cup orange blossom honey

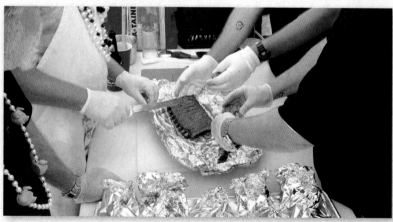

All hands on deck for the RIBS.

Motley Que American Royal Invitational First Place Chicken

When the Motley Que team does competition barbecue chicken, it's all hands to battle stations. Someone's seasoning, someone's barbecuing, and someone's basting.

MAKES: 10 to 12 servings

TIME: 2 hours (plus overnight marinating time)

YOU'LL NEED: Fire pit, Royal Oak lump charcoal, small split log of wild Ozark cherry wood, heavy-duty aluminum foil, 2 aluminum half sheet pans

PREP-AHEAD TIP: Make the finishing sauce up to a week ahead of time. The night before, season the chicken thighs and place them in half sheet pans to marinate overnight.

1. Place the chicken thighs on a half sheet pan and spread a light coating of Slabs Birds & Bones Rub. Refrigerate overnight, uncovered, to marinate.

2. Start a fire pit and get the temperature to about 275°F. Place the wild Ozark cherry wood on top of the coals.

3. Lightly season the thighs again with Head Country rub. Put ½ stick of margarine in the sheet pan, then place it over the pit so the margarine melts and coats the pan evenly. Remove the pan from the pit and place the chicken thighs back on the pan, skin side up. Top each with a pat of margarine. Cover the pan tightly with foil and place it back over the pit. Cook for 45 minutes, then remove the foil and lightly reseason the chicken with Head Country rub. Cook for 45 minutes more. When done, the chicken will be tender and have a nice deep color.

4. Meanwhile, combine the ingredients for the finishing sauce and set aside.

5. Remove the foil and baste the chicken generously with finishing sauce. Dust a second, clean half sheet pan with The Slabs Birds & Bones Rub. Transfer the chicken to the new pan and place it in the pit, uncovered, for 7 to 10 minutes, until the sauce sets and coats the chicken nicely. Remove from the pan and serve.

I think Unyawn names every one of them.

24 organic, air-chilled chicken thighs (about 7 pounds)

2½ cups (about 8 ounces) The Slabs Birds & Bones Rub

2½ cups (about 8 ounces) Head Country All-Purpose Championship Seasoning

2 sticks (1 cup) Parkay

Finishing sauce

3 cups Guy Fieri Pacific Rim Barbeque & Wok Sauce

1 cup honey

Motley Que American Royal Brisket

Our brisket takes forever, low and slow. We tend to the barbecue like a night watchman at Fort Knox, because what lies inside may just be championship gold.

MAKES: 1 large brisket, 10 to 12 servings

TIME: About 48 hours

YOU'LL NEED: Fire pit, Royal Oak lump charcoal, 5- to 6-inch split log of wild Ozark cherry wood, heavy-duty aluminum foil, meat bag, injector (meat syringe), large basting brush or BBQ mop, instant-read meat thermometer

PREP-AHEAD TIP: Make the finishing sauce up to 1 week ahead. Make the Motley Que Brisket Marinade one day ahead of time. Inject the meat and leave it in the bag, refrigerated, the night before cooking.

1. Begin by trimming the meat and removing all the silverskin from the meat side of the brisket. Leave the fat cap on to protect the meat as it cooks and keep it moist and flavorful.

2. Fill a meat syringe (injector) with the Motley Que Brisket Marinade and inject it into different points all over the meat, ensuring that it's evenly dispersed. Place the brisket in a meat bag, seal, and refrigerate overnight.

3. Start a fire pit and get the cooking temperature to 240°F. Remove the brisket from the meat bag and paint on a thin coat of yellow mustard (to help the rub adhere). Apply a light seasoning of garlic pepper, followed by a liberal amount of Head Country seasoning over the entire brisket. The coating of Head Country Rub should be so thick that you can't see the meat through the rub.

4. Place the brisket on the pit, fat side down, to cook. Place the log of wild Ozark cherry wood on top of the charcoal. The cook time is about 1 to 1½ hours per pound of meat, so the total cook time is about 20 hours (about 10 hours per side). At the halfway point, flip the meat so it's fat side up. The brisket is cooked when the internal temperature reaches 165°F to 170°F.

5. Place the brisket (fat side up) on a large sheet of foil and pour the beef broth over it. Seal tightly and place back over the pit. Cook for 1 to 2 hours longer, until the internal temperature of the brisket reaches

195°F to 205°F. When done, the brisket should have the softness and feel of Jell-O when lightly pressed.

6. Partially unwrap the brisket to vent for 15 to 20 minutes to stop the cooking process. Rewrap the meat in the foil and hold it in a cooler for 1 to 3 hours. This will allow it to firm up and slice cleanly. Slice the brisket across the grain ¼ inch thick. Cutting across the grain of the meat ensures super-tender pieces of already tender brisket!

7. In a saucepan over medium heat, combine the finishing sauce ingredients and heat through. Baste the sliced brisket with the finishing sauce and keep warm until serving.

One 16-pound Creekstone Premium Prime Angus brisket

Motley Que Brisket Marinade (recipe follows)

Yellow mustard, as needed

6 ounces garlic pepper

8 ounces Head Country All Purpose Championship Seasoning

1¾ cups beef broth

Finishing sauce

Guy Fieri Brown Sugar Bourbon Sweet and Sticky Sauce

¼ cup orange blossom honey

Motley Que Brisket Marinade

MAKES: Enough for 1 brisket

In a saucepan over medium heat, mix all ingredients together. Heat just enough for the butter to melt. Keep warm and mix well again before you inject the mixture into the meat.

1 cup beef broth

2 tablespoons Worcestershire sauce

½ teaspoon onion powder

½ teaspoon garlic powder

½ teaspoon white pepper

1 stick (½ cup) unsalted butter

½ teaspoon Colman's mustard powder

¼ cup Butcher BBQ Brisket Rub or other brisket rub

BBQ Brisket Hash with Roasted Red Pepper Hollandaise

Breakfast at a barbecue competition may be the only solid meal you get all day. Ingredients are limited and waste is not allowed. That's why the barbecue brisket hash is a staple on our team.

½ pound asparagus,
tough ends trimmed

1 tablespoon extra-virgin olive oil,
plus more for the pan

Kosher salt and freshly ground
black pepper, to taste

1 pound cooked BBQ brisket,
sliced (such as our American
Royal Brisket, page 126)

½ pound Yukon gold potatoes,
scrubbed and cut into ¾-inch dice

1 small yellow onion, sliced

½ red bell pepper,
seeded and sliced

½ green bell pepper,
seeded and sliced

2 garlic cloves, minced

Roasted Red Pepper Hollandaise
(recipe follows)

Chopped scallions, for garnish

Sliced avocado, for garnish

Smoked paprika, optional

MAKES: 4 servings

TIME: 50 minutes

YOU'LL NEED: Grill, heavy griddle, large cast-iron skillet

PREP-AHEAD TIP: Roast the red peppers for the hollandaise a couple days in advance, and you'll be a step ahead if you have leftover American Royal Brisket.

1. Preheat grill to high. Toss the asparagus with olive oil, salt, and pepper. Set a heavy griddle pan over high heat and wipe it down with olive oil. When hot, place the asparagus on the pan and cook for 2 to 3 minutes, then turn and cook 1 to 2 minutes on the other side. Remove from the grill and set aside.

2. Slice the brisket into thin, bite-size strips. Heat a large cast-iron skillet over high heat, coat with olive oil, add the brisket, and cook until crisped around the edges, 4 to 5 minutes. Season lightly with salt and pepper. Remove the brisket and set aside to keep warm.

3. Reduce the heat under the skillet by moving to the cooler side of the grill and add ¼ cup olive oil. Add the diced potatoes, season with salt and pepper, and brown on all sides. When the potatoes are about three-fourths of the way cooked, about 8 minutes, add the onion, bell peppers, and garlic. Cook for 5 to 7 minutes more, until the vegetables are cooked and caramelized. Taste for seasoning.

4. To serve, cut the asparagus into 1-inch pieces and toss with the potato mixture. Plate the hash with sliced, crisped brisket on top, drizzle with the hollandaise, and garnish with chopped scallions and sliced avocado. Dust with smoked paprika, if desired.

Roasted Red Pepper Hollandaise

1. Over a stovetop gas flame or under a broiler, char the red peppers on all sides. Put the peppers in a bowl and cover tightly with plastic wrap. After 10 minutes, remove the plastic and peel or rub the skin off each pepper. Core and seed the peppers, then set aside.

2. Put the egg yolks, lemon juice, salt, cayenne, and paprika in a blender. Blend at medium speed until the mixture lightens in color, about 25 seconds. Lower the speed and slowly begin to drizzle in the melted butter. Add the charred peppers and blend until the mixture is completely smooth. Taste for seasoning and add more salt, cayenne, or lemon juice, if desired.

MAKES: About 1 cup

TIME: 15 to 20 minutes

YOU'LL NEED: Blender

2 red bell peppers

3 large egg yolks

1 tablespoon fresh lemon juice

½ teaspoon kosher salt

Pinch of cayenne pepper

½ teaspoon smoked paprika

1 stick plus 2 tablespoons unsalted butter, melted

Red Wine Beef Stroganoff with Buttered Noodles

When cooking for a big crew of hungry dudes who've been sleeping in a parking lot, do not think you can get away with fettuccine Alfredo. You've got to think about big flavor and big portions, and noodles and beef hits the mark.

MAKES: 4 to 6 servings

TIME: 40 minutes

YOU'LL NEED: Propane burner, Dutch oven, large pot

PREP-AHEAD TIP: Mushrooms are time-consuming to clean and prep, so do those 1 day ahead of time or at least before you head out to a tailgate. Clean and portion them and hold in a paper bag in the fridge.

1. Clean the mushrooms and slice them into bite-size pieces.

2. Heat the olive oil in a large Dutch oven over medium-high heat. Add the onion, garlic, mushrooms, and thyme and sauté for 4 to 5 minutes, or until the mushrooms are golden brown and the onion is caramelized. Add the ground beef and cook until browned, breaking it up with a wooden spoon as it cooks. Season with salt and pepper.

My Beef with Lori's Noodles

One of the first things, and maybe one of the only things, that Lori was really interested in cooking for me when we first met was this dish called Noodles and Beef, which consisted of egg noodles, ground beef, and canned gravy. Now, as ridiculous as this may sound and as simple as this dish may be, sometimes when I just wasn't interested in cooking or I was getting home late, there was something comforting about having her Noodles and Beef. Hunter loved Noodles and Beef; Ryder loved Noodles and Beef; everybody loved Noodles and Beef. So one day I decided I would show Hunter how to make noodles and beef the "correct" way, with a roux and all. I finished the dish and served it up, Hunter looked at me and said, "Man, this noodles and beef is really good, but Mom's is better." I was crushed. Culinarily speaking, mine was superior. But if you're brought up on something, it just doesn't matter.

Red wine beef stroganoff

1¼ pounds assorted mushrooms (such as cremini, white button, portobello, shiitake, oyster, chanterelle)

1 tablespoon extra-virgin olive oil

1 large yellow onion, diced

2 garlic cloves, minced

2 fresh thyme sprigs

1½ pounds ground beef (80/20 blend)

Kosher salt and freshly ground black pepper

2 tablespoons all-purpose flour

1½ cups dry red wine

1 bay leaf

2 cups low-sodium beef broth

2 teaspoons Worcestershire sauce

1 cup sour cream

1 tablespoon Dijon mustard

Buttered noodles

1 pound egg noodles

2 tablespoons unsalted butter

2 tablespoons extra-virgin olive oil

2 tablespoons chopped fresh parsley

Kosher salt and freshly ground black pepper, to taste

3. Sprinkle in the flour and stir to combine and create a roux. Add the red wine, scraping any brown bits from the bottom of the pan and stirring to avoid lumps. Add the bay leaf, broth, and Worcestershire, stir well, and bring to a simmer. Reduce the heat to medium-low and cook for 20 minutes, or until the sauce has come together and is rich and silky.

4. Meanwhile, cook the egg noodles according to package instructions. Drain and immediately toss with the butter, olive oil, parsley, salt, and pepper. The warm pasta will melt the butter and soak it up as you toss together. Set aside and cover to keep warm.

5. Remove the beef stroganoff from heat. Add the sour cream and Dijon mustard and stir well. Taste and give it a final season with salt and pepper. Serve with the warm buttered noodles.

Smoked Chicken Tacos with Roasted Red Pepper Salsa

When we're cooking for competition there's always some chicken that doesn't make the cut for "turn-in" to the judges, and when that happens (and hopefully it does), this dish is on the menu that night. The touch of smoke on the chicken thighs along with the roasted red pepper salsa will change the way you think of chicken tacos forever.

TIME: 45 minutes

MAKES: 4 to 6 servings

YOU'LL NEED: Grill or burner, sauté pan

PREP-AHEAD TIP: Make the salsa 2 or 3 days ahead of time and store in the fridge. This recipe is great for leftover chicken, so the chicken can be done 2 to 3 days beforehand.

1. To roast the red peppers, rub the outside of the peppers with a teaspoon of the olive oil. Place the peppers directly over an open flame and char all sides, about 2 minutes. Place the peppers in a large bowl and cover with plastic wrap. After 2 minutes, remove the peppers and peel off the charred skin. Remove the core and seeds. Roughly chop and set aside.

2. To make the red pepper salsa, in a sauté pan over medium heat, sauté the onion and garlic in 1 tablespoon olive oil until lightly browned, about 5 minutes. Stir in the balsamic vinegar and pour the entire mixture into the food processor. Add the roasted red peppers, tomatoes, and cumin and season with a little salt and pepper. Pulse to combine and slowly drizzle in the ¼ cup olive oil. The salsa should remain slightly chunky.

3. In a small bowl, combine the avocado, mango, and red onion with a squeeze of lime juice and a pinch of salt. Set aside.

4. In a nonstick pan over high heat, add 2 teaspoons olive oil and sear chicken for 2 to 3 minutes to reheat—this also browns and crisps the chicken a little.

5. To assemble, warm up the tortillas, either on a grill or in a dry sauté pan—about 45 seconds per side over high heat. Use 2 tortillas per taco to form a sturdy base. Place the cabbage in the center of the tortilla, followed by a heaping spoonful of the chicken. Drizzle the red pepper salsa over the top along with a few small dollops of sour cream. Garnish with the avocado mixture and a sprinkle of cilantro. Serve with the lime wedges.

Roasted red pepper salsa

2 medium red bell peppers

1 tablespoon plus 1 teaspoon olive oil, divided

½ red onion, sliced

3 garlic cloves, minced

3 tablespoons balsamic vinegar

¼ cup fire-roasted tomatoes

½ teaspoon ground cumin

Kosher salt and freshly ground black pepper

¼ cup olive oil

Chicken tacos

2 teaspoons olive oil

2 cups BBQ chicken, pulled (see page 124)

Twelve 6-inch corn tortillas

Garnish

1 ripe avocado, finely diced

1 mango, finely diced

½ red onion, finely diced

1 lime, juiced

Pinch of kosher salt

¼ head green cabbage, thinly sliced

½ cup sour cream

¼ cup chopped cilantro

2 limes, cut into small wedges

Smoked Chicken, Sausage, and Andouille Gumbo

Recipe courtesy of Ron Walker

I judge every gumbo I eat off of one of the best gumbos I've ever had, and that's this one—which comes from our team brother Ron "UnYawn" Walker.

MAKES: 6 to 8 servings

TIME: 1½ hours, plus 4 hours smoking time

YOU'LL NEED: Smoker, propane burner, pecan wood, large stockpot

PREP-AHEAD TIP: This recipe works great with leftover American Royal Chicken (page 124)—just be sure you've reserved the bones to make the stock.

1. Prep smoker, heat wood until smoldering and smoking at about 275°F.

2. To prepare the chicken (unless you're using leftover smoked chicken), cut the chicken in half and season with granulated garlic, salt, and black pepper. Smoke the bird with pecan wood for 4 hours, until the chicken is almost falling apart. Debone the chicken, keeping the pieces of meat as large as possible, and reserve the bones. Refrigerate the meat in a sealed container until needed.

3. To prepare the stock, put the chicken bones in a large pot with 1 gallon of cold water. Add 2 teaspoons kosher salt and set over high heat. Bring to a boil, lower the heat, and simmer for at least 2 hours (or until you've got a deep, smoke-flavored chicken stock). Strain the bones out of the stock and set aside.

4. To make the gumbo, start by making a roux.* In a large pot over medium-high heat, combine the flour and oil. Cook, stirring con-

---

* Important Roux Tip (or You'll Ruin the Day): Keep stirring the roux to keep the flour moving; it will burn very fast! If you see any black specks or if it smells burned . . . it is burned! Throw it away and start over. This roux will have a nutty aroma, so don't be confused. You want to slowly brown your roux to a dark chocolate color, which will result in a dark, rich gumbo!

stantly, for 15 to 20 minutes, until it turns a dark chocolate brown. (A flat-bottom wooden spatula works best, as you can scrape the flour from the bottom of the pot and move it around easily.)

5. Push the roux to one side of the pot and add the onions, celery, bell pepper, and garlic. Sauté for 5 to 6 minutes, then add 1 cup of the reserved chicken stock and mix together well. This keeps things from sticking. Cook until the vegetables are translucent, about 7 to 8 minutes.

6. Add the smoked sausage and andouille sausage to the pot and cook for a few minutes, until the sausage browns a little. Add 3½ cups of the chicken stock and stir well with a whisk to ensure that there are no lumps. When the mixture is smooth, bring to a simmer, then reduce the heat to low. Simmer for about 1 hour, or until the gumbo is nice and thick. The sauce should be smooth and thickened, the sausage and vegetables tender, and the color a rich dark brown. Add salt, black pepper, and cayenne to taste.

7. Add the chopped scallions and parsley and serve over steamed white rice, with sliced French bread and butter on the side.

Smoked chicken

One 4- to 5-pound chicken

1½ tablespoons granulated garlic

Kosher salt and freshly ground black pepper

Gumbo

⅓ cup all-purpose flour

⅓ cup vegetable oil

2 large onions, chopped

4 celery stalks, chopped

1 green bell pepper, chopped

⅓ cup minced garlic

1 pound smoked sausage, cubed

12 ounces andouille sausage, cubed

Cayenne pepper

⅓ cup chopped scallions

2 tablespoons chopped fresh flat-leaf parsley

Steamed white rice, for serving

French bread and butter, for serving

Chicken, Pork, and Sausage Jambalaya

Recipe courtesy of Ron Walker

I pride myself on my jambalaya: the ingredients, the technique, the spirituality, the mojo, and the bon temps. But I gotta be honest—the man who taught me how to do it, right there on the grounds of the American Royal, is none other than my team member, Mr. Jambalaya himself, Mr. Ron "UnYawn" Walker.

The beginning of ten years of trouble!

MAKES: 16 to 18 servings

TIME: 1 hour

YOU'LL NEED: Propane burner, stock pot

PREP-AHEAD TIP: This one you're gonna want to cook at the tailgate start to finish, so it's all about the prep and mise en place beforehand to make life easier. Chop all your vegetables and proteins and measure everything else so all you have to do is cook and assemble on-site.

1. In a large heavy pot over medium heat, fry the bacon until it's crisp and the fat has rendered. Transfer the bacon to a plate and set aside. Add the pork butt to the fat and fry hard and fast until it's dark brown and just starting to stick, 8 to 10 minutes. Keep stirring and scraping the pot to make the "graton" (little crumbs of highly caramelized pork), another 2 to 3 minutes. Add the onions, celery, bell pepper, and garlic and sauté until browned and the onions are translucent, about 5 minutes. Add the chicken and cook until browned, 4 to 5 minutes. Add the sausage and cook for 2 to 3 minutes to brown a little as well.

2. Add 1 cup water to deglaze the pan, then bring it to a boil. Scrape up any brown bits from the bottom of the pan and add the thyme and bay leaves. When the liquid is boiling, reduce the heat to medium, then whisk in the roux, stirring vigorously to keep lumps from forming. Once fully incorporated, reduce the heat to a simmer and cook for 10 minutes, stirring occasionally or until the sauce is smooth and lightly thickened. Season with the salt, pepper, and cayenne.

3. Add the rice and 2 quarts water to the pot and mix well. Increase the heat to high and bring it to a simmer, giving the pan a shake to level the rice. Reduce the heat to medium-low so it stays at a steady simmer. Cook for 15 to 20 minutes, stirring every 4 or 5 minutes, scraping to get the rice off the bottom of the pot. If the rice starts to dry out too much (it varies depending on how much moisture is in the vegetables and the size of the pot), add up to 2 cups more water as required (but no more than 10 cups total). Cook until almost all the liquid is cooked off.

4. Add the scallions and parsley, stir one last time, turn off the heat, and cover. Let the jambalaya sit for 30 minutes undisturbed—do not uncover! Your patience will be rewarded. Okay, now you can open the lid and enjoy.

¼ pound thick-cut applewood smoked bacon

2½ pounds boneless Boston pork butt, cut into 1-inch cubes

2 large yellow onions, diced

4 celery stalks, finely diced

1 large red bell pepper, diced

2 teaspoons minced garlic

2½ pounds boneless chicken thighs, cut into 1-inch pieces

2½ pounds smoked sausage, sliced

¼ pound andouille sausage, sliced

1 tablespoon fresh thyme leaves

2 bay leaves

1 cup roux (see page 134)

1 tablespoon plus 1 teaspoon kosher salt

1 tablespoon freshly ground black pepper

½ teaspoon cayenne pepper, or to taste

5 cups (about 2½ pounds) converted rice (such as Uncle Ben's)

½ cup sliced scallions

½ cup chopped fresh flat-leaf parsley

Since I was ten years old, our lake cabin in Northern California has been one of the greatest places in the world for my entire family. The day after we leave, we look forward to returning. Now, let me just explain a few things about the setup: We don't have running water or electricity, and up until about fifteen years ago we didn't even have a cabin—we had a bunch of decks built on a steep slope at the end of the lake and a dock sitting on the water. But even though we didn't have amenities like walls, windows, doors, and refrigeration, it's always been my family's favorite place. Canoeing, wake boarding, fishing, campfires—and of course, cooking—were the staples of my upbringing.

This rustic setting might seem culinarily challenged, but my family, friends, and I have made some of the greatest meals ever on a propane stove and a charcoal grill. This is my hallowed ground, where my culinary experiences and creativity started in earnest. There were very few things in the pantry, very limited resources, and the store was a fifteen-minute boat ride and a forty-five-minute drive away. So, trust me, you didn't want to screw it up and burn the pork chops.

We spent weeks at a time at the lake—and that only increased everyone's expectations for creative menus. So cross-utilizing ingredients, properly applying leftovers, and making menu planning a priority only added to the unbelievable spreads we served up. Just as in tailgating, there's a lot of pride in the menu you make at your cabin up on the lake. When you run into people while you're getting gas at the marina, you're sure to be asked, "What did you guys make for dinner?" When I was a kid I don't think people believed us half the time, 'cause *nobody* makes *egg rolls* when they're camping at the lake. Now, this could be a whole book about cooking at the lake, but it's just one chapter of my experiences in outdoor cooking. I hope you enjoy some of the lake's greatest hits.

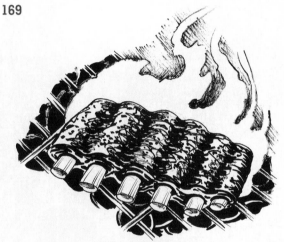

The Menu Rules

A week before we leave for the lake, Lori will be all over me with, "What is the *menu?*" With good reason, as certain tricks of the trade must happen when we prepare to leave, starting with the proteins. For example, when we're going to be there for seven to ten days and we're taking pork (frozen pork loin, say) we have to determine when we're going to use it. We'll have one cooler set up to hold its temperature for a long time, along with three or four frozen chickens and maybe some frozen tri-tip. The goal will be to keep it properly iced, and layering the cooler with what's going to be used last on the bottom and first on the top is key. In addition, how we ration the milk, the cream for the coffee, the pasta—everything we bring—is decided ahead of time. A menu has to be determined and followed. There's nothing worse than someone going off the path and taking the cabbage to make some coleslaw when it was supposed to be used in the Moroccan Chicken Tagine. And remember, we have to bring it all across on the boat, restocking for ice first at the marina and then the store—and then haul it all up the hill to the cabin. (That last part sucks.)

Chicken-Fried Steak with Mushroom Gravy

Although it's sunny and hot at the lake, when the sun goes down some of the nights are a little bit chilly, and with the level we play at, people are hungry. So this recipe is a mainstay for dinner when we've had a day packed with activity.

1. Cut the beef into 4 equal thick slices. Put each slice between sheets of plastic wrap or thick resealable bags and use the textured side of a meat mallet to pound it ¼ inch thick. Put the meat in a shallow glass or plastic dish and cover with the buttermilk, turning to coat. Set the meat aside.

2. Next, prepare the dredging station. Put the flour in a large baking dish, and season generously with salt and pepper. In a second dish, whisk the eggs and milk. Season with salt and pepper. In a third dish, combine the crushed breading mix and the panko. Season with salt and pepper as well.

BBQ MVP

A zip-top bag is second to none when it comes to cheap, super-useful BBQ gear to have on hand. The thicker the better, and get the strongest reseal you can find. They're great for marinating, as piping bags, for tenderizing, and for coating and dredging, not to mention one of my all-time favorites, cracker smashing. They also do double duty for transporting ingredients, such as marinated meat. Plus, a thick, resealable bag can even work for reheating meals or sous vide, if you want to get fancy with your cooking techniques.

MAKES: 4 servings

TIME: 25 minutes

YOU'LL NEED: Stovetop or propane burner, oven, cast-iron pan

PREP-AHEAD TIP: Pound out the top round the day before, then wrap in plastic and refrigerate until you're ready to dredge and cook. Collect leftover bread products before and during the trip to make "Whatever You Have" Breading.

1 pound boneless top round, trimmed

1½ cups buttermilk

2 cups all-purpose flour

Kosher salt and freshly ground black pepper

3 large eggs

¼ cup milk

2 cups "Whatever You Have" Breading (recipe follows)

1½ cups panko (Japanese breadcrumbs)

1 cup canola oil

1 lemon, cut into wedges

Chopped fresh flat-leaf parsley, for garnish

Mushroom gravy

2 garlic cloves, minced

1 medium shallot, minced

½ cup morel mushrooms, cleaned

2 cups cremini mushrooms, cleaned and cut into ⅜-inch slices

1 teaspoon fresh thyme leaves

½ cup dry white wine

Pinch of cayenne pepper

Kosher salt and freshly ground black pepper

3 tablespoons unsalted butter

¼ cup all-purpose flour

1½ cups whole milk

1 cup low-sodium chicken broth

1 teaspoon Dijon mustard

3. Remove the steaks from the buttermilk, then dip each piece in the flour to coat, shaking off the excess flour. Next, coat them in the egg wash, then dip them in the cracker and panko mixture, gently pressing the crumbs into the steak. Set the steaks aside to rest for 10 minutes.

4. Preheat the oven to 325°F.

5. Heat the canola oil in large cast-iron pan over high heat. When the oil is shimmering, add one steak to the pan and cook for 3 minutes on the first side, until golden brown. Cook one steak at a time so as not to overcrowd the pan, and do not move the steak around, so that the coating stays intact and gets nice and crsipy. Use tongs to turn the steak very carefully, then cook for 2 to 3 minutes on the second side, or until the meat is cooked through and the coating is crispy. Repeat with the remaining steaks. As you finish the steaks, transfer them to a paper towel–lined baking sheet to remove the excess oil. Keep warm in the preheated oven while you make the mushroom gravy.

6. Pour the oil out of the pan into a heatproof bowl. Wipe out any crumbs from the pan with a paper towel and discard. Pour 3 table-spoons of the cooking oil back into the pan and set it over medium-high heat. Add the garlic, shallot, mushrooms, and thyme and sauté for 5 to 7 minutes, or until the mushrooms are golden brown. Deglaze the pan with the white wine and simmer until the liquid is almost completely reduced. Season with cayenne, salt, and pepper, then add 2 tablespoons of the butter and the flour and cook, stirring, for 2 to 3 more minutes to make a roux. Whisk in the milk and chicken broth and simmer until the gravy is thickened, about 4 to 5 minutes. Taste for seasoning. Finish with the remaining 1 tablespoon butter and the mustard.

7. Arrange the steaks on a serving platter and smother with the mush-room gravy. Serve with a wedge of lemon and garnish with parsley.

"Whatever You Have" Breading

This is what we call cross-utilization: The idea is to be resourceful when you're out camping. Use whatever crispy, crunchy bread, crackers, or savory snacks you have to create a delicious crispy coating on this awesome chicken-fried steak (or anything else that deserves a crunchy coating). Here are some examples of what you can crush up, or toast and then crush:

Butter crackers (e.g., Ritz)

Saltines

Wheat crackers (e.g., Triscuits)

Unsweetened plain granola

Bread (e.g., sliced and toasted sourdough, baguette, or any loaf bread)

Pretzels

Potato chips

Place the mixture in a resealable plastic bag and crush it to the texture of breadcrumbs, then fortify it by mixing in panko breadcrumbs for a super-convenient crunchy bread coating. Just remember that crackers and pretzels often have salt, so adjust your seasoning accordingly.

Bone-In Double-Cut Pork Chops with Brie and Apples

Pork is like my canvas; it takes on all the great flavors inspired by the imagination. That's my way of saying you can do just about anything with pork. Here's one of my favorites. On a night at the lake when we're really celebrating or doing something special, a brined bone-in double-cut pork chop makes people feel like they're eating at a restaurant even while roughing it in the great outdoors. And the beauty of it is, as fancy as it seems, this is practically a one-fry-pan dish.

Brine and pork chops

½ cup light brown sugar

¼ cup apple cider vinegar

2 tablespoons kosher salt, plus more for sprinkling

1 tablespoon granulated garlic

1 tablespoon black peppercorns

1 tablespoon dried thyme

1 teaspoon mustard powder

Pinch of dried red pepper flakes

2 cups ice cubes

2 double-cut, bone-in pork loin chops (1 bone per chop), about 1½ inches thick, approximately 1 pound each

Kosher salt and freshly ground black pepper

Extra-virgin olive oil

4 ounces Brie cheese, sliced

MAKES: 2 to 4 servings

TIME: 1 hour 55 minutes

YOU'LL NEED: Stovetop or propane burner, large saucepan, cast-iron pan, kitchen twine, foil or lid, instant-read thermometer

PREP-AHEAD TIP: Brine the chops for 2 or 3 hours, but no longer. Remove them from the brine and tie the chops. At this stage you can store them in the fridge or transport to where you need them and keep chilled until ready to cook.

1. To make the brine, combine 2 cups water, the brown sugar, vinegar, 2 tablespoons salt, garlic, peppercorns, thyme, mustard powder, and red pepper flakes in a large saucepan and set it over high heat. Bring to a simmer and stir until the sugar has dissolved. Remove from the heat and add the ice cubes to bring down the temperature. When the ice cubes have melted, pour the brine into a resealable plastic container or freezer bag and add the pork chops. Refrigerate for at least 1 hour and up to 3.

2. Preheat a cast-iron pan over high heat.

3. Remove the pork chops from the brine and discard the brine. Pat the chops dry with paper towels (removing the excess moisture on the surface allows the pork to sear and caramelize). Tie each chop around the perimeter with a piece of kitchen twine. This will help the chops retain a nice, round shape while cooking. Sprinkle lightly with salt and pepper.

4. Coat the pan with oil and when it starts to smoke, add the pork chops to the pan. Cook over high heat until well browned, 8 to 10 minutes. Turn the chops over and reduce the heat to medium to allow the chops to cook through until golden brown, about 8 minutes.

5. Divide the slices of Brie between the chops, layering them evenly so the meat is well covered. Place a metal bowl or sheet of foil loosely over the chops and cook until the Brie has just melted and the pork has cooked to 140°F. Transfer the chops to a platter to rest while you make the sauce.

6. Add a drizzle of olive oil to the pan and raise the heat to high. Add the apple and onion and saute for 4 to 5 minutes, then add the apple brandy. Allow the alcohol to cook off (you can flambé at this stage if desired by igniting the brandy in the pan). Once the brandy has reduced, add the broth and simmer. Season with salt and pepper to taste. Allow the sauce to reduce for 2 to 3 minutes, then remove from the heat and swirl in the cold butter cubes. This will thicken the sauce and give it a nice sheen. Serve the Brie-topped pork chops with the sauce.

Pan sauce

Extra-virgin olive oil

1 green apple, such as Granny Smith, unpeeled, cored, and sliced

½ sweet onion, such as Vidalia, roughly sliced

¼ cup apple brandy (such as Calvados) or plain rum

½ cup low-sodium chicken broth

Kosher salt and freshly ground black pepper

2 tablespoons cold unsalted butter, cubed

Pancakes, Sweet and Savory

I'm not a guy who can eat breakfast at dinnertime. It's always driven me crazy that people can do that. But sometimes you find yourself with limited ingredients and you need to improvise. A pancake is a medium that you can take sweet or savory, call it a thick crepe or a wide Johnny cake. But when you make a lot of pancake batter, you can improvise all you like. It's a good, hot base for breakfast, lunch, or dinner, and very outdoor cooking friendly.

MAKES: 16 pancakes

TIME: 15 minutes

YOU'LL NEED: Stovetop, propane burner, or grill, nonstick skillet or griddle

PREP-AHEAD TIP: When packing this one up to go (or simply trying to get ahead of the game), mix the dry ingredients together and store, and mix the wet ingredients together and refrigerate. This can be done the night before, and then the morning of, mix both together to make your pancake base.

Basic Sweet Pancakes

2 cups all-purpose flour

2 teaspoons baking powder

1 teaspoon baking soda

2 tablespoons sugar

1 teaspoon salt

1½ cups buttermilk

2 large eggs

¼ cup unsalted butter, melted, plus more for cooking

Maple syrup, for serving

1. Combine the flour, baking powder, baking soda, sugar, and salt in a medium bowl. Pour the buttermilk into a large bowl, then whisk in the eggs and melted butter. Pour the flour mixture into the wet mixture and whisk until the lumps are gone.

2. Heat a large skillet or griddle over medium heat (on a stovetop, propane burner, or grill) and brush with melted butter.

3. Use a ¼-cup measure to pour the batter onto the hot skillet. Cook the pancakes until bubbles appear on the surface. Flip with a spatula and cook until browned on the other side.

Ricotta-Orange Pancakes

1. Mix 1 teaspoon of the orange zest into the sweet pancake batter.

2. Using a hand mixer, whip the ricotta, powdered sugar, and remaining orange zest for 30 to 60 seconds, until the mixture is light and fluffy.

3. Serve the pancakes with a heaping tablespoon of whipped ricotta, a few orange segments, and maple syrup. Dust with more powdered sugar.

Basic Sweet Pancakes batter (preceding recipe)

1 orange, grated zest and segments

1 cup ricotta cheese

¼ cup powdered sugar, plus more for dusting

Maple syrup, for serving

MORE SWEET VARIATIONS

- Top with sautéed sliced peaches and toasted pecans.

- Mix in peanut butter and top with raspberry preserves and crushed peanuts.

- Mix in poppy seeds and lemon zest and top with blackberries.

Basic Savory Pancakes

1. Combine the flour, baking powder, baking soda, and salt in a medium bowl. Pour the buttermilk into a large bowl, then whisk in the eggs and melted butter. Pour the flour mixture into the wet mixture and whisk until the lumps are gone.

2. Heat a large skillet or griddle over medium heat (stovetop, burner, or grill) and brush with melted butter. Use a ¼-cup measure to pour the batter onto the hot skillet. Cook the pancakes until bubbles appear on the surface. Flip with a spatula and cook until browned on the other side.

2 cups all-purpose flour

2 teaspoons baking powder

1 teaspoon baking soda

1 teaspoon salt

1½ cups buttermilk

2 large eggs

½ stick (¼ cup) unsalted butter, melted, plus more for cooking

Turkey, Green Chile, and Swiss Pancakes

Basic Savory Pancakes batter
(preceding recipe)

½ cup diced roasted green chiles

1 tablespoon butter, melted

1 cup shredded Swiss cheese

1 cup diced roasted turkey

Sour cream, for garnish

Chopped scallions, for garnish

1. Fold the green chiles into the pancake batter.

2. Heat a large skillet or griddle over medium heat (stovetop, burner, or grill) and brush with melted butter. Use a ¼-cup measure to pour the batter onto the skillet, scatter 1 tablespoon of cheese and 1 tablespoon of turkey atop each pancake, and cook until bubbles appear on the surface. Flip with a spatula and cook until browned on the other side.

3. Serve with a dollop of sour cream and chopped scallions.

MORE SAVORY VARIATIONS

- Fold some browned, crumbled sausage with sautéed red peppers and grated Fontina cheese into the savory pancake batter.

- Serve sautéed leeks and mushrooms over basic savory pancakes.

- Fold crumbled bacon into the basic savory pancake batter. Top the cooked pancakes with sliced Brie cheese, pop under the broiler to melt, then serve.

- Fold diced ham, sliced scallions, and grated pepper Jack cheese into the basic savory mix.

- Spoon warmed leftover chili onto the pancakes, top with grated cheese, and broil to serve.

Maple Nut Granola and Other Variations

I have many great childhood memories from the lake, and one of them is my mother's homemade granola. The great thing about granola is that—a lot like an omelet or a stew—whatever you have on hand can go in there.

1. Preheat the oven to 325°F. Line 2 large rimmed sheet pans with aluminum foil.

2. Combine the oats, nuts, salt, and cinnamon in a large bowl. In a small saucepan over low heat, warm the oil, butter, and maple syrup. Add the vanilla and pour over the oats and nuts. Toss to combine and coat evenly.

3. Spread the mixture evenly on the sheet pans and bake until fragrant and golden brown, about 20 minutes, stirring once. Cool, then mix in the dried fruit. Store in an airtight container.

OTHER GRANOLA FLAVOR VARIATIONS:

Use the basic granola recipe above and add the following ingredients for three different variations.

MAKES: 10 servings

TIME: 25 minutes

YOU'LL NEED: Oven, sheet pans

PREP-AHEAD TIP: This granola can be made ahead and stored for 2 to 3 weeks in an airtight container.

3 cups rolled oats

½ cup pecans, roughly chopped

½ cup almonds, roughly chopped

½ teaspoon kosher salt

1 teaspoon ground cinnamon

½ cup canola oil

2 tablespoons unsalted butter

¼ cup maple syrup

1 teaspoon vanilla extract

½ cup golden raisins

½ cup chopped dried apricots

Healthy Granola

¼ cup flax seed

¼ cup oat bran

¼ cup sunflower seeds

¼ cup pepitas (pumpkin seeds)

3 tablespoons agave syrup (in place of the maple syrup)

3 tablespoons wheat germ

Add the flax seed, oat bran, sunflower seeds, and pepitas to the original mix before roasting. Replace the maple syrup with agave. Fold in the wheat germ at the finish when mixing in the fruit.

Peanut Butter and Jelly Granola

1 cup unsalted peanuts, roughly chopped

½ cup good-quality strawberry jam

½ cup chunky peanut butter

½ cup dried cranberries

½ cup dried strawberries

Add the peanuts to the base mixture. Replace the maple syrup in the wet mixture with jam when melting the butter, and also add peanut butter at that stage. Substitute dried cranberries and dried strawberries for the dried apricots and raisins in original recipe.

Tropical Granola

½ cup cashews

½ cup macadamia nuts

1 cup flaked coconut

6 tablespoons brown sugar

¼ cup chopped dried pineapple

¼ cup chopped dried mango

½ cup banana chips

Add the cashews, macadamias, and coconut to the base mixture before baking. Use brown sugar in place of maple syrup in the wet mixture. Add the dried pineapple, mango, and banana chips in place of raisins and dried apricots.

Queso Fundido with Fresh Tortilla Chips

If there's one thing we love to do when we're at the lake, it's snack. And nothing is better than a little melted cheese, chorizo, jalapeño, beans, and green chile all mixed together as a dip for fresh-fried tortilla chips.

MAKES: 6 to 8 servings

TIME: 30 minutes

YOU'LL NEED: Stovetop and oven, cast-iron skillet or pot

PREP-AHEAD TIP: You can brown the chorizo the night before. You can also make the cheese sauce the day before, but when you reheat it, just thin it out with a bit more beer to loosen it. Don't fold the chorizo in until you're ready to serve— you need to keep that great contrast in texture.

3 or 4 medium poblano peppers

1 link fresh chorizo, casing removed

½ yellow onion, minced

1 serrano chile, seeded and minced

2 garlic cloves, minced

½ cup shredded Oaxaca cheese

½ cup shredded mozzarella cheese

1 cup shredded sharp Cheddar cheese

1 tablespoon all-purpose flour

½ cup dark beer

½ cup pinto beans, drained and rinsed

Chopped scallions, for garnish

Diced Roma (plum) tomato, for garnish

Homemade Tortilla Chips (recipe follows)

1. Begin by roasting the poblanos. Place them over an open flame on the stovetop or grill and char all over. Cook until completely blackened on all sides (3 or 4 minutes per side). Remove from heat, place in a large bowl, and cover tightly with plastic so they sweat. Let sit for 5 minutes, then remove from the bowl and rub off the skins. Discard the skins, remove the seeds and stems, and dice the chiles. Set aside.

2. Preheat the oven to 400°F.

3. In a large cast-iron skillet, cook the chorizo over medium heat, breaking it up with a wooden spoon as it renders, 7 or 8 minutes. Add the onion, serrano, and garlic and cook until the chorizo is crisp and onion is translucent, 6 or 7 minutes. Transfer the mixture to a bowl (reserve the skillet).

4. In a medium bowl, toss the cheeses with the flour.

5. Add the beer to the skillet, stirring and scraping up any brown bits on the bottom. Whisking constantly, add the cheese a bit at a time, until the mixture is smooth and well-blended. Stir in the beans, roasted poblanos, and chorizo mixture. Finish in the oven until hot and bubbly, about 12 minutes. Garnish with chopped scallions and diced tomato and serve with tortilla chips.

Homemade Tortilla Chips

MAKES: 4 servings

TIME: 20 minutes

YOU'LL NEED: Stovetop or propane burner, cast-iron skillet, frying thermometer

Vegetable oil, for frying

8 flour or corn tortillas

Fine sea salt

Ground cumin, optional

Fresh lime juice, optional

1. Heat 1 inch of oil in a large cast-iron skillet to 350°F. Stack the tortillas and, using a knife or pizza cutter, slice each into 6 or 8 wedges, depending on the desired size. Once the oil is up to temperature, fry a few chips at a time, turning with a slotted spoon, until crisp and lightly browned, about 1 minute per side.

2. Drain the chips on a paper towel–lined plate and immediately season with salt. If desired, sprinkle lightly with cumin and finish with a squeeze of fresh lime juice.

My camping culinary arsenal.

Beef Ribs with Orange BBQ Sauce

I don't think beef ribs get enough BBQ love, usually because people don't cook them long enough, so they are too chewy. Well, not these babies, they're fall-off-the-bone tender.

MAKES: 6 to 8 servings

TIME: 3 to 3½ hours (plus overnight marinade)

YOU'LL NEED: Grill, 3 roasting trays, basting brush, spice grinder, heavy-duty aluminum foil

PREP-AHEAD TIP: Make the dry rub ahead of time and keep in an airtight container. Dry-rub the ribs the night before and store in the fridge. The BBQ sauce can be made 1 or 2 days in advance and stored in an airtight container in the fridge.

1. Begin by toasting the fennel seeds in a dry pan over medium-high heat. Toast for 4 or 5 minutes, until they become fragrant; toss occasionally as they toast so they don't burn. Transfer to a spice grinder and grind to a fine powder.

2. Rinse the ribs in cool water and pat dry with paper towels. Unless your butcher has already done so, remove the membrane from the back and trim off any excess fat. Combine the dry rub ingredients in a small bowl and mix well. Coat both sides of the meat with a heavy layer of the dry rub. Refrigerate overnight, uncovered.

3. Heat half the grill to medium to create indirect heat.

4. Set out a few large sheets of foil (one for each slab). Divide the sliced onion and thyme between the sheets and spread them out evenly. Place 1 rack on each sheet, meat side down, and fold the foil over to form a sealed pouch around each rack. Place each pouch on a roasting tray (to keep foil from getting pierced and letting steam out) and grill it over indirect heat for 2 hours.

3 racks center-cut beef ribs (8 or 9 pounds total)

1 sweet onion, peeled and cut into ¼-inch rings

6 fresh thyme sprigs

Dry rub

2 teaspoons fennel seeds

¼ cup kosher salt

¼ cup dark brown sugar

¼ cup cracked mustard seed

½ cup paprika

2 tablespoons freshly ground black pepper

2 tablespoons cayenne pepper

¼ cup granulated garlic

5. Open the foil and peel it back so the ribs are exposed. Carefully turn the meat over so the meat side is on top, then cook for 1½ hours with the foil open. When done, the ribs will be tender and the meat will have shrunk back from the bones.

6. For the last 10 minutes, remove the ribs from the foil and place them directly on the hot side of the grill. Brush with the Orange BBQ Sauce and allow the heat to caramelize the sauce and crisp the exterior, then flip the ribs and brush the other side for the final 5 minutes. Serve with additional sauce.

Orange BBQ Sauce

1 cup ketchup

¼ cup apple cider vinegar

¼ cup molasses

1 cup orange juice

1 tablespoon onion powder

2 garlic cloves, minced

1 teaspoon honey

2 tablespoons Worcestershire sauce

1 tablespoon balsamic vinegar

2 tablespoons orange marmalade

1 teaspoon dried red pepper flakes

MAKES: About 1½ cups

Whisk together all the ingredients in a medium saucepan and simmer over medium-low heat for 25 to 30 minutes, until it reaches a ketchup-like consistency.

Beef Ribs with Orange BBQ Sauce.

Moroccan Chicken Tagine with Spicy Tahini Sauce

On the cooler days at the lake, I like to make the lunches more substantial than your typical deli sandwiches and hot dogs. This one will get them to show up. And if you're worried about spending all morning explaining what in the world a tagine is, just tell them it's awesome stewed chicken and get back to your hiking and swimming.

Spice mixture

1 preserved lemon, pulp removed, peel chopped and reserved for garnish (see page 63)

2 teaspoons paprika

1 teaspoon ground cumin

1 teaspoon ground ginger

1 teaspoon ground cinnamon

1 tablespoon kosher salt

1½ teaspoons freshly ground black pepper

Hunter rockin' the wave surf.

Campfire Dutch Ovens

Look at how a lot of Dutch ovens are made and you'll see that the lid can be turned upside down while still keeping a seal on the pot. The whole thing is so thick and solid that you can stick the pot directly down into the fire and put a few coals on top of the flipped lid. If you're tackling this method, build the fire in a three-quarter circle, and place the Dutch oven in the middle of it. You surround it with heat, but you also need a spot to reach in without having to reach over the fire. Just remember to rotate the pot every once in a while. The Dutch oven is made for campfire cooking.

MAKES: 4 to 6 servings

TIME: 2 hours 30 minutes

YOU'LL NEED: Grill, stovetop or propane burner, Dutch oven (or tagine, if you have one), instant-read thermometer

PREP-AHEAD TIP: Spicy Tahini Sauce can be made a week in advance and stored in the fridge. You can also marinate the chicken in the spice mixture ahead of time (overnight if you want) and transport it in a resealable bag so it's ready to cook.

1. Combine the lemon pulp, paprika, cumin, ginger, cinnamon, salt, and pepper. Put the chicken pieces in a large resealable bag along with the spice mixture, rubbing the meat to coat every piece. Refrigerate for 1 hour (or up to 24 hours) to marinate.

2. Preheat a grill to medium-high heat. Grill the chicken for 3 to 4 minutes per side, just to mark the skin (the chicken will not be cooked through at this point). Remove and set aside.

3. Meanwhile, heat the canola oil in a Dutch oven over medium-high heat; add the onion, carrot, garlic, ginger, and turmeric. Season with salt and pepper. When the vegetables have softened and the spices are fragrant, 7 to 8 minutes, add the chicken pieces, stock, and apricots, scraping up any browned bits at the bottom of the pan. (Tuck the

Chicken tagine

One 3- to 4-pound whole chicken, cut into 8 pieces (or 3 to 4 pounds of legs and thighs)

2 tablespoons canola oil

1 large yellow onion, diced

1 large carrot, diced

4 garlic cloves, minced

1-inch piece fresh ginger root, minced

1 teaspoon turmeric

Kosher salt and freshly ground black pepper

1 cup low-sodium chicken stock

½ cup dried apricots, roughly chopped

Two 15½-ounce cans chickpeas, rinsed and drained

1 cup pitted green olives

3 cups finely shredded green cabbage

Pitas, warmed, for serving (see "How to Treat a Yo Pita")

Chopped fresh cilantro, for garnish

Slivered almonds, for garnish

Spicy Tahini Sauce, for serving (recipe follows)

chicken pieces into the pan to try to fit them in a single layer.) Bring to a boil, then reduce to a simmer; cover and cook for 1 hour. When the chicken is cooked (it should register 165°F), remove and set aside under foil to keep warm. Increase the temperature to medium-high and add the chickpeas, olives, and cabbage. Cook, uncovered, until the stew has thickened slightly, about 10 minutes. Taste for seasoning.

4. Serve the chicken and vegetables with warm pitas, garnished with thinly sliced preserved lemon peel, cilantro, almonds, and the tahini sauce.

Spicy Tahini Sauce

1 cup tahini

1 garlic clove, peeled and minced

1 teaspoon toasted sesame oil

2 teaspoons chili garlic sauce (e.g., sambal)

½ teaspoon ground cumin

Juice of 1 lemon

2 tablespoons seasoned rice vinegar

½ teaspoon kosher salt

MAKES: 1 cup

YOU'LL NEED: Blender

Combine all the ingredients in a blender along with 3 tablespoons water and puree until smooth. Scrape down the sides if necessary and add extra water as needed to achieve a light, smooth consistency.

How to Treata Yo Pita

Brush the pita with a little bit of oil if available, but the real key is to put a little toast to it, a few grill marks, and then wrap it up in a towel, in foil, any way you can. Let the heat steam it to life. A warm, soft pita is much more enjoyable and palatable then a hard, dry, cold pita.

Chorizo and Polenta Casserole with Crispy Kale

Think about this as a large Italian-Mexican tamale without a husk, in a casserole dish. Wow, that's tough to imagine. Anyway—sounds weird, tastes awesome. What more do you want?

MAKES: 6 servings

TIME: 1 hour 50 minutes

YOU'LL NEED: Stovetop or propane burner, oven, large sauté pan, 8 by 8 by 2-inch gratin dish or oval 9-inch cast-iron dish, foil, sheet pan

PREP-AHEAD TIP: Make the polenta and chorizo a day in advance. You can assemble it in the gratin dish, cover in foil, and refrigerate if you're heading out to the lake and want a dish that's ready to simply throw in the oven. For the kale, wash, prep, and dry the leaves before transporting in an airtight bag or container. Then all you have to do is dress the leaves and roast them in the oven.

Kale

1 bunch kale

Extra-virgin olive oil

Kosher salt

Polenta

1 quart low-sodium chicken stock

1¼ cups quick-cooking polenta

1½ teaspoons kosher salt

2 tablespoon unsalted butter, melted

1. Preheat the oven to 350°F.

2. Wash and drain the kale. Remove the tough stems and ribs and tear the leaves into large bite-size pieces. Spread out on a sheet pan and drizzle with a little olive oil. Season lightly with salt. Roast in the oven for 15 minutes, or until crispy and dehydrated around the edges. When done, remove and set aside.

3. While the kale is cooking, make the polenta. Bring the chicken stock to a boil in a large pot over high heat. Add the polenta and whisk until fully incorporated, 3 to 4 minutes. Sprinkle with the salt and cook, covered, over medium heat for 5 to 6 minutes. Finish by folding in the melted butter. Keep the polenta warm.

4. To make the chorizo, coat a large sauté pan with olive oil and set it over medium-high heat. Add the onion and cook until almost translucent, then add the ground pork. Brown for 4 to 5 minutes, breaking up the pork with the back of a wooden spoon as it cooks. Add the paprika, granulated garlic, onion powder, chili powder, and cumin and sprinkle with salt and pepper. Cook for 1 minute to toast the spices, then add the vinegar, garlic, and tomatoes. Simmer until the sauce is thickened and reduced, 8 to 10 minutes. Taste and season as needed with salt and pepper. Keep warm.

5. To assemble the casserole, grease an 8 by 8 by 2-inch gratin dish or an oval 9-inch cast-iron pan. Pour half of the polenta in the dish and spread it out evenly. Top with all the chorizo, then sprinkle with half the Fontina and mozzarella. Repeat with a layer of the remaining polenta, then the remaining fontina and mozzarella. Cover with foil, place the dish on a sheet pan, and bake for 30 minutes. Remove the foil and bake until the cheese is golden and bubbly, 15 minutes more. Let sit 25 minutes to set up, then top with crispy roasted kale and grated Parmesan and serve.

Chorizo

2 to 3 tablespoons extra-virgin olive oil

1 small onion, diced

1 pound ground pork

2 tablespoons paprika

1 tablespoon granulated garlic

1 tablespoon onion powder

1 teaspoon chili powder

1 teaspoon ground cumin

Kosher salt and freshly cracked black pepper

2 tablespoons red wine vinegar

4 garlic cloves, minced

One 14½-ounce can fire-roasted diced tomatoes (such as Muir Glen)

½ cup grated Fontina cheese

½ cup grated mozzarella cheese

2 tablespoons grated Parmesan cheese

Volcano Chicken with Maui Onion Straws

Volcano chicken has been a staple at my Johnny Garlic's restaurants for the past fifteen years, and it's highly requested up at the lake. The great thing about this one? Very few ingredients make a super-flavorful dish.

2 tablespoons kosher salt, plus more to taste

1 teaspoon black peppercorns

4 garlic cloves, smashed

4 large boneless, skinless chicken breasts

Freshly ground black pepper

2 cups Maui Onion Straws (recipe follows)

Sliced scallions, for garnish

Volcano sauce

2 cups Kansas City–style BBQ sauce

½ cup fresh lemon juice

2 tablespoons Dijon mustard

½ cup chipotles in adobo sauce

1 teaspoon dried red pepper flakes

½ teaspoon cayenne pepper

½ teaspoon freshly ground black pepper

½ cup canola oil

MAKES: 4 servings

TIME: 1 hour 30 minutes

YOU'LL NEED: Grill, stovetop or propane burner, blender, frying thermometer

PREP-AHEAD TIP: Volcano sauce can be made a week in advance and refrigerated. Maui onion straws should be made fresh, but 1 or 2 hours before serving is okay—just let cool and store them in an airtight container.

1. To make the brine, bring 6 cups water to a boil in a large pot. Add the 2 tablespoons salt, peppercorns, and garlic. Let cool for 30 minutes, then add the chicken and refrigerate for 30 minutes to brine. Remove the chicken from the brine and pat dry. Season with salt and pepper.

2. Meanwhile, make the volcano sauce. Combine all the ingredients in a blender and puree until smooth. (If you don't have a blender, chop chipotles as finely as possible.)

3. Preheat a grill to medium-high heat. Place the chicken breasts on the grill. After 3 minutes, rotate the breasts half a turn to create cross-hatch grill marks. After about 6 minutes, turn the chicken over to finish cooking, about another 6 minutes, basting with volcano sauce.

4. To serve, drizzle with more volcano sauce and top with crispy Maui onion straws. Store any leftover volcano sauce in an airtight container in the refrigerator. It's great with roasted vegetables, pork chops, steaks, and even tacos!

Maui Onion Straws

1. In a large saucepan, heat the oil to 350°F.

2. Whisk the eggs and milk in a medium bowl. In a separate bowl, combine the flour, cayenne, paprika, garlic powder, salt, and pepper.

3. Cut the onion in half and then into ⅛-inch-thick half-rings; separate the half-rings into short, straw-like pieces. Place the onions in the milk mixture to soak for at least 15 minutes.

4. Once the oil is hot enough, remove the onions from the milk mixture, shake off the excess, and dredge in the flour mixture, 4 to 5 pieces at a time. Fry until golden brown, then drain on a paper towel–lined plate.

MAKES: 4 cups

2 cups canola oil

1 large egg

½ cup milk

2 cups all-purpose flour

1 teaspoon cayenne

1 teaspoon paprika

1 teaspoon garlic powder

½ tablespoon kosher salt

½ teaspoon freshly ground black pepper

1 sweet onion (Maui or Vidalia)

Captain Ryder of the USS Fieri.

Chicken Paillard Salad with Mustardy Vinaigrette

Here's something light and simple to serve as a salad or on top of some grilled dough as a rustic pizza. (Sorry for the fancy name.)

4 boneless, skinless chicken breasts

¼ cup fresh lemon juice

¼ cup extra-virgin olive oil

¼ teaspoon dried red pepper flakes

1 shallot, grated

½ teaspoon kosher salt

¼ teaspoon freshly ground black pepper

2 cups lightly packed baby arugula

2 cups torn red-leaf lettuce

2 cups torn frisée

Dijon Vinaigrette (recipe follows)

½ cup thinly sliced roasted red bell peppers

2 Roma (plum) tomatoes, sliced into small wedges

½ cup shaved Parmesan cheese

1 lemon, cut into wedges

MAKES: 4 servings

TIME: 40 minutes

YOU'LL NEED: Stovetop or propane burner, griddle or cast-iron pan

PREP-AHEAD TIP: Pound the chicken breast the night before and store tightly wrapped in plastic in the fridge. The Dijon vinaigrette can be made 1 or 2 days in advance and stored in an airtight container in the fridge. Washing salad greens ahead of time is also a great time saver. Don't do it any earlier than the night before and simply store in a resealable plastic bag or airtight container with a damp paper towel over the greens. Keep refrigerated until you're ready to assemble and dress the salad.

1. Begin by pounding the chicken breasts. Working with one breast at a time, place between two sheets of plastic wrap. Using the smooth side of a meat tenderizer, pound the chicken to a ¼-inch even thickness.

2. Combine the lemon juice, olive oil, red pepper flakes, shallot, salt, and pepper in a large freezer bag. Add the chicken breasts and marinate in the refrigerator for 30 minutes.

3. Preheat a large cast-iron griddle or barbecue (work with 2 pans simultaneously if you have them) to medium-high heat. Cook the chicken paillards 3 to 4 minutes per side, until golden brown and just cooked through. Reserve any accumulated pan juices.

4. In a large bowl, toss the arugula, red leaf lettuce, and frisée with just enough vinaigrette to coat the leaves. Place the chicken breasts on a large plate and drizzle the pan juices over the chicken. Top with a big handful of salad greens and garnish with sliced red peppers, tomatoes, and shaved Parmesan. Serve with fresh lemon wedges.

My favorite view in the world.

Dijon Vinaigrette

MAKES: About ½ cup

In a medium bowl, whisk the lemon juice, mustard, garlic, honey, salt, and pepper until combined. While whisking constantly, add the olive oil in a thin, steady stream until the dressing lightly emulsifies. Add the chives and stir.

3 tablespoons fresh lemon juice

1 tablespoon Dijon mustard

1 small garlic clove, minced

½ teaspoon honey

Kosher salt and freshly ground black pepper, to taste

⅓ cup olive oil

1 tablespoon minced fresh chives

Lamb Curry with Chickpeas and Spinach

After many days at the lake, barbecue sauce, tomato sauce, and ketchup and mustard start to lose their zest, so it's nice to mix things up with a little warm curry. Serve it up with steamed rice, boiled potatoes, or warm pitas.

3 pounds boneless lamb shoulder, excess fat trimmed, cut into 1-inch cubes

Kosher salt and freshly ground black pepper

3 tablespoons canola oil

1 tablespoon coriander seeds

2 large yellow onions, diced

3 tablespoons minced fresh ginger root

7 garlic cloves, minced

2½ tablespoons ground cumin

1 teaspoon ground cinnamon

3½ tablespoons curry powder

1 teaspoon mustard powder

2 bay leaves

Two 14½-ounce cans fire-roasted diced tomatoes

3 cups low-sodium chicken stock

2 russet potatoes, peeled and diced

One 15½-ounce can chickpeas, rinsed and drained

3 cups fresh baby spinach

1 cup plain Greek yogurt

Chopped fresh cilantro, for garnish

MAKES: 4 to 6 servings

TIME: 1 hour 15 minutes

YOU'LL NEED: Stovetop or propane burner, Dutch oven

PREP-AHEAD TIP: *Mise en place* all the ingredients ahead of time so all you have to do is brown and stew everything in the pot.

1. Season the lamb with salt and pepper. Heat the canola oil over medium-high heat in a large Dutch oven; brown the lamb on all sides, 8 to 10 minutes. Remove and set aside.

2. In a small dry skillet, toast the coriander seeds until fragrant, 3 to 4 minutes, stirring often.

3. In the same Dutch oven, pour off all but 2 tablespoons of any accumulated fat (if you have less than this, add more canola oil). Add the onion, ginger, and garlic and sweat until translucent, 6 or 7 minutes. Add the cumin, toasted coriander, cinnamon, curry, mustard, and bay leaves. Cook for 2 to 3 minutes and season with salt and pepper. Return the lamb to the Dutch oven, add the diced tomatoes and chicken stock, and simmer for 1 hour and 10 minutes. Add the potatoes and chickpeas and simmer for 20 minutes, or until the potatoes are tender. Stir in the spinach and heat until it's just wilted.

4. Serve the lamb curry garnished with a dollop of yogurt and some chopped cilantro.

Spicy Carbonara with Pancetta and Parm

When we're at the lake, there are a few staples we're guaranteed to have on hand: bacon, eggs, some sort of pasta, Parmesan cheese, and a little bit of spice. What does that spell? Some really weird acronym (BEPPS?), or, as it's more commonly known, Spicy Carbonara with Pancetta and Parm.

1. In a large sauté pan over medium heat, cook the pancetta until tender-crisp, 6 or 7 minutes. Add the chiles and cook for 1 minute or so, until they sizzle and become fragrant, then transfer both pancetta and chiles to a paper towel–lined plate and set aside. Reserve the pan with the drippings.

2. Separate 4 of the eggs and put the yolks in a large bowl, reserving the 4 whites for another use. Crack the fifth egg and add it whole to the yolks (this gives the richness of mostly yolks and the lightness of a little egg white). Add the cheese, black pepper, and cayenne and whisk to combine.

3. Bring a large pot of water to a boil and cook the pasta until al dente. Add the peas to the pasta water when the pasta is just about finished, then strain both into the pan with the reserved pancetta drippings. Reserve about ¾ cup of the pasta water to fortify the sauce.

4. Add the egg mixture to the hot pasta and toss well with tongs for about 1 minute to distribute it. Stir in the reserved pasta water in ¼-cup increments until the desired sauce consistency is reached. If the mixture gets too watery, place the pan back over the heat briefly to help cook off some of the liquid.

5. Add the parsley, pancetta, and chiles and gently toss together. Pour the pasta into a serving dish and season with salt to taste. Garnish with grated Parmesan and chopped parsley.

MAKES: 6 servings

TIME: 30 minutes

YOU'LL NEED: Stovetop or propane burner, sauté pan, large pot for pasta

PREP-AHEAD TIP: Make the egg mixture ahead of time—just store it in the fridge in an airtight container.

1½ cups ¼-inch-diced pancetta (or bacon)

1½ Fresno chiles, seeded and diced (or jalapeño)

5 large eggs, organic if possible

½ cup grated Parmesan cheese, plus more for garnish

½ teaspoon freshly ground black pepper

⅛ teaspoon cayenne pepper

1 pound bucatini (or spaghetti)

1 cup frozen peas

Kosher salt to taste

1 tablespoon chopped fresh flat-leaf parsley, plus more for garnish

Pork Chile Verde

2 dried pasilla chiles,
stems removed

2 pounds tomatillos,
husks removed

2 tablespoons canola oil

1 large sweet onion, diced

2 Anaheim chiles,
seeded and diced

2 poblano peppers,
seeded and diced

2 jalapeño peppers,
seeded and minced

6 garlic cloves, minced

4 pounds boneless pork butt,
trimmed of fat and cut into
1½-inch cubes

Kosher salt and freshly
ground black pepper

½ cup white wine

3 tablespoons white vinegar

1 quart low-sodium chicken stock

2 tablespoons dried oregano

2 tablespoons ground cumin

1 bay leaf

⅓ cup masa harina
(yellow corn flour)

1 lime, halved

Chopped fresh cilantro,
for garnish

Crispy Tortilla Strips (recipe
follows), for garnish

Shredded jalapeño Jack cheese,
for garnish

Chopped scallions, for garnish

Probably my favorite piece of meat is the pork shoulder, or Boston butt. It's tough and riddled with fat and connective tissue, but when cooked down, low and slow, it is amazing. Plus, pork is one of the most economical proteins you can buy. When I go to the lake I never know who's going to show up looking for something to eat. Pork Chile Verde works perfectly.

MAKES: 12 servings

TIME: 1 hour 40 minutes

YOU'LL NEED: Stovetop or propane burner, Dutch oven or cast-iron pot, grill, frying thermometer

PREP-AHEAD TIP: Grill the chiles and tomatillos the day before. Store in an airtight container in the fridge.

1. Begin by rehydrating the pasillas. Place them in a bowl with ¾ cup warm water and let sit for 20 minutes.

2. Grill the tomatillos over an open flame (or under a broiler) until lightly charred all over—this will give the finished tomatillos a rich, smoky flavor. Set aside to cool, then roughly chop. Tear up the hydrated pasilla peppers and reserve the soaking water.

3. In a large Dutch oven over medium heat, heat the oil. Add the onion; the Anaheim, poblano, and jalapeño peppers; and garlic. Sauté until translucent but not brown. Remove from the pan and set the mixture aside.

4. Season the pork with salt and pepper to taste. Add to the Dutch oven and cook over high heat until browned on all sides, about 8 minutes. Return the onion-pepper mixture to the pan. Mix thoroughly, then deglaze with the wine and vinegar. Cook the mixture for 5 minutes to reduce, then add the chicken stock, oregano, cumin, bay leaf, tomatillos, torn pasilla, 2 cups water, and reserved pasilla water. Season with salt and pepper to taste. Bring to a boil, then lower the heat to a simmer.

5. Simmer, covered, for 30 minutes. Whisk in the masa harina, which will thicken the chile. Simmer for 30 minutes more, or until the sauce is thickened and the pork is tender.

6. Finish with a squeeze of fresh lime juice. Serve in bowls and garnish with fresh cilantro, crispy tortilla strips, shredded cheese, and chopped scallions.

Crispy Tortilla Strips

In a heavy pot, heat 3 inches of oil to 350°F. Stack the tortillas, cut them in half, then slice into ¼-inch strips with a sharp knife. Fry them in small batches until crisp and golden, 3 to 4 minutes, stirring as they cook to separate them. Drain on paper towels and season with salt.

Canola oil, for frying
6 to 8 fresh corn tortillas
Kosher salt

Campfire Baked Ziti as you've never experienced it before . . .

Baked Ziti

At the lake, most of the days are hot and some of the nights are cold. Nothing warms you up by the campfire like a hearty helping of baked ziti.

MAKES: 10 to 12 servings

TIME: 45 minutes

YOU'LL NEED: Stovetop or propane burner, oven, Dutch oven, large pot for pasta, large cast-iron pan or ceramic baking dish

PREP-AHEAD TIP: All of the components can be made the night before. Parcook the pasta and toss in a little olive oil to prevent sticking. Make the ricotta mixture and red sauce. Refrigerate all the components in separate containers and assemble the morning of the day you want to serve.

2 tablespoons extra-virgin olive oil

1 large yellow onion, diced

3 garlic cloves, minced

1 pound Italian pork sausage

1 pound ground beef (80/20 blend)

Two 28-ounce cans crushed fire-roasted tomatoes, with juice

Kosher salt and freshly ground black pepper, to taste

1 tablespoon dried thyme

1 tablespoon dried basil

½ teaspoon dried red pepper flakes

1 pound ziti (or penne)

1 pound fresh mozzarella cheese, grated

1½ cups ricotta cheese

1 large egg

½ cup grated Parmesan cheese

2 tablespoons chopped fresh parsley, for garnish

2 tablespoons chopped fresh rosemary, for garnish

1. Heat the olive oil in a Dutch oven over medium-high heat. Add the onion and garlic and sauté for 4 to 5 minutes, until the onion starts to soften. Add the sausage and beef, breaking it up with a wooden spoon, and sauté until it's cooked through, 7 to 8 minutes. Drain off extra fat if needed. Add the tomatoes with their juice, salt, pepper, thyme, basil, and red pepper flakes. Simmer, stirring occasionally, for 25 minutes. Set the meat mixture aside to cool.

2. Preheat the oven to 375°F.

3. Cook the pasta in a large pot of boiling, salted water until just short of al dente—it will continue to cook in the oven. Drain the pasta and reserve.

4. In a large bowl, combine three-fourths of the mozzarella, the ricotta, egg, ½ teaspoon salt, and 2 or 3 grinds of black pepper and mix well. Toss the pasta with the cheese mixture. Add the cooled meat sauce and toss all ingredients to combine completely.

5. Pour the mixture into a large cast-iron pan or ceramic baking dish. Top the ziti with the remaining mozzarella and the Parmesan. Bake for 20 minutes, until bubbly and golden brown. Garnish with the herbs.

Blackened Trout with Shrimp Sauce

Some of the greatest dinners I've had at the lake have been made from fresh fish caught by Hunter, Ryder, and my nephew Jules.

Spice blend

1 tablespoon paprika

2 teaspoons mustard powder

1 teaspoon cayenne

1 tablespoon garlic powder

1 teaspoon ground cumin

1 teaspoon dried thyme

1 teaspoon dried basil

1 tablespoon kosher salt

1½ teaspoons freshly ground black pepper

MAKES: 4 servings

TIME: 20 minutes

YOU'LL NEED: Stovetop or propane burner, large cast-iron skillet

PREP-AHEAD TIP: Make the spice blend ahead of time. It can also be used on chicken or pork chops.

1. To make the spice blend, combine all the spices in a bowl. Sprinkle the spice mixture generously over both sides of the fish.

2. Melt 2 tablespoons of the butter in a cast-iron skillet over medium-high heat until frothy. Add the trout and cook for 3 to 4 minutes on the first side. Turn the fillets and cook until opaque, about 1 more minute. With a spatula, carefully transfer the fillets to a serving platter; tent with foil to keep warm.

3. To the same skillet, add the shrimp and sauté for 2 to 3 minutes, until pink. Season with salt and pepper and set aside on a plate. To the same pan, add the celery, bell pepper, onion, and garlic and cook until just softened, 2 to 3 minutes. Add the fish or shrimp stock and bring to a simmer. Add the cream and continue to simmer until slightly reduced, 3 to 4 minutes. Return the shrimp to the pan and cook until opaque. Finish with the remaining 1 tablespoon butter and a squeeze of lemon juice. Spoon the shrimp sauce over the trout and garnish with sliced scallions and lemon wedges.

Trout for Aunt Patty

When I was growing up in Ferndale, California, they would stock Francis Creek with trout. On the first morning it was open for fishing, my friends and I would attack the creek. With fishing poles, tackle boxes, and fireball salmon eggs (the best bait for trout), we would cover every mile of that creek, some of us in rubber boots, some in tennis shoes, some even in bare feet. From dusk till dawn that weekend, nobody slept, everybody fished. Now, I don't know what it feels like to be in a big bass tournament, but in my era in my town, you could spot a kid riding down the street with a string of trout hanging from his handlebars.

I prided myself in my fishing ability and my understanding of the elusive trout. One particular Saturday I hit it big, yanking in five monster trout. If you had asked me then how big they were, I'd have said they were all about two feet long. But in reality they were probably a good twelve to thirteen inches. Back then it was no big deal for a kid to clean a fish (catfish skinning is another story—see page 180).

My aunt Patty lived in Ferndale at the time, and somehow I got the idea that she would want trout for her birthday. I'm not even sure it was her birthday, but I remember cleaning her trout on the front porch. I went in to get aluminum foil from the kitchen . . . and what happened next was right out of *A Christmas Story* or any slapstick comedy. I came out to find a squadron of barn cats devouring my trophy fish.

I lost it. The cats had eaten four of the trout down to the cartoon head and tail. One trout was left, and the largest of the big calico barn cats grabbed it by the tail and ditched under the house to finish it off. I was so out of my mind I scrambled under the house and was screaming and yelling trying to get the trout from the cat, who was now willing to fight back because I was less intimidating on my belly. All my dad could hear coming from underneath the kitchen floor was me screaming and swearing. He ran out to see what was wrong and dragged me out by my feet as I continued to scream hysterically that the cats had eaten all the fish that I was going to give to Aunt Patty. I was devastated. I was never sure if Aunt Patty ever knew about the trophy fish she missed out on receiving. (Well, I guess she does now.)

Trout and shrimp sauce

Four 6-ounce trout fillets, pin bones removed

3 tablespoons unsalted butter

½ pound medium shrimp, peeled and deveined, roughly chopped

Kosher salt and freshly ground black pepper

2 celery stalks, finely diced

1 small green bell pepper, seeded and finely diced

1 small yellow onion, finely diced

2 garlic cloves, minced

1 cup fish stock (or Shrimp Stock, page 178)

1 cup heavy cream

Lemon wedges

Sliced scallions, for garnish

Hunter's First Trout

Depending on the region of the country or the background of the family, different kids are accustomed to eating different foods. I know some kids who love seafood but hate lamb, kids who enjoy Mexican food but not Chinese, kids who will eat foie gras but not sushi. There are different ways to encourage a love of fish, and one is to teach them to fish.

So, there we were at the lake at just about dusk and Hunter (I think about age 6) was out fishing with his buddy Jessie. All of a sudden, I heard screaming and yelling that made me think they were being attacked by a wild animal. I ran down the path to the lake only to be met by Hunter holding . . . wait for it, wait for it . . . a beautiful thirteen-inch rainbow trout. The hook still in the mouth, the pole still in hand, fish just a-flappin', and he'd come to show me what he'd caught. Hunter was so excited I thought he was going to eat it hanging from the line. We took it down to the water, cleaned it, came back up, and prepared it. Even though Hunter had already eaten a full dinner, he sat down and enjoyed his bounty of the county. Watching my kid catch, cook, and eat his first fish was one of the greatest moments I've had at the lake.

Hunter with some bass he caught. If I'd known he was going to be this good, I'd have named him Fisherman.

Roasted Shrimp and Crab Étouffée

Kinda like short ribs, when étouffée is good, it's really good, and when it's bad, it's still pretty good. I don't know what it is about Cajun cooking, but to me there's almost nothing better. You would think that there would be a Cajun joint on every corner across America, and this étouffée is one of the reasons why. It's rich, flavorful, and comforting.

MAKES: 4 to 5 servings

TIME: 1 hour 15 minutes

YOU'LL NEED: Stovetop or propane burner, oven, Dutch oven, roasting pan, stockpot

PREP-AHEAD TIP: Prep the seafood and toss it in the seasonings a few hours beforehand. Store it in the fridge until ready to roast. Shrimp stock can be made well in advance and kept frozen until ready to use.

1. Melt the butter in a Dutch oven over medium heat. When it's melted and frothy, add the onions, celery, green pepper, and garlic. (Holy Trinity refers to the Creole/Cajun culinary world trinity, which is onion, bell pepper, and celery.) Cook, stirring often, until the vegetables have softened, about 5 minutes. Add the flour and stir to create a roux; cook, stirring constantly, until the roux is golden brown, 5 to 7 minutes. Season lightly with salt and pepper. Add the tomatoes, bay leaf, thyme, and 1½ tablespoons of the Cajun seasoning. Cook for 3 minutes more, then whisk in the shrimp stock. Bring the mixture to a boil, then lower the heat and simmer for 30 minutes, stirring occasionally.

2. While the mixture simmers, preheat the oven to 400°F. Place the shrimp and drained crab on a roasting pan and season with the remaining 1½ tablespoons Cajun seasoning, the granulated garlic, and salt and pepper to taste. Roast for 10 to 12 minutes, until the shrimp and crab are lightly charred around the edges. (If you can do this over

½ stick (¼ cup) unsalted butter

2 cups diced onions

1 cup diced celery

1 cup diced green bell pepper

1 tablespoon minced garlic

¼ cup all-purpose flour

Kosher salt

Freshly ground black pepper, or cayenne pepper for additional heat

1 cup diced (plum) Roma tomatoes

1 bay leaf

1 tablespoon chopped fresh thyme

3 tablespoons Cajun seasoning

2 cups Shrimp Stock (recipe follows)

1½ pounds 21/25 count shrimp (peeled, tail on)

1 pound jumbo lump crabmeat, drained

2 teaspoons granulated garlic

½ lemon

Steamed white rice, for serving

Chopped fresh flat-leaf parsley, for garnish

Chopped scallions, for garnish

charcoal, you'll love the smoky taste.) Transfer the shrimp, crab, and pan juices to the Dutch oven with the vegetables. Stir and season with salt, pepper, and a squeeze of lemon juice.

3. Serve the étouffée over white rice, topped with parsley and scallions.

Shrimp Stock

2 teaspoons canola oil

4 cups shrimp shells

1 yellow onion, chopped

1 carrot, chopped

2 celery stalks, chopped

2 tablespoons tomato paste

3 garlic cloves, smashed

Handful of fresh parsley

2 or 3 fresh thyme sprigs

1 tablespoon black peppercorns

2 bay leaves

MAKES: 1 quart

TIME: 1 hour

In a large stockpot, heat the canola oil over medium heat. Add the shells, onion, carrot, and celery and cook until the shrimp shells have turned pink and the vegetables have softened, 5 to 6 minutes. Stir in the tomato paste, garlic, parsley, thyme, peppercorns, and bay leaves. Cover with water (about 6 cups) and bring to a boil; lower the heat and simmer, uncovered, for 45 to 50 minutes. Strain and discard all the solids, cool the stock, and refrigerate (or freeze) until ready to use.

ROUX the Day

There's light roux and there's dark roux . . . in Australia there's kanga-roux (sorry, just had to). Roux is a basic ratio of equal parts flour and fat. The fat can be butter or animal fat, such as bacon or sausage fat, or you can even make it with vegetable oils for a healthier spin. You throw the fat and flour together in a pan and whisk it as it cooks; the idea is that you're cooking the flour—as the fat melts, it toasts the flour.

The first stage that develops is called a blond roux—it has a nice golden blond color and the texture of wet sand. That's the most common roux, used as the base for a béchamel, which you use when you make mac and cheese or a thick soup. But if you keep cooking the roux past the blond stage, it gets browner and becomes a dark roux—it's what makes New Orleans cooking distinctive. You take it to a really dark stage before adding your holy trinity (onion, carrot, and celery), your seasonings and spices, and the liquid. Just as you can change out the fats, so you use different liquids—stock, milk, or even beer. But keep in mind that as the roux gets darker, its thickening properties diminish.

Here's my theory on roux: Make more than you need, 'cause if you find it isn't thickening as much as you want, it's a real pain to go back in the middle of your cooking to make more, and the last thing you want to do is substitute a cornstarch slurry. If you make too much, you can always hold it in the refrigerator for 3 weeks, or freeze it for up to 6 months.

Catfish (or Any Fresh-Caught Fish) and Peppers en Papillote

I like to bring catfish on lake or camping trips because it's inexpensive and can handle being transported without breaking apart. Whether you catch it fresh or pack it, you'll find that catfish takes on great flavor. *En papillote* is the French technique of wrapping fish in parchment paper before cooking. The method really seals in all the juices and flavors of the fish and vegetables—and needless to say, the *en papillote* presentation is not something you expect to see at the lake.

MAKES: 4 servings

TIME: 40 minutes

YOU'LL NEED: Oven, heavy-duty aluminum foil, parchment, sheet pan

PREP-AHEAD TIP: If you're bringing fish to the lake: Assemble the pepper mixture and fish in the parchment pouches the morning before you head out. You don't want to do it too far ahead of time, as the fish will over-marinate if it sits too long. Because you won't be in the comfort of your own kitchen, wrap each pouch in foil for durability and to handle any mishaps that may occur. Stack 'em, wrap 'em in plastic, and keep 'em cold so they're ready for you to simply add marinade, reseal, throw in the oven (or on the campfire!) when you're ready.

If you're planning on catching fresh fish: To make the on-site prep that much easier, mix the marinade together and pop it in a jar, then chop up the peppers and onions and put them in a resealable plastic bag to transport in the cooler.

1. Preheat the oven to 350°F.

2. To make the marinade, combine the balsamic vinegar, lemon juice, thyme, and garlic in a small mixing bowl. Season with salt and pepper. Set aside.

3. To make the peppers, heat the oil in a medium sauté pan over high heat. Add the onion and sauté until translucent, about 3 minutes. Add the peppers and continue to cook to get a little color on the vegetables,

Marinade

½ cup balsamic vinegar

2 tablespoons fresh lemon juice

1 teaspoon finely chopped fresh thyme

¼ teaspoon finely minced garlic

Kosher salt and freshly cracked black pepper

Peppers

2 tablespoons extra-virgin olive oil

1 small red onion, julienned

1 medium yellow pepper, seeded, membrane removed, and julienned

1 medium red pepper, seeded, membrane removed, and julienned

Kosher salt and freshly cracked black pepper

The Catfish Crucifixion

I remember catching my first catfish when I was a kid, and it was done the old-school way by taking a piece of line tied onto a piece of leftover meat and hanging it over the side of the boat dock. The catfish would come and bite on the meat and you'd catch it. I can't say that this method was incredibly successful, but I remember the day I caught my first catfish and the process of cleaning it . . . OMG. Now, those of you who are a little bit squeamish, move on to the next recipe. But those of you who remember catching a catfish as a kid, you know there was only one way to clean it. First you gut the catfish as you would any fish. But catfish are bottom feeders with notoriously tough thick skin . . . that you have to remove. So my dad took me to the tree next to the dock and showed me how to nail the catfish through the head to the tree. Then I had to make the incision behind the gills and remove the skin—with pliers. The catfish was delicious, but I think that may have been my last wild-caught catfish experience. Not that I was squeamish, but wow, it was a tremendous amount of work to tackle when you're ten—and I didn't want it *that* bad! But today I can't look at that tree without remembering the catfish-nailing incident.

Catfish

Four 6- to 8-ounce catfish (or other fish) fillets, cleaned and skin removed

½ teaspoon paprika

Olive oil, as needed

1 tablespoon chopped fresh parsley

2 tablespoons sliced scallions

1 lemon, cut into wheels

about 2 minutes. Season with salt and pepper and sauté until just fragrant, about 30 seconds. Remove from the heat and reserve.

4. To make the catfish, lay four 12 by 12-inch sheets of parchment paper on a clean work surface. Working with one packet at a time, begin by folding a piece of parchment paper in half to make a crease down the middle. Open it back up and spoon about ⅓ cup sautéed peppers and onions onto the middle of the paper. Place a fish fillet on top. Drizzle 2 tablespoons of the marinade over the fish and sprinkle with salt, pepper, and a pinch of paprika. Fold the parchment back over the fish to enclose. Working from one corner and around the fish to the other corner, make small folds that overlap one another so the packet gets tightly sealed. Continue to fold crease over crease until the packet is sealed. Tuck the last fold under the packet to hold in place. Brush the paper with a little olive oil to help keep it from burning.

5. Repeat to make 4 packets. Place them on a sheet pan and bake until the packets puff up completely, 10 to 12 minutes.

6. To serve, open the parchment packet tops with scissors and garnish with parsley, scallions, and lemon wheels.

Catfish and Peppers en Papillote,
giving some proper respect to
the catch of the day.

Turkey and Quinoa-Stuffed Peppers
with Roasted Tomatillo Avocado Sauce
backing them up.

Turkey and Quinoa–Stuffed Peppers with Roasted Tomatillo Avocado Sauce

With all the snacks and overindulgence that we experience at the lake, it's nice to eat something light, healthy, and clean like these turkey and quinoa–stuffed peppers.

Don't have quinoa on hand? This dish loves to take on all types of grains, rices, and even leftover starches. Don't be afraid to adapt it to your cabin's pantry.

MAKES: 4 servings

TIME: 1 hour 15 minutes

YOU'LL NEED: Oven, roasting pan or large sauté pan, saucepan

PREP-AHEAD TIP: The quinoa can be cooked 1 or 2 days in advance and the filling recipe can be made the night before. Don't stuff the peppers until you're ready to cook them or they can go soft. Roasted Tomatillo Avocado Sauce can be made a day in advance; just chill it down straightaway and store it in the fridge. Taste and reseason before using.

1. Preheat the oven to 425°F.

2. To make the quinoa, over medium-high heat, bring the broth to a boil in a medium saucepan. Add the quinoa, stir, and cover. Reduce the heat to a simmer and steam until the grains pop, about 10 minutes. Remove from the heat and let stand for 10 minutes, covered. Fluff with a fork.

3. To make the peppers, set a large sauté pan over medium-high heat. Add a drizzle of olive oil and the turkey, onion, red pepper flakes, and garlic. Sprinkle with salt and pepper. Cook until the turkey is well browned, 5 to 7 minutes, stirring with a wooden spoon to break up the meat. Deglaze with the wine.

Quinoa

2 cups low-sodium chicken broth

1 cup red quinoa

Peppers

Extra-virgin olive oil

1 pound lean ground turkey

½ cup diced sweet onion

½ teaspoon dried red pepper flakes

1 garlic clove, minced

Kosher salt and freshly ground black pepper

¼ cup white wine

2 large red bell peppers

2 large green bell peppers

2 cups lightly packed stemmed and julienned kale leaves

¼ cup toasted pepitas (pumpkin seeds)

1½ cups finely ground panko (Japanese breadcrumbs)

¼ cup grated Parmesan cheese

Roasted Tomatillo Avocado Sauce, for serving (recipe follows)

4. While the turkey is browning, rinse the peppers and pat dry. With a pepper lying down on its side, cut in half through the stem and remove the seeds and membrane. Repeat with the remaining peppers, to give you 8 pepper halves. Leave the stem on the top for presentation. Set aside.

5. When the turkey is browned, shut off the heat and fold in the quinoa, kale, and pepitas. Mix to incorporate all ingredients thoroughly. Check the seasoning and add salt and pepper as needed.

6. In a small mixing bowl, combine the panko and Parmesan. Add a drizzle of olive oil to lightly moisten and season with salt and pepper. Set the peppers cut side up on a roasting pan and stuff each with about ⅓ cup of filling. Sprinkle each pepper half with about 2 tablespoons of the panko-Parmesan topping. Cover loosely with foil, place in the center of the oven, and bake for 15 minutes. When the peppers are tender and cooked through, remove the foil and turn on the broiler. Set under the broiler to brown the panko and crisp up, 2 to 3 minutes. Keep a careful eye on them to keep them from burning. Remove the peppers from the oven and allow them to rest for a few minutes. Serve with Roasted Tomatillo Avocado Sauce.

Roasted Tomatillo Avocado Sauce

MAKES: About 2 cups

1. Preheat the oven to 350°F.

2. Place the tomatillos on a baking sheet and toss them with a bit of olive oil. Season with salt and pepper and roast until nicely charred, about 10 minutes. Set aside to cool.

3. Combine the tomatillos, ¼ cup water, 1 teaspoon salt, cumin, avocado, garlic, jalapeño, onion, lime juice, and cilantro in a blender and puree until completely smooth (or use a mortar and pestle if you are without power). Allow the sauce to settle for 2 to 3 minutes before serving.

6 medium tomatillos (about 8 ounces), husks removed

Extra-virgin olive oil

Kosher salt and freshly ground black pepper

1 teaspoon ground cumin

1 ripe avocado, diced

1 garlic clove, minced

½ jalapeño pepper, seeded and coarsely chopped

½ sweet onion, roughly chopped

Juice of 1 lime

Handful of fresh cilantro leaves

Serving it up to my mom and Morgan at the lake.

Lamb Barbacoa Tacos

If I say tacos you might first think of beef . . . okay. Then fish . . . all right. Then chicken. But for most people, lamb won't come to mind at all. That is, unless they've tasted this recipe with ancho and chipotle chiles and lamb—a combo that was meant to be. Wrapped up in banana leaves, rich and tender and way outside the box, they're an adventure to cook and eat by the lake. That's right—lamb is so much more than just chops.

Marinade

2 dried ancho chiles

2 dried chipotle chiles

1 tablespoon paprika

2 teaspoons dried oregano

¼ teaspoon ground cinnamon

5 garlic cloves, crushed

½ cup vegetable oil

Lamb

3 pounds tied boneless lamb shoulder (prepared by your butcher)

Kosher salt and freshly cracked black pepper

6 banana leaves

2 limes, cut into wedges

10 to 12 flour tortillas, warmed (see page 111)

1 cup fresh cilantro leaves

1 cup crumbled queso fresco

1 cup shaved radishes

1 red onion, finely sliced

MAKES: 6 servings

TIME: About 9 hours

YOU'LL NEED: Oven, large roasting pan, large nonstick sauté pan, blender, heavy-duty aluminum foil

PREP-AHEAD TIP: You can make the lamb 1 or 2 days in advance, up to the roasting and pulling part. Then all you have to do is crisp it up in a sauté pan when ready to serve. The lamb actually crisps up better when it goes into the pan cold (it will break up less).

1. Place the anchos and chipotles in a bowl and cover with boiling water. Soak the chiles until soft and rehydrated, about 20 minutes.

2. To make the marinade, drain the chiles (reserve the soaking liquid) and put them in a food processor along with the paprika, oregano, cinnamon, and garlic. Pour in the oil and process until smooth. If the puree is too thick, add 1 or 2 tablespoons of the chile soaking liquid to thin to the desired consistency.

3. Place the lamb in a roasting dish and sprinkle all over with salt and pepper. Pour the marinade on top, cover with plastic wrap, and refrigerate for at least 3 hours or overnight.

4. Preheat the oven to 275°F. Thaw the banana leaves (if frozen) by running them under warm water. Line a turkey roaster or braising dish with the banana leaves, slightly overlapping them.

5. Remove the lamb from the marinade and place it on the leaves. Wrap up the lamb with the banana leaves, tucking in the edges so it is completely covered. Add 1½ cups water to the baking dish and cover the entire pan with aluminum foil. Roast until the meat is tender and falling apart, 4 hours. Remove the foil and open the banana leaves. Shred the lamb with a fork and season with salt and lime juice. Place in the fridge to cool.

6. When ready to serve, heat a large nonstick sauté pan and pan-fry the pulled lamb until crisp, about 5 minutes. Season and serve with the warm flour tortillas, cilantro leaves, queso fresco, radishes, and onion.

Banana Leaves

Banana leaves are usually found in the frozen food section of a specialty store or Asian food market. They are as durable as all get-out. As a matter of fact, I think this is nature's original foil and plastic wrap. Not only do they seal in moisture, they also enhance food with their own unique flavor. Buy a pack, use a few, and the rest will last in your freezer for quite a while.

It's so rustic where we camp that the sheets are made of banana leaves!

Farro Salad with Citrus Vinaigrette

Farro is one of the oldest grains known to mankind. I make a double batch of this hearty salad and keep it in the cooler for a quick, high-protein snack during the day. But this dish is a meal in itself: The veggies, the tender farro, and the zesty vinaigrette are all you need.

Farro

1 cup farro

2 teaspoons kosher salt

2½ cups water or vegetable stock

Vinaigrette

Zest of 1 orange

2 tablespoons minced shallot

2 teaspoons Dijon mustard

3 tablespoons white balsamic vinegar

⅓ cup extra-virgin olive oil

Kosher salt and freshly ground black pepper

Salad

1 cup lightly packed baby arugula

½ cup diced red bell pepper

1 orange, peeled and cut into wheels

½ cup Marcona almonds

⅓ cup prunes, chopped

⅓ cup dried cherries, chopped

¼ cup ¼-inch-diced red onion

½ cup ¼-inch-diced tart apple or firm pear

MAKES: 8 servings

TIME: 55 minutes

YOU'LL NEED: Stovetop or propane burner, large heavy saucepan

PREP-AHEAD TIP: You can boil the farro 1 day in advance, then store it in an airtight container in the fridge. The vinaigrette can be made a day ahead as well.

1. TO MAKE THE FARRO: In a large heavy saucepan over medium-high heat, combine the farro, salt, and water (or stock, if using). Bring to a simmer, cover, and cook, stirring occasionally, until the farro is tender, 35 to 45 minutes. Check a few times while it is cooking; you want it to be al dente. Remove from the heat, drain any excess water, and set aside to cool.

2. WHILE THE GRAINS ARE SIMMERING, MAKE THE VINAIGRETTE: Whisk together the orange zest, shallot, mustard, vinegar, and olive oil. Add salt and pepper to taste and set aside.

3. To serve, toss the farro with 3 tablespoons dressing and transfer it to a large serving bowl. In the same bowl, combine the arugula with the diced pepper, orange wheels, almonds, prunes, cherries, onion, and apple and gently toss with 3 tablespoons of the dressing, adding more as needed.

Yeah! Healthy never
looked so good.

Chipotle Corn Salad with Grilled Bacon

If there's a vegetable that loves the grill, it's corn. Caramelizing the natural sugars, adding a little bit of chipotle heat, then kissing it with a little bacon . . . the only thing I warn you is that you cannot live on this alone. You must eat other things.

6 ears of corn, in the husk

4 slices applewood smoked bacon

2 poblano peppers

2 scallions

¼ cup diced red bell pepper

¼ cup diced sweet onion

Dressing

½ cup sour cream

½ cup ranch dressing

2 tablespoons fresh lime juice

1 tablespoon ground cumin

1 teaspoon agave syrup

1 chipotle in adobo, minced, plus 1 tablespoon adobo sauce

Kosher salt and freshly ground black pepper, to taste

MAKES: 4 servings

TIME: 30 minutes

YOU'LL NEED: Grill

PREP-AHEAD TIP: Mise en place everything ahead of time on this one—chop everything, roast the poblanos, and cook the bacon. The dressing can be made 1 or 2 days ahead and stored in the fridge. But cooking and shucking the corn is best left to the last minute, as the corn will stay nice and bright and juicy.

1. Carefully peel back the husks from the corn without detaching them from the bottom. Remove the silk from the corn, fold the husks back around the ears, and soak the ears in water for 30 to 45 minutes. Weigh down the ears so they are fully submerged.

2. Preheat a grill to medium-high. Drain the corn, open the husks, and dry the ears with paper towels. Fold the husks back over the corn and grill, turning often, for 3 to 4 minutes per side, turning 3 times.

3. While the corn is grilling, grill the bacon on the other half of the grill until crispy and golden brown and the poblanos and scallions until charred. Remove all items and set aside.

4. Once the corn is cool enough to handle, cut the kernels from the cob, finely dice the scallions, seed and dice the poblano, and chop the bacon into bite-size pieces, placing everything in a large bowl. Mix in the bell pepper and onion.

5. Whisk together all the dressing ingredients in a medium bowl. Dress the salad lightly and serve.

Corn salad done my way, with chipotle and grilled bacon.

Wild Mushroom Risotto

Risotto is the perfect canvas. It's starchy, rich, and creamy with some chewiness to its texture. If you use fresh mushrooms and have the diligence to prepare the risotto right, it will make anyone a mushroom fan.

3 ounces dried porcini mushrooms

6 cups low-sodium chicken stock

1 tablespoon unsalted butter, plus ½ stick (¼ cup), cubed

3 tablespoons olive oil

2 shallots, minced

1 pound cremini mushrooms, sliced

½ pound oyster mushrooms, sliced

1 teaspoon fresh thyme leaves

Kosher salt and freshly ground black pepper

2 garlic cloves, minced

1½ cups Arborio rice

½ cup dry white wine

½ to ¾ cup grated Parmesan cheese

3 tablespoons chopped fresh parsley

MAKES: 4 servings

TIME: 35 minutes

YOU'LL NEED: Stovetop or propane burner, large saucepan

PREP-AHEAD TIP: Clean and prep the mushrooms the night before. Washing them ahead of time and letting them sit uncovered in the fridge allows them to dry out, and they'll sauté much better. If you want to prep risotto ahead of time, a technique we use in restaurants is to parcook the rice to just before the al dente stage, spread it out in a single layer on a sheet pan, and then refrigerate it—this stops the cooking process, and spreading it out keeps it from clumping. When you're ready to cook, add the risotto back to the pot and warm it through with more stock, which finishes the cooking and heats it up at the same time!

1. In a medium bowl, rehydrate the porcini mushrooms in ½ cup warm water for 15 minutes. Drain, reserving the liquid for later.

2. In a medium saucepan, warm the chicken stock over low heat and keep warm.

3. In a large saucepan, heat the 1 tablespoon butter and 1 tablespoon of the olive oil over medium heat. Add the shallots and sauté for 1 minute. Add the porcini, cremini, and oyster mushrooms and the thyme and sauté until the mushrooms have softened and turned golden brown, 7 to 8 minutes. Season with salt and pepper, then transfer to a plate and set aside.

4. In the same saucepan, add the remaining 2 tablespoons olive oil. Add the garlic and cook for 30 seconds. Add the rice, stirring to coat in the oil, and toast until golden brown, about 5 minutes. Deglaze with white wine and the reserved porcini liquid, stirring constantly until the liquid is completely absorbed.

5. Ladle ½ cup of warm stock into the rice, stirring constantly until absorbed. Continue adding stock in this manner until the rice is al dente, 18 to 20 minutes. Fold in the mushrooms and taste for seasoning. Just before serving, stir in the cubed butter, Parmesan cheese to taste, and parsley.

Swiss Family Robinson, Northern California style.

Roasted Poblano Skillet Cornbread

If there's one thing that a cast-iron pan was born to do, it's make skillet cornbread. The consistent heat is exactly what cornbread needs. My version here is camping cornbread gone wild. Roasted poblanos? Are you kidding me? This cornbread eats like a meal, and goes great with chili (see page 40) or Old-School Baked Beans (see page 254)!

CONVENTIONAL COOKING METHOD

Bake in a preheated 350°F oven for 20 to 25 minutes, uncovered.

½ cup all-purpose flour

1 cup stone-ground yellow cornmeal

1 teaspoon kosher salt

1 tablespoon baking powder

½ teaspoon baking soda

½ cup buttermilk

1 cup milk

1 large egg

1 stick (½ cup) unsalted butter, melted, plus 2 tablespoons

8 ounces Monterey Jack cheese, shredded

½ cup diced roasted poblano peppers

1 cup frozen corn kernels, thawed

MAKES: 8 to 10 servings

TIME: 45 minutes

YOU'LL NEED: Campfire with grill grate, 12-inch cast-iron skillet with lid

PREP-AHEAD TIP: Roast, seed, and dice the peppers. Shred the cheese and measure everything so all you have to do is mix it all together when out camping.

1. Start a campfire with wood and wait until the flames die down and the coals glow red with white ash. Place a 12-inch cast-iron skillet adjacent to the coals to heat up.

2. Combine the flour, cornmeal, salt, baking powder, and baking soda in a large bowl. In a separate bowl, combine the buttermilk, milk, egg, and melted butter. Make a well in the dry ingredients and slowly stir the wet ingredients into the dry, mixing gently until the lumps are dissolved. Fold in the cheese, poblanos, and corn.

3. Remove the cast-iron skillet from the fire and put the 2 tablespoons butter in the hot pan so it sizzles. Roll the butter around the pan to coat it evenly, then pour the cornbread batter into the hot skillet. Top with a lid and place back in the spot adjacent to the coals. Using a metal shovel, place hot coals on top of the lid and cook for 25 to 30 minutes, or until the bread is golden and firm. Rotate the pan every 7 to 8 minutes so the cornbread cooks evenly. Carefully remove the coals and lid and let the cornbread cool slightly in the pan, about 5 minutes. Slice and serve warm.

Cornbread takes to cast-iron like a fish to water.

Banana Split with Rum-Roasted Pineapple

What was the quintessential ice cream experience when you were a kid? For me, it was the banana split. Three scoops of ice cream, the banana cut in half, the whipped cream, the cherry on top—it was the ultimate finale to the celebration dinner if you did really well in school. Nowadays kids get so many different kinds of treats it doesn't seem that special, but back in the day, the banana split was *it*. So here's a little fancied-up version for your old-school memories.

Roasted pineapple

1½ cups ½-inch pineapple chunks

2 tablespoons dark rum
(or fresh-squeezed orange juice
for alcohol-free desserts)

½ vanilla bean, split, caviar
scraped out

1 tablespoon light brown sugar

Chocolate sauce

¼ cup sugar

¼ cup light corn syrup

1 teaspoon instant coffee powder

5 tablespoons unsweetened
cocoa powder

1 ounce semisweet chocolate,
chopped

Banana splits

¼ cup walnuts

2 bananas, split in half lengthwise

1 teaspoon canola oil

Vanilla, chocolate, and strawberry
ice cream

1 cup strawberries,
hulled and sliced

Whipped cream

MAKES: 4 servings

TIME: 30 minutes

YOU'LL NEED: Grill, oven, cast-iron skillet

PREP-AHEAD TIP: You can toast the walnuts the night before and store in an airtight container. You can also mix and marinate the pineapple a few hours before cooking and leave it in the fridge so all you have to do is roast it when ready or roast it the morning of and set aside. The chocolate sauce can be made 1 to 2 days in advance. Store it in a squeeze bottle wrapped in plastic in the fridge until ready to use.

Ryder presents the ultimate in banana splits.

1. Preheat the oven to 425°F. In a cast-iron skillet, mix together the pineapple, rum, vanilla bean pod and scrapings, and brown sugar. Roast until caramelized, 18 to 20 minutes. Remove the vanilla bean pod. Preheat the grill to medium.

2. While the pineapple is roasting, make the chocolate sauce. In a medium saucepan over medium heat, whisk together ½ cup water, the sugar, corn syrup, instant coffee, and cocoa powder. Bring to a boil, remove from the heat, and stir in the chopped chocolate until completely melted.

3. To prep the walnuts, crush the nuts in a resealable plastic bag, then toast them in a hot, dry skillet for 6 to 7 minutes, stirring often, until dark brown.

4. Meanwhile, brush the banana halves with canola oil and grill over medium heat, 2 or 3 minutes per side, until caramelized.

5. TO SERVE: Lay a grilled banana half at the bottom of 4 sundae dishes. Place 1 scoop each of vanilla, chocolate, and strawberry ice cream on top of the banana. Scatter strawberries around the sundae dish, spoon roasted pineapple across the ice cream, and drizzle chocolate sauce on top. Garnish with whipped cream and toasted walnuts.

Pineapple Upside-Down Cake with Rum Blueberries

This is another one of those staples in dessert history, and the great thing about it is that it's actually camping friendly as well. So when you have some extra time on your hands and you want to blow everybody away, this is a wow 'em dessert over a campfire.

One 12-ounce package frozen blueberries

¾ cup spiced rum

½ pineapple, peeled, cored, quartered, and cut into ¼-inch pieces (about 4 cups pineapple chunks)

¾ cup rum (not spiced)

2 sticks (1 cup) butter, at room temperature

¾ cup granulated sugar

5 large eggs

2 teaspoons vanilla extract

1½ cups all-purpose flour

1 teaspoon kosher salt

¾ teaspoon baking powder

1 tablespoon dark brown sugar

1 pint crème fraîche

Grated zest of 1 lime

Grated zest of 1 orange

MAKES: 10 servings

TIME: 1 hour (plus 8 hours marinating time)

YOU'LL NEED: Oven or campfire; Dutch oven

PREP-AHEAD TIP: Cut and prep the pineapple ahead of time and store it in the fridge. Combine the dry ingredients beforehand but keep them separate from the wet ingredients if you're traveling. Combine them to make the cake batter right before cooking. The crème fraîche with zest can be made a day in advance and kept refrigerated.

1. In a medium bowl, combine the blueberries and the spiced rum. In another bowl, combine the pineapple and the regular rum. Cover and refrigerate for 8 hours or overnight.

2. Preheat the oven to 350°F. (Or prepare your campfire.)

3. In a large bowl, cream together 1¾ sticks of the butter and the granulated sugar until pale yellow, about 2 minutes. Beat in the eggs, one at a time. Stir in the vanilla extract and set aside.

4. In a separate bowl, combine the flour, salt, and baking powder. Add the dry ingredients to the wet ingredients and stir until a smooth batter forms.

5. In a Dutch oven over medium heat (on a stove or on a grate over a campfire), heat the remaining ¼ stick butter until just melted. Add the brown sugar and, using a slotted spoon, add the pineapple pieces, reserving the rum. Sauté until the pineapple begins to caramelize, about 4 minutes. Add the blueberries and the rum they soaked in.

6. Remove the Dutch oven from the heat and light the rum with a long kitchen match. When the flames subside, return the pan to the heat and cook until most of the alcohol has evaporated. Remove the Dutch oven from the heat and set aside to cool for 6 to 10 minutes.

7. Add the batter to the Dutch oven and put in the oven (if camping, top with a lid, place hot coals on top, and set over to the side of the fire pit, in an area where the side of the Dutch oven is heated. Rotate the Dutch oven every 15 minutes a quarter turn). Bake for 30 to 45 minutes, or until a toothpick inserted into the center comes out clean.

8. Set aside to cool for about 5 minutes before unmolding. To unmold, run a small knife around the edge of the cake, place a large serving plate over the Dutch oven, and carefully flip the Dutch oven and plate over. Let the Dutch oven sit for a couple of minutes until the cake releases itself onto the plate.

9. Put the crème fraîche in a small bowl and stir in the zests. Cut the cake into wedges and serve with a dollop of crème fraîche.

Bourbon Blueberry and Peach Cobbler

I enjoy a fresh peach cobbler as much as anybody, but let's face facts, that old-school peach cobbler experience we all remember was most likely achieved with canned peaches. If you're going old-school and packing cans, the key is to lighten up on the sugar so it isn't too sweet. But even made with fresh peaches, as I do here, this is a surprisingly easy, portable dessert when you're camping.

Filling

6 cups sliced ripe yellow peaches (about 5 peaches)

¾ cup ripe blueberries

¼ cup bourbon (or dark rum if you prefer)

¼ cup sugar

2 tablespoons cornstarch

1 teaspoon ground cinnamon

¼ teaspoon grated lemon zest

1 teaspoon fresh lemon juice

½ teaspoon vanilla extract

Topping

1 cup all-purpose flour

1 cup rolled oats

½ cup sugar

½ teaspoon kosher salt

1½ sticks (¾ cup) cold unsalted butter, cut into small cubes

2 tablespoons heavy cream

1 quart good-quality store-bought vanilla yogurt, for serving

MAKES: 4 to 6 servings

TIME: 45 minutes

YOU'LL NEED: 12-inch skillet

PREP-AHEAD TIP: Prepare the filling and topping ahead of time and store them in airtight containers in a cooler.

1. Preheat the oven to 375°F.

2. To make the filling, in a large bowl, combine the peaches, blueberries, bourbon, sugar, cornstarch, cinnamon, lemon zest and juice, and vanilla. Mix well to coat the peaches and blueberries evenly. Set aside.

3. To make the topping, in a second large bowl, combine the flour, oats, sugar, and salt. Add the cold butter cubes and cut the butter into the flour (either with a pastry blender, two knives, or your hands). Mix until the texture is coarse and clumps in your palm when you squeeze a handful. Add the heavy cream and mix just until the dough comes together a bit more.

4. Bake the cobbler for 30 to 35 minutes, or until set.

CAMPFIRE COOKING METHOD

Pour the filling into a 12-inch cast-iron Dutch oven (with a fitted cast-iron lid) and spread it out evenly. Spoon the topping mixture evenly over the filling, then cover with the lid. Place the Dutch oven adjacent to hot coals in a place where it will get a good amount of radiant heat so the batter cooks through evenly without burning. Use a metal shovel to pile hot coals on top of the lid (this will distribute heat from the top). Cook for 45 to 50 minutes, rotating the Dutch oven 90 degrees every 10 minutes so the cobbler cooks evenly. Change out the hot coals on top 2 or 3 times during cooking so the top stays hot throughout and the cobbler cooks evenly. Bake the cobbler for 30 to 35 minutes, or until the fruit is bubbling around the edges and the topping is light and fluffy, serve the cobbler straight from the pan, with vanilla yogurt on the side.

A juicy, crunchy cobbler spooned up old-school.

Guy's Lemongrass-Ginger Julep

I love going to the Kentucky Derby, and there's something about drinking a mint julep at the Derby that you never forget. But not everyone is a fan of the julep because it can be so sweet. My way has a lot of unique flavors, and the little bit of spice from the ginger makes it really refreshing.

**2 fresh mint sprigs,
plus 1 for garnish**

Ice

**1½ ounces (3 tablespoons)
Kentucky bourbon**

**¾ ounce (1½ tablespoons)
Lemongrass-Ginger Simple Syrup
(recipe follows)**

Cold club soda

Lime wedge

MAKES: 1 serving

TIME: 5 minutes (1 hour if making syrup)

YOU'LL NEED: Cocktail shaker, Collins or Mason jar or equivalent glass

PREP-AHEAD TIP: Make the simple syrup up to a week in advance.

Combine the 2 mint sprigs and ice in a cocktail shaker and muddle. Add the bourbon and the simple syrup and shake vigorously to combine. Pour into a Collins glass filled with ice. Top with club soda and a squeeze of lime juice and garnish with a sprig of mint.

Lemongrass-Ginger Simple Syrup

MAKES: 2 cups

**6 stalks lemongrass (can be
found in the freezer aisle at an
Asian grocery)**

2 cups sugar

1-inch slice of fresh ginger root

1. Trim the lemongrass stalks so you have the bases only. Bash with the back of a knife (or a meat mallet) so the oils and aroma release more easily.

2. Combine the lemongrass, sugar, 2 cups cold water, and the ginger in a medium saucepan over medium heat. Simmer until the sugar dissolves. Reduce the heat and steep the lemongrass and ginger until the syrup is fragrant, 30 to 40 minutes, then strain. If not using immediately, keep in an airtight container in the refrigerator for up to 4 weeks.

It's the Kentucky Derby at the lake!

I have done just about every kind of camping you can imagine: on horseback, on the beach, around the lake, in the back of a truck . . . it almost starts to sounds like Dr. Seuss, in a boat on a moat with a goat. Growing up with my parents, there was no avoiding it—we camped. We camped across the country when I was two months old in a square-backed VW, moving from Columbus, Ohio, to Whittier, California; we camped in a green Econoline van up and down the coast of California when I was two years old and we hadn't yet settled in Ferndale. And later on we camped in the Marble Mountains, eight miles in, with only the food and equipment we could pack onto our horses. I always loved to camp, and I still do. Sometimes we even go camping in our RV just thirty minutes out of town at Doran Beach. There's just something about sitting outside and smelling the campfire, with no TV, no cell phones, and no computer.

Now, please don't let me fool you—I've also made chili in cans stuck into the fire and simple potatoes wrapped in foil and set in the coals. I have burned it, spilled it, knocked it over, screwed it up, and added dirt where dirt wasn't desirable any number of times. But that is what makes the culinary adventure in camping so much fun. It's not about just enjoying the culinary creations; it's conquering the kitchen stadium of cooking in the outdoors.

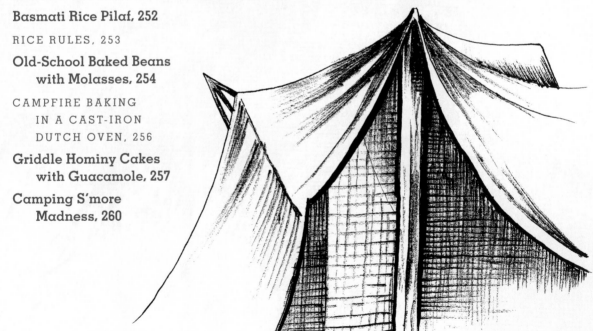

Prepare for Bears

Camping is all about versatility and adaptability. There are a million variables when you camp, and when I talk to people about whether or not they appreciate camping, their feelings usually have to do with their level of preparedness, amount of experience, and the company they keep. If you were a Boy Scout or Girl Scout, you probably do better at camping than most. The task of building a fire that's not in your fireplace at home, where you have a variety of fuel sources and paper supplies, can be a daunting one—as can putting up a livable tent on the uneven forest floor. A lot of factors can create a negative experience, but when camping is done right it's an adventure that kids and adults alike will never forget.

I pride myself on being a good camper: picking the right spots and bringing the right equipment. I can't say I always know the right weather—I've had my share of camping in the rain—but one of the keys to my camping success has always been the food. Why would I set up this amazing experience in beautiful surroundings and then subject myself to subpar food? Don't get me wrong—I like weenies and beans as much as anyone—but not cold ones, and not just weenies and beans. I want a menu and variety. My culinary expectations come from my dad, who famously made chicken and dumplings up in the middle of the Marble Mountains. There was nothing more

This is the meadow with the bees!

My cousins the Prices, Morgan, my dad, and me.

comforting or more appreciated while watching a sunset in the mountains, sitting on a log alongside the lake, with horses grazing in a nearby meadow, than chicken and dumplings: creamy, tender, doughy, amazing, stick-to-your-ribs kind of food. That's when I realized that if my dad could figure out how to get a cast-iron pot, fresh chicken, vegetables, and the fixings to make dumplings into the Marble Mountains, packing on horseback all day long, then I could prepare anything, anywhere, as long as I was prepared, organized, and educated.

There were bears in the Marble Mountains, and you had to do certain things to secure your food—first, leaving food out is dangerous, and second, you want the food for yourself not the bears and racoons. But there was a system in place to keep the bears at bay: You tied all the food into a tarp and used ropes to hoist the tarp so that it was suspended between two trees about fifty feet apart. First, all the coolers and food were placed on the tarp, and it was tied off kind of like a piece of saltwater taffy. Then the ropes were tied around the horns of the saddles of two horses and the horses pulled in unison in opposite directions to hoist all those perishables up into the air. If you just tied the tarp up in a tree, the bear could climb that tree and get it, but not if you suspended it in midair.

When I was about twelve we rode up into the mountains on horseback with our friends the Andersons and the Dunns and their kids. Following protocol, we put all our belongings into the tarp once we reached the campsite. I was on my horse, Rebel, and my dad told me to "dally," or wrap the rope around the horn of my saddle multiple times. He said to be sure I'd done it several times, and I told him not to worry about it—I had it covered (I prided myself on my horsemanship). We proceed to pull the package thirty feet into the air . . . and all of a sudden the rope came loose off my saddle. You could hear that rope buzzing like a zip line as it unwound. So, one end of the tarp stayed thirty feet in air and the other end let loose, crashing onto the forest floor with all our belongings shooting out.

Needless to say, my dad was pissed. He started chasing me, and I went straight for the only place I knew I would be safe—the middle of the lake. And of course I was fully clothed. Dad paced back and forth on the shoreline, but I stuck it out. Finally at dusk my mom called me over to the shore by the cattails and brought me in and put me into my sleeping bag with no dinner . . . and I was just fine with that. We didn't speak of the incident for the rest of that trip.

P.S. And for the next book, remind me to tell you the story about the bees and the horse through the meadow—that was a doozy. . . .

Smoked Salmon Hash

Smoked salmon has so much great flavor, it parties well with other ingredients. Here's a great way to let them hash it out with international seafood.

CONVENTIONAL COOKING METHOD

Same method, just cook it on the stovetop.

2 tablespoons canola oil

1 pound Yukon gold potatoes, cut into ½-inch dice

2 garlic cloves, minced

1 large yellow onion, cut into ½-inch dice

1 large red pepper, cut into ½-inch dice

½ teaspoon smoked paprika

Kosher salt and freshly ground black pepper

8 ounces smoked salmon, cut into bite-size strips

1 cup frozen peas, thawed

Thick-cut sourdough bread

Extra-virgin olive oil, for the bread

Sour cream–Dijon sauce

¾ cup sour cream

¼ cup Dijon mustard

1 teaspoon fresh lemon juice

Kosher salt and freshly ground black pepper

2 tablespoons chopped fresh dill

1 tablespoon chopped fresh chives

1 tablespoon chopped fresh parsley

MAKES: 4 servings

TIME: 35 minutes

YOU'LL NEED: Campfire with grill grate, cast-iron skillet

PREP-AHEAD TIP: This hash can be made with any protein or meat you have left from other camping meals, such as chicken or beef; simply substitute it for the salmon. That's what camping is all about—being resourceful and using what you have. When it comes to frozen peas, throw them in a bag in the cooler. This takes care of two things: helps keep stuff cool initially, then by the time you use the peas 2 or 3 days later, they should be partially thawed and ready to use.

1. Start a wood campfire and wait until the flames die down and the coals glow red with white ash. Place a grilling grate so that it sits just above the coals and you have medium-high heat to cook with.

2. Heat the canola oil in a cast-iron skillet on the grill grate. Add the potatoes and cook for 10 minutes. Add the garlic, onion, and pepper and cook until all the vegetables are tender and charred, about 10 more minutes. Season with smoked paprika, salt, and pepper.

3. Gently fold in the smoked salmon and peas; cook for 1 to 2 minutes to warm through.

4. To grill the bread, drizzle slices of sourdough with olive oil, then place them on the grill grate over the fire. Turn the bread frequently when grilling over the open flame until it is crisp and slightly charred around the edges, 60 to 90 seconds per side.

5. To make the sauce, whisk together the sour cream, Dijon mustard, and lemon juice, season with salt and pepper, and fold in the chopped herbs. Serve the hash straight from the pan and drizzle with the sauce.

Ham and Grits with Red-Eye Gravy

Now, I'll be honest, this recipe is not really that dynamic. But this is, without question, my favorite thing to eat for breakfast. Not just for breakfast—for lunch and/or dinner. It's Sunday football in a bowl; it's childhood memories on a plate. Okay, it may not be for everybody, but to be true to myself and true to you all, this is what I eat when I go camping. Love it or leave it—this is ham and grits.

Grits

2 cups milk

2 cups low-sodium chicken stock

1 cup stone-ground grits

1 cup grated sharp white Cheddar cheese

½ cup grated Parmesan cheese

2 tablespoons unsalted butter

Kosher salt and freshly ground black pepper

2 or 3 dashes of hot sauce

Ham

2 tablespoons unsalted butter

1 pound cooked country ham, cut into ¼-inch slices

Red-eye gravy

1 cup strong brewed coffee

1 tablespoon unsalted butter

Kosher salt and freshly ground black pepper

MAKES: 4 to 6 servings

TIME: 1 hour

YOU'LL NEED: Campfire with grill grate, large cast-iron skillet, medium saucepan, whisk

PREP-AHEAD TIP: Grits can be made the night before, just use a little extra milk to loosen and reheat.

1. Prepare a wood campfire and wait until the flames die down and coals glow red with white ash. Lower a grilling rack so it sits just above the coals.

2. To make the grits, in a medium saucepan, bring the milk and chicken stock to a boil over medium-high heat. Slowly stir in the grits, whisking constantly. Once the grits are incorporated and there are no lumps, reduce the heat to low. Whisking frequently, continue cooking for 25 to 30 minutes or until the grits are creamy and soft. Gradually stir in both cheeses and top with the butter. Season with salt, pepper, and hot sauce to taste.

3. For the ham, melt the butter in a large cast-iron skillet over medium-high heat. Add the ham and sear it until golden brown on both sides, about 2 to 3 minutes on the first side and 1 to 2 minutes on the second side. Transfer the ham to a plate and keep it warm next to the fire. Deglaze the pan with the coffee and use a wooden spoon to scrape the bottom and release any brown bits. Simmer for 2 to 3 minutes. Remove from the heat and stir in the butter. Season with salt and pepper to taste. Set the sauce aside in a bowl and wipe out the skillet.

4. For the eggs, melt the 2 tablespoons of butter in the cast-iron skillet over medium heat. Break the eggs into separate vessels. Carefully, one at a time, slip the eggs into the pan and move the pan to a cooler area. Once the outside of the egg whites begin to set, cover with a lid. Cook for 2 to 3 minutes, or until desired doneness. Season with salt and pepper.

5. To serve, place a heaping ladleful (or two) of the grits on the bottom of a shallow bowl or rimmed plate. Chop up the ham and top the grits with some ham and a fried egg, if desired, and finish with spoonful of red-eye gravy.

Fried egg (optional)
(very optional . . . jk)

2 tablespoons unsalted butter

4 to 6 large eggs

Kosher salt and freshly ground black pepper

Red-Eye Gravy

When I was a kid this is what my mom would make me: grits, ham steak, and an egg with red-eye gravy. (Although there was a time I called it one-eye gravy and another era where I called it brown-eye gravy, but my parents corrected me.) Today I'll admit that when someone asks me what one of my last meals would be, I say ham and grits with red-eye gravy.

Take a really good slice of ham and cook it in a cast-iron skillet; after the fat renders from the rind and the ham browns on both sides, remove the ham and deglaze the pan with a cup of strong, hot, black coffee. When friends see me chop up the ham, put it on the grits, and then pour what looks like brown greasy sludge on top of that, they think something has really gone wrong. You either love it or hate it. Salt, pepper, and a pat of butter in those grits with the red-eye gravy—that's what it's all about. I've seen red-eye gravy made around the country on Triple D, and every time I have to do a taste test, but nobody makes it as good as mine. Black coffee, pan drippings, that's it. I hope you dig this.

Campfire Cooking Basics

Back in the day campfires were used for light, to keep warm, and to keep predators away. These instincts to huddle around the campfire run deep, and it's not a camping trip without a fire. What isn't quite as instinctual anymore is the ability to cook over a campfire. So here are a few basics to keep in mind:

1) If you use the direct heat of the flame of the fire, you're likely to burn your food.

2) The key is to build a strong fire, then patiently wait for it to burn down to hot coals. We're striving to establish a solid coal bed, as it's the radiant heat of the coals that do the real cooking for you.

3) Adjust the heat level, from low to high, by using a grate over the coals that can be raised or lowered using rungs or even piles of bricks, or establish a "cooler" side of your grill grate by piling the coals on one side. If you have a campfire ring, a cooler heat level for cooking can be established by swinging the grate out, away from the main heat source. Whatever your setup, the lower heat level can be used for simmering and braising, while the hotter level can be used for searing and boiling.

4) Cooking over a campfire is not an exact science, so use the stated cooking times as guidelines but pay extra attention to visual cues to establish when your food is done.

That's the whole foundation. If you have the convenience of a camp stove or propane burner, by all means use it, but for the big volume cooking and flavor, if you can manage your coals that's where you're going to get your return on your campfire-building investment.

1. Dry kindling and firewood

2. Make a tepee with lots of crumpled paper to start

3. Make sure there's good ventilation

4. Once the coals are established, add more medium wood

5. Those are cookin' coals

Stout-Braised Short Ribs with Pearl Barley

I think the Dutch oven was made for short ribs and a campfire. I mean, how else are you going to get it done? If you don't have a grill grate, surround the pot with coals, drop a few on the top, and let the meat cook down till it's tender.

CONVENTIONAL COOKING METHOD

You can cook this on the stovetop using the method in this recipe, or braise it in the oven: After browning and bringing to a simmer, place the covered Dutch oven in a 350°F oven and cook for 2 hours, or until the ribs are fall-apart tender.

4½ pounds bone-in short ribs (4-inch pieces)

Kosher salt and freshly ground black pepper

¼ cup canola oil

2 medium carrots, roughly chopped

2 celery stalks, sliced

2 medium onions, roughly chopped

4 garlic cloves, thinly sliced

6 fresh thyme sprigs

2 bay leaves

2 fresh rosemary sprigs

Two 12-ounce bottles stout beer, such as Guinness

1 quart low-sodium beef broth

One 14½-ounce can diced tomatoes

1 cup pearl barley

2 teaspoons mustard powder

MAKES: 6 servings

TIME: 4 hours 15 minutes

YOU'LL NEED: Campfire with grill grate, Dutch oven

PREP-AHEAD TIP: The short ribs can be braised a day ahead of time. Once they're cooked, cool them and refrigerate them overnight in the braising liquid—they're even more tender and more flavorful the next day when reheated.

1. Start a wood campfire and wait until the flames die down and the coals glow red with white ash. Place a grilling grate so that it sits above the coals and you have medium-high heat.

2. Season the short ribs all over with salt and pepper, then grill so they are well charred all over, 2 to 3 minutes per side. You want a deep brown color on the meat, as this will give the stew its rich flavor and color. Remove the ribs and set them aside on a tray. Move the grill so it's 4 to 5 inches above the coals (medium heat).

3. Set a Dutch oven or large heavy pot on the grill and pour in the canola oil. Add the carrots, celery, and onions. Sauté the vegetables until caramelized and wilted, 8 to 10 minutes. Add the garlic and

If You Wouldn't Drink It, Don't Cook with It

Everybody has been around with that bottle of wine that's opened and someone says, "Oh, it's terrible. But don't throw it out; we'll cook with it." Well, cooking only intensifies it, so you just end up with more pronounced bad flavors. And by the way, the same goes for beer—if you wouldn't drink it, don't cook with it. My personal favorites to cook with are sauvignon blanc for whites and cabernet sauvignon for reds—I'm not a big chardonnay fan, and I'll take cabernet over merlot.

toss to combine and heat through. Place the ribs in the pot and nestle them among the vegetables. Add the thyme, bay leaves, rosemary, stout, broth, and tomatoes. Season lightly with salt and pepper, then stir and bring to a boil. Cover with a lid and simmer the ribs for 2½ hours. Periodically skim any excess fat on the surface and discard. Because you're simmering for so long, you'll need to keep the campfire fueled, so throw more coals or wood on the fire every time you skim the surface.

4. After 2½ hours, mix in the pearl barley and mustard powder, then cook 45 more minutes, uncovered (this will help reduce and intensify the broth). Remove the bay leaf and thyme and rosemary sprigs. Taste, season with salt and pepper, and serve with rice or Camping Baked Potatoes with Herbed Sour Cream (page 249).

Zing Zang Flank Steak

So, here's the beauty of this dish—you can prep this filling ahead of time and take a full-flavored steak experience on your next camping trip. All you need is a hot grill.

CONVENTIONAL COOKING METHOD

Use the same method with your home grill or a grill pan on the stovetop.

Extra-virgin olive oil

4 garlic cloves, minced

1 medium onion, sliced

2 teaspoons dried Italian seasoning

2 teaspoons fresh thyme leaves

6 medium peperoncino Calabrese peppers (dried hot red peppers in oil), sliced thin

Kosher salt and freshly cracked black pepper

Two 1½-pound flank steaks

2 Roma (plum) tomatoes, thinly sliced

½ cup panko (Japanese breadcrumbs)

1 cup shredded provolone cheese

½ cup fresh basil leaves

MAKES: 4 servings

TIME: 45 minutes

YOU'LL NEED: Campfire with grill grate, large sauté pan, propane burner, 2 metal or thick bamboo skewers (see sidebar)

PREP-AHEAD TIP: Prepare the stuffing mixture the night before and keep refrigerated or in a chilled cooler.

1. Start a wood campfire and wait until the flames die down and the coals glow red with white ash. Place a grilling grate so that it sits just above the coals and you have medium-high heat to cook with.

2. Set a large sauté pan on the grill grate. Coat with olive oil and add the garlic, onion, Italian seasoning, and thyme. Fold the peppers into the onion mixture. Season with salt and pepper and sauté until the onion is well caramelized, 7 to 8 minutes. Set aside to cool and divide in half evenly.

3. Trim the steaks of any excess fat and remove any tough silverskin with the tip of a knife. Working with one steak at a time, place the steak on a clean cutting board (so the grain runs up and down). Using a sharp knife, carefully make a flat cut down one long side of the steak and cut it open parallel to the board so you can open the steak like a book.

4. On one side of the steak, spread half of the onion mixture. Top with half of the tomato slices, panko, and shredded cheese. Tear up the

Zing Zang Flank Steak

Skewers

Invest in a good set of metal skewers, preferably with wide flat-edge blades, as it's less likely that your food will spin and flip. If you're using bamboo skewers, the thicker the better, and please soak them in water for at least an hour before cooking with them. If bamboo or round skewers are all you have and you're experiencing the food Ferris wheel, especially with heavy medallions of meat (you know what I mean—the meat's on the skewer, you pick it up, and it rolls around on the skewer right back to where it was, so you can't flip it—it has a mind of its own), then try the double-skewer method. It takes a little bit of time, but it's well worth the effort as it will give you much more consistent cooking—and less of a headache. (See the illustration on page 225.)

basil leaves and scatter on top for the last layer of filling. Fold the flap of beef over the top to cover. Using a bamboo skewer, thread the steak along the cut edge to seal the steak back together and hold in the filling. Repeat with the second steak.

5. Wipe down the grill grates with some oil-blotted towels to clean and create a nonstick surface. Season the stuffed flank steaks with salt and pepper on both sides, then place on the hot grill. Cook for 7 to 8 minutes on the first side (turn 90 degrees to create crosshatch marks halfway through), then use a large spatula to carefully flip the steaks and cook for 5 minutes more on the second side for medium-rare.

6. Remove the steaks from the grill and set aside to rest for 5 minutes. Use a sharp knife to cut them into 1-inch-thick slices and serve.

Warm Taco Salad with Spicy, Smoky Ranch

When I was a kid, taco salad night at my house was my favorite night of the week. And guess what—it's no different with Hunter, Ryder, and Jules. Wait till your kids get a load of this.

CONVENTIONAL COOKING METHOD

Use the same method on your stovetop.

MAKES: 6 servings

TIME: 25 to 30 minutes

YOU'LL NEED: Campfire, propane burner, cast-iron skillet, frying thermometer

PREP-AHEAD TIP: Make the smoky ranch dressing 1 or 2 days before you head out camping and keep it refrigerated or chilled in a cooler until you need it. You can fry the tortilla strips 2 or 3 hours ahead of time, drain well, and store in an airtight container. In place of the beef, you can substitute any leftover protein, such as smoked chicken, sliced tri-tip, brisket, or ground turkey.

"Ryder, this is how you dig a fire pit."

Canola oil, for frying

8 medium corn tortillas, cut into ¼-inch strips

Kosher salt

3 garlic cloves, minced

1 medium yellow onion, diced

1 jalapeño pepper, seeded and minced

1 pound lean ground beef (or ground turkey)

1 teaspoon tomato paste

1 tablespoon smoked paprika

1 tablespoon ground cumin

1 teaspoon dried oregano

1 tablespoon chipotle chile powder

1 tablespoon ancho chile powder

Freshly ground black pepper

2 romaine lettuce heads, chopped into 1-inch pieces

1½ 15½-ounce cans black beans, drained and rinsed

2 cups diced Roma (plum) tomatoes

1 cup ¼-inch cubes Cheddar cheese

4 to 6 radishes, sliced

Smoky Ranch Dressing (recipe follows)

¼ cup sliced scallions, for garnish

2 tablespoons chopped fresh cilantro, for garnish

¼ cup crumbled Cotija cheese, for garnish

1. Start a wood campfire and wait until the flames die down and the coals glow red with white ash. Place a grilling grate so that it sits above the coals and you have good, consistent medium-high heat.

2. Begin by deep-frying the tortilla strips. This is easier to do over a camping burner than a campfire, as the oil temperature will come up faster and be more consistent. In a medium pot, heat 2 to 3 inches of canola oil to 350°F over medium-high heat. Add the tortilla strips in batches and fry for 2 to 3 minutes, until crisp and golden. Drain on paper towels and season with salt. Set aside.

3. Lightly coat a cast-iron skillet with oil and set it over medium-high heat on the grate over the campfire. Add the garlic, onion, and jalapeño and sauté until softened and lightly caramelized, 5 to 6 minutes. Add the ground meat, tomato paste, paprika, cumin, oregano, and chili powders and brown the meat while breaking it up with the back of a large wooden spoon. Taste and season with salt and pepper. When the meat is cooked through, drain any excess fat from the skillet, add 1 cup water, and reduce until the meat mixture has thickened slightly.

4. Assemble the salad with layers of sliced romaine, black beans, tomatoes, Cheddar cubes, radish slices, and tortilla strips. Pile on the warm meat mixture as the top layer to prevent the lettuce from wilting, and drizzle the salad with the ranch dressing. Garnish with sliced scallions, chopped cilantro, and crumbled Cotija.

Smoky Ranch Dressing

MAKES: Approximately 2 cups

TIME: 5 minutes

Whisk together the buttermilk, mayonnaise, and lime juice. Add the remaining ingredients and whisk until smooth. Taste for seasoning. Refrigerate until ready to use.

1 cup buttermilk

¾ cup mayonnaise

Juice of 1 lime

1 chipotle in adobo, finely chopped, plus 2 tablespoons adobo sauce

¼ teaspoon ground cumin

1 teaspoon garlic powder

½ teaspoon agave syrup

Kosher salt and freshly ground black pepper

Jules, Hunter, and our other son, Cowboy.

Green Onion and Flank Steak Yakitori

One of the things you've got plenty of when you're camping is time. Time to spend together talking, telling stories, and cooking . . . and if you decide you're making this dish, grab everybody together to help you assemble the roll-ups and skewers. Trust me, it's worth it.

CONVENTIONAL COOKING METHOD

Cook the steak on a cast-iron griddle on the stovetop.

1 pound flank steak, trimmed

½ cup soy sauce

3 tablespoons canola oil

2 tablespoons mirin

1 teaspoon toasted sesame oil

1 tablespoon toasted sesame seeds, plus more for garnish

2 tablespoons light brown sugar

2 garlic cloves, minced

1 teaspoon sambal (or any Asian chili-garlic sauce)

1-inch piece fresh ginger root, grated

6 scallions

Kosher salt and freshly ground black pepper

MAKES: 4 servings

TIME: 2 hours 15 minutes

YOU'LL NEED: Campfire with grill grate, small saucepan, skewers

PREP-AHEAD TIP: Cut the flank steak and marinate it in a plastic bag or container, chilled in a cooler. It can marinate for up to 24 hours, as the beef is very robust. If using bamboo skewers, soak them in water overnight.

1. Cut the flank steak into 4 by 4-inch pieces and place them in a resealable plastic bag. Whisk together the soy sauce, 2 tablespoons of the canola oil, mirin, sesame oil, sesame seeds, sugar, garlic, sambal, and ginger. Pour the marinade over the steak, seal the bag, and marinate for at least 2 hours or overnight.

2. Start a wood campfire and wait until the flames die down and the coals glow red with white ash. Place a grilling grate so that it sits right on the radiant coals and you have high heat.

3. Remove the flank steak from the marinade and pat dry. Pour the marinade into a saucepan and bring to a boil over high heat. Reduce to a simmer by moving the pot to the edge of the grill where it is farther

away from the hottest coals. Simmer for 5 to 10 minutes to thicken the sauce until it lightly coats the back of a spoon.

4. Toss the scallions with the remaining 1 tablespoon oil, salt, and pepper, and grill on the grate over the fire until charred, 1 to 2 minutes per side. Trim them into 5-inch pieces and set aside.

5. To assemble the skewers, lay 2 or 3 grilled scallion pieces in the center of each piece of steak. Tightly roll up each steak around the scallions, into a log. Using 2 parallel bamboo skewers, skewer 3 of the logs together, piercing through each side of the log at the seam. Repeat with the remaining beef and scallions until you have 6 rolled pieces of beef, for 2 double skewers.

6. Wipe down the grill grate with an oil-blotted paper towel to clean and create a nonstick surface. Grill the skewers for 4 to 5 minutes per side for medium rare, glazing with the reduced marinade. Garnish with toasted sesame seeds.

Crispy Veal Schnitzel with Garlic-Onion Gravy

I know the title sounds ambitious for camping, but if you pound out that veal at home, you can dredge it on-site, and all you need is a hot fire and a cast-iron skillet.

CONVENTIONAL COOKING METHOD

Cook on a stovetop burner following the same method. You can even use a large nonstick skillet if you have a full range of equipment to work with.

MAKES: 4 servings

TIME: 1 hour 10 minutes

YOU'LL NEED: Campfire with grill grate, cast-iron skillet

PREP-AHEAD TIP: Gather crackers, toast, and so on in a resealable bag for "Whatever You Have" Breading (see page 145), then make crumbs by bashing the bag with the back of a pan. Pound out the veal cutlets before you head out camping and keep them chilled, wrapped tightly in plastic.

1. Start a wood campfire and wait until the flames die down and the coals glow red with white ash. Place a grilling grate so that it sits above the coals and you have nice, even, medium heat.

2. Working with 2 cutlets at a time, place them between 2 sheets of plastic wrap. Using the flat side of a meat tenderizer, gently pound out each piece (working from the center outward) to an even ¼-inch thickness. Work carefully to keep them even and not tear the veal. Repeat with the remaining cutlets.

3. Set up a breading station. Place the flour in a shallow bowl, season with salt and pepper, and mix well. Pour the buttermilk into a second shallow bowl, season with salt and pepper, and mix well. In a third shallow bowl, combine the breadcrumbs and Parmesan, season with salt and pepper, and mix well.

4. Dredge each cutlet lightly in the flour. Shake off any excess, then dip it in the buttermilk. Finally, dredge in the breadcrumb mixture. Cover evenly on both sides, gently patting the crumbs into the veal to help them stick.

5. To cook the cutlets, set a large cast-iron skillet (work with 2 if you have them so you can cook all 4 cutlets at once) on the grate over the campfire. Heat 2 tablespoons of the oil in the skillet and cook the cutlets for 3 to 4 minutes per side. If the cutlets start to brown too quickly, move the skillet to a cooler part of the grate. You want the cutlets to be golden brown, crispy, and cooked through. Transfer the cutlets to a paper towel–lined plate to drain. Season with salt while warm and set aside.

6. To make the gravy, set the same skillet over the heat again. Use a paper towel to wipe out any brown bits or debris but leave the fat (this will add flavor to the gravy). Add the butter, garlic, onions, and thyme, season with salt and pepper, and sauté until the onions are lightly caramelized and tender, 7 to 8 minutes. Dust the mixture with the flour, stirring constantly to make a roux. Cook the roux until just golden, then add the wine to deglaze the pan, whisking to ensure that no lumps form. Add the chicken broth, mix well, and simmer for 5 to 6 minutes, or until the gravy is thickened. Serve the schnitzel with the gravy. Garnish with the parsley, tomato, and lemon wedges.

Cutlets

Four 6-ounce veal cutlets

2 cups all-purpose flour

Kosher salt and freshly ground black pepper

2 cups buttermilk

2 cups "Whatever You Have" Breading

½ cup grated Parmesan cheese

¼ cup olive oil, for pan-frying

2 tablespoons chopped fresh flat-leaf parsley, for garnish

¼ cup seeded and finely diced Roma (plum) tomato, for garnish

Lemon wedges, for garnish

Garlic-onion gravy

3 tablespoons unsalted butter

3 garlic cloves, minced

1 medium onion, finely diced

1 teaspoon fresh thyme leaves

Kosher salt and freshly ground black pepper

2 tablespoons all-purpose flour

¼ cup dry white wine

1 cup low-sodium chicken broth

Grilled Huli Huli-Style Chicken

Huli Huli warning: After trying this chicken you may experience the immediate urge to fly to Oahu.

CONVENTIONAL COOKING METHOD

Cook on the grill at home. Traditional method: Cook on a Huli Huli machine or rotisserie.

MAKES: 4 servings

TIME: 2 hours 25 minutes

YOU'LL NEED: Campfire with grill grate, flat wire grilling basket, silicone pastry brush

PREP-AHEAD TIP: Spatchcock and brine the chicken ahead of time. Transport it in a zip-top bag in an iced cooler, so all you have to do at the campground is toss it in the dry rub. Huli Huli sauce can be made 1 or 2 days in advance.

1. Start a wood campfire and wait until the flames die down and the coals glow red with white ash. Place a grilling grate so that it sits above the coals and you have nice, even, medium heat. You can skip the grate on this one and just hold the wire baskets over the coals, but you might get tired and want to rest the baskets, so the grate is a good option if you have one.

2. PREPARE THE SPATCHCOCK CHICKEN: Place the whole chicken, breast side down, on your preparation surface. Using kitchen shears, remove the backbone by cutting up from the tailbone to the neck on both sides. Open the bird and remove the breastbone and wishbone. Tuck the wings under the breast so that the chicken sits in one flat layer.

3. To make the brine, in a small saucepan, combine 1 cup water, the salt, sugar, bay leaves, and garlic. Bring to a simmer to dissolve the salt and sugar. Turn off the heat and add the ice. Once the liquid is cool, pour it into a resealable bag over a bowl and add the chicken, making sure it is completely submerged. Brine the chicken for 1 hour and keep chilled in the fridge or a cooler (this can be done ahead of time before you head out camping).

4. For the Huli Huli sauce, in a small saucepan over medium-low heat, combine the pineapple juice, ketchup, soy sauce, and sherry vinegar. Once the liquid simmers, whisk in the brown sugar and ginger.

Continue to simmer until the liquid begins to thicken, about 5 minutes. Remove from the heat and let stand (or prepare ahead and chill). Reserve 1 cup sauce for serving.

5. Remove the chicken from the brine and pat dry. To make the dry rub, thoroughly mix the garlic powder, salt, paprika, cayenne, onion powder, cumin, and black pepper to taste in a small bowl. Coat the chicken with the dry rub, making sure to sprinkle well inside the cavity. Lay the chicken in a medium rectangular wire-mesh grilling basket, making a neat, rectangular package with the thighs tucked next to the breasts. Place the basket on the grill grate over the campfire breast side down and char for 7 to 8 minutes. Turn once and grill the other side for 15 minutes.

6. Squeeze the lemon juice over the chicken and continue to cook, turning frequently so that the chicken develops a deep golden brown skin without burning. When the chicken is done, the skin will be thoroughly crispy and browned and a digital instant-read thermometer reached an internal temperature of 165°F. The total cook time will be 35 to 40 minutes. Using a heat-resistant silicone pastry brush, glaze the chicken with the Huli Huli sauce the last 5 minutes. Remove the chicken from the basket and set aside to rest for 6 to 8 minutes.

7. To serve, carve the chicken into breasts, thighs, and wings. Arrange on a large serving dish alongside the reserved Huli Huli sauce.

Chicken and Huli Huli brine

One 5- to 7-pound whole chicken

1 cup kosher salt

½ cup sugar

3 bay leaves

3 garlic cloves, peeled and smashed

3 cups ice

Huli Huli sauce

1 cup pineapple juice

½ cup ketchup

½ cup soy sauce

2 tablespoons sherry vinegar

½ cup light brown sugar

2 teaspoons ground ginger

Dry rub

2 tablespoons garlic powder

2 tablespoons kosher salt

1 tablespoon plus 1 teaspoon paprika

1 tablespoon cayenne pepper

1 tablespoon onion powder

1 teaspoon ground cumin

Freshly cracked black pepper

1 lemon, halved

The Legend of the Huli Huli Chickenfest

When we were on the island of Oahu shooting *Diners, Drive-ins and Dives*, we pulled into Haleiwa. I didn't know where to eat, so I did what I tell everyone else to do: slow down and take a look around. I parked the rental car and Lori and Ryder went off to the restroom while Hunter and I went for a walk. I found the most local-looking person I could and asked, "Where's a good place to eat?"

The guy said, "What kind of food do you like?"

I said, "Local."

"You sure?"

"Yeah, why?"

"'Cause it ain't no indoor sit-down restaurant."

"All the better." My mouth starting watering. "What do they serve?"

"Chicken."

"What else?"

"Just chicken. Some sauce, too."

He pointed to a vacant parking lot with an enormous trailered barbecue that had thirty spit rotisseries, each holding six chickens. There was a line of at least forty people standing in the hot Hawaiian sun waiting to receive Styrofoam boxes full of cut-up Huli Huli (which means *turn turn*) chicken. I couldn't believe it. So I waited in line and watched as they removed chickens from the spit, cut them in half, and served the sauce in little plastic containers. Once I'd gotten my chicken I went to sit down, but the tables were occupied, so I proceeded to walk away from the barbecue with my purchase. Only then did I get the true aroma of the Huli Huli chicken. I must've looked like someone who hadn't eaten in weeks as I dug into this hot Styrofoam box in a plastic bag, in the heat of Hawaii while crossing the road, with Hunter reaching over my shoulder trying to grab his piece of chicken. It was so fall-apart tender that when I pulled the drumstick out of the bag it had only a tiny piece of meat left on it. The Styrofoam container couldn't withstand the heat of the bird, and the juice was running down and out of the flimsy plastic bag. We got across the street and Lori and Ryder were trying to flag us down from the restaurant they'd gone to, but we just hunkered down there in the parking lot like dogs with a doggie bag. As we finished the chicken we walked over to Lori and Ryder, licking our fingers, chicken juice all over us, and as we sat down Lori asked, "Did you save me any?" And the choice at this point was to answer no, we didn't save you any, or no, you wouldn't have liked it.

So, shhhhhhhhh—don't tell Lori she woulda liked it.

Later that week on Oahu, we were shooting Triple D at a place called Fresh Catch. I asked the owner, and now great friend, Reno, where I could get a Huli Huli machine. He said, "You get it from your uncle."

I said, "My uncle doesn't have one of these!"

And he said, "No, you don't buy it, you get it from a person—these things are passed down."

So I made countless requests for the phone number of someone I could buy one from, or the measurements of one so I could make one myself, but I got nothing.

Then one day Reno called me and said, "Hey, Triple D guy, I'm coming to visit you, and I have something for you." Crazy Reno, the chicken man, wearing his chicken headband, had gotten together with his friends and built me a Huli Huli chicken machine . . . and shipped it from Hawaii! After Reno got it delivered from the port of Oakland, I was so excited that we loaded up the machine with thirty-six chickens at nine o'clock at night.

Not everybody has the Huli Huli rotisserie program, but I can offer here a good Huli Huli take-off that we featured on *Guy's Big Bite*.

Slamma Jamma Chicken Parmigiana

The key to any good chicken parm is balance, which for me means: a little bit of time in the brine, a properly diluted egg wash, crispy seasoned panko breadcrumbs, and the right temperature oil. I call these the critical success factors. If you don't brine the chicken, you don't get the moisture you need; if the egg wash is too thick, it clumps up and makes a thick batter; if the breadcrumbs aren't crispy-crunchy, they're too dense and heavy and soak up oil; if the oil isn't at the right temperature either the chicken will be soggy or it will brown too fast and be raw in the middle. Another key factor: The chicken has to be the right thickness to cook correctly. Trim the thicker side a bit so that it will pound out evenly.

CONVENTIONAL COOKING METHOD

If you're making this on the stove top at home, melt the cheese on the crisped chicken under the broiler for 30 to 40 seconds.

MAKES: 4 servings

TIME: 2 hours 15 minutes

YOU'LL NEED: Campfire with grill grate, cast-iron skillet, sheet pan

PREP-AHEAD TIP: The tomato sauce can be made 1 or 2 days in advance; keep refrigerated until ready to use. The chicken breast can be pounded out before you head out on your adventures. Transport it in an iced cooler, wrapped tightly in plastic. Use my "Whatever You Have" Breading method (see page 145) to gather up the crunchy coating over the course of the trip.

1. Start a wood campfire and wait until the flames die down and the coals glow red with white ash. Place a grilling grate so that it sits above the coals and you have nice, even, medium heat.

2. Lightly pound the chicken breasts to ½-inch thickness. Combine the kosher salt, sugar, and 1 quart water in a 1-gallon resealable plastic bag; shake until dissolved. Add the chicken breasts and soak at room temperature for 30 minutes.

3. Place the flour in a medium bowl. Remove the chicken from the brine. Shake off the excess moisture and, with tongs, lightly dredge the chicken in the flour. Shake off the excess flour and transfer the chicken to a large plate.

4. Mix the eggs and milk in a medium bowl and whisk thoroughly. In a separate bowl, combine the breadcrumbs, oregano, basil, parsley, sea salt, and pepper. Dredge the chicken in the egg and milk mixture

Chicken Parm and Elvis Duran, Z100

One of my favorite radio morning shows is Elvis Duran on Z100 in New York. The dude and his team are hysterical—nothing is safe and everything is fun. I wish I could go on this show every day. They treat me like family, and my stomach hurts from laughing after I leave. The relationship runs deep because they were there for one of the first media experiences I had with Food Network. For *Next Food Network Star*, we had to make chicken Parmesan and bring it to these guys to try, like a cook-off. Now, I have held my chicken Parmesan closely—I'm dedicated to it, and quite frankly I think it's one of the best. But I was worried taking it to these guys. Here I was in New York, and we're going to be under the gun; maybe they liked it old-school, a little soggy under the sauce, where mine is crunchy? But they loved my chicken Parmesan, and that was the beginning of the momentum that led to my winning the *Next Food Network Star* competition. I'll never forget it.

Every time I see Elvis and the team it takes me back to that day. Thanks so much, guys, for all the great love and support—you're an amazing group of people with a hysterical show. I look forward to many more adventures.

Four 5-ounce boneless, skinless, trimmed chicken breasts

½ cup kosher salt

½ cup sugar

1½ cups all-purpose flour

2 large eggs

¼ cup milk

3 cups "Whatever You Have" Breading

¼ teaspoon dried oregano

¼ teaspoon dried basil

1 teaspoon dried parsley

1 teaspoon fine sea salt

½ teaspoon freshly ground black pepper

1 pound penne rigate

Canola oil, for frying (about 2 cups)

1 pound fresh mozzarella cheese, sliced

¼ pound Parmigiano-Reggiano, plus extra for garnish, grated

Tomato Sauce (recipe follows)

¼ cup minced fresh flat-leaf parsley, for garnish

and let the excess drain off. Then dredge the chicken in the breadcrumb mixture, lightly patting in the breadcrumbs to adhere. Let the breaded chicken sit for 5 minutes before frying. Bring a large pot of salted water over high heat to boil and cook pasta according to package directions until al dente.

5. In a cast-iron skillet set on a grate over the campfire, add enough canola oil to come a quarter of the way up the sides of the chicken. Test the heat of the oil by sprinkling a few breadcrumbs into it. They should sizzle and float and turn a nice golden brown when the oil is ready to go (about 350°F). Carefully place the chicken in the pan, cook-

ing it in batches until golden brown on both sides, 3 to 4 minutes per side. Remove from the pan and place on a paper towel–lined plate to drain. Repeat with the remaining chicken.

6. Place mozzarella slices and sprinkle Parmesan evenly on top of each piece of chicken, reserving some Parmesan for garnish. Place the chicken on a sheet pan over the flame and rotate until the cheese melts.

7. Serve the chicken over pasta and ladle tomato sauce on top. Garnish with additional Parmesan and parsley.

Tomato Sauce

2 tablespoons extra-virgin olive oil

1 yellow onion, minced

4 garlic cloves, crushed

6 cups peeled and diced Roma (plum) tomatoes

1 tablespoon thinly sliced fresh basil leaves

1½ teaspoons chopped fresh oregano leaves

Salt and freshly ground black pepper

MAKES: About 5 cups

Heat the olive oil over medium heat in a saucepan. Add the onion and cook until translucent, about 3 to 4 minutes. Add the garlic and cook until almost brown, 1 or 2 minutes, then add the tomatoes. Simmer for 30 minutes over medium-low heat. Add the basil and oregano and cook for 30 minutes more, until fragrant. Mash with a potato masher to break up the tomatoes so you have a rustic tomato sauce, perfect for camping. Season with salt and pepper to taste.

Pastrami Burger with Caraway Coleslaw

I make great burgers, as you will discover at Guy's Burger Joint if you take a Carnival Cruise. I think my method is "the" method, but when I made a "pastrami burger" I realized this method was worth adding to my repertoire. The key to this is really thin high-quality pastrami. The combination of the burger and pastrami seasoning is what makes this work. The burger benefits from the pastrami flavor and the pastrami benefits from the burger fat.

CONVENTIONAL COOKING METHOD

Follow the same method on a stovetop.

MAKES: 4 servings

TIME: 45 minutes

YOU'LL NEED: Campfire with grill grate, cast-iron skillet

PREP-AHEAD TIP: Form the burgers and place a sheet of parchment paper between each. Wrap in plastic and keep refrigerated or chilled in a cooler. The caraway coleslaw can be made 1 or 2 days in advance. Keep it refrigerated or on ice.

½ stick (¼ cup) unsalted butter, softened

2 garlic cloves, minced

Kosher salt and freshly ground black pepper

Canola oil, as needed

1 sweet onion, finely sliced

12 ounces good-quality pastrami, sliced

2 pounds ground beef (80/20 blend)

8 slices Muenster cheese

4 soft brioche hamburger buns, cut in half

2 kosher dill pickles, finely sliced

2 heirloom tomatoes, finely sliced

8 Boston lettuce leaves, separated (about 1 small lettuce head)

1. Start a wood campfire and wait until the flames die down and the coals glow red with white ash. Place a grilling grate so that it sits above the coals and you have nice, even, medium heat.

2. Place the butter and garlic in a cast-iron skillet. As the butter melts, the garlic will infuse the butter and become fragrant. Stir well, season with salt and pepper, transfer garlic butter to a small bowl, and set aside to cool.

3. Place the same skillet back over medium heat to warm up. Add enough canola oil to coat the skillet, then add the onion. Cook over medium heat, stirring, until the onion caramelizes, 6 to 7 minutes. Season with salt and cook until soft and evenly brown. Transfer the onion and garlic to a plate and set aside.

Classic Katz's

So let me tell you about one of my favorite pastrami sandwiches, at Katz's Deli in New York. It was the first week of *The Next Food Network Star*, and we had a day off. Fellow contestant Andy Schumacher—who now owns Cobble Hill Restaurant in Cedar Rapids, Iowa—and I went on a pastrami pilgrimage. He told me there was a place called Katz's Deli. Remember the deli in the movie *When Harry Met Sally*? It's that place. I thought, if it's in a movie, it's probably not that great. Oh, was I wrong. When you walk into Katz's they give you a ticket—a ticket that's like a carnival ride ticket. And when you order a pastrami sandwich (which, yes, is as big as your head), they mark it off on your ticket. We ordered everything, and I had it all filled out on my ticket because I decided that I was going to treat since he was showing me the joint. So after we finished our pastrami feast and beers we went up to the counter and waited in line; I gave them my ticket and I paid the bill. As we were walking out, the lady asked Andy, "Where's your ticket?" We explained that his ticket didn't have anything on it. But she said, "No, where's your ticket?" That's when we notice the big sign that says Lost Ticket $150. And it's all cash . . . I tell the lady, go over and ask the guys doing the meat; I had all of it on my ticket. And she says, I understand, but you have to have the ticket. Next thing I know we're on our hands and knees searching for the ticket, underneath the legs of the people now seated at our table. And then, just by chance, I see the corner of the ticket under a table four tables away from us under a big dude's boot. It was gnarled, stepped on, and wet. But we handed her the ticket and got out of there without paying the ticketless toll. (Don't let the story scare you, you *have* to go to Katz's Deli, because it's the bomb.)

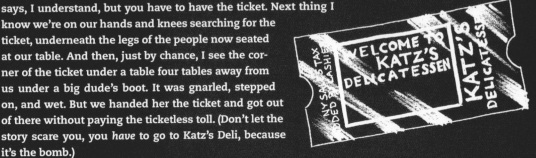

4. Raise the heat level by moving the skillet to the center of the grill over the coals, or lower the grill grate so that it's closer to the coals. Add enough canola oil to coat the pan. Add the pastrami and cook turning a few times, until crisp, 7 to 8 minutes total. Remove the pastrami and set aside, leaving any accumulated pan juices in the skillet.

5. Divide the ground beef into 4 equal portions and form them into 4 tight balls. Sprinkle them all over with salt and pepper. Place the hamburger balls in the skillet and sear for 30 to 40 seconds, then use a strong, flat metal spatula to flatten them to about ⅓-inch thick. Continuing to press with a spatula, cook until the burgers develop a crust on the bottom, about 2½ minutes. Flip and cook to develop a

crust on the second side, 1 minute. Use a spoon to baste the burgers with the pastrami fat in the pan.

6. Top each burger with 2 slices of cheese. Pour 1 tablespoon water into the pan and cover the skillet with a lid or foil or another pan to seal in the steam (this will help melt the cheese). Leave covered for 30 to 40 seconds, or until the cheese has melted, then remove the lid. When the burgers are at the desired point of doneness and the cheese is completely melted, top each with a pile of crispy pastrami, then set the burgers aside.

7. Brush the cut sides of the buns lightly with the garlic butter. Toast the buns directly on the grill over the campfire until golden and crisp around the edges, 15 to 20 seconds. Flip and lightly toast the outsides, another 15 seconds. Assemble the burgers by layering the base with pickle slices and caramelized onions, then the hamburger/pastrami patty. Next layer the tomato and lettuce and finish with the top half of the bun. Serve with caraway coleslaw.

Caraway Coleslaw

MAKES: 4 to 6 servings

TIME: 25 minutes

½ cup mayonnaise

½ cup sour cream

1 teaspoon Dijon mustard

3 tablespoons apple cider vinegar

2 teaspoons caraway seeds

1 tablespoon mustard seeds

Kosher salt and freshly ground black pepper

4 cups shredded green cabbage

2 cups shredded red cabbage

½ sweet onion, thinly sliced

2 carrots, grated

1. In a large mixing bowl, whisk together the mayonnaise, sour cream, Dijon, and vinegar. In a dry medium skillet over medium heat, toast the caraway and mustard seeds until golden brown and fragrant, 2 to 3 minutes. Add to the bowl with the dressing, season with salt and pepper, and stir well.

2. Add the cabbages, onion, and carrots and mix well, massaging in the dressing to coat the slaw evenly and tenderize the vegetables. Cover and set aside to marinate for at least 10 to 15 minutes before serving.

White Turkey and Bean Chili

When I'm on the road and not able to cook for the family, one of the requests is for me to make chili, because it's quick and easy for Lori to heat up. (Before I leave there's usually an inventory of chili and tomato sauce stacked in the freezer.) But since it's a hearty one-pot meal, of course it's also a Fieri camping favorite.

CONVENTIONAL COOKING METHOD

Use the same method, just cook on a stovetop.

MAKES: 6 to 8 servings

TIME: 1 hour

YOU'LL NEED: Propane burner, Dutch oven or large cast-iron pot

PREP-AHEAD TIP: Instead of ground turkey, you can swap in any leftover protein you have on hand, such as pulled pork shoulder, roasted chicken, grilled chicken breast, or cubed steak.

1. Start a wood campfire and wait until the flames die down and the coals glow red with white ash. Place a grilling grate so that it sits above the coals and you have even, medium-high heat.

2. In a large Dutch oven set over the middle of the grate where there is medium-high heat, combine the olive oil and garlic and sauté for 1 minute. Add the ground turkey and cook for 5 to 7 minutes, or until almost cooked, breaking up the meat with a large wooden spoon. Add the onion, celery, and jalapeño and cook until softened, 7 to 8 minutes. Add the poblano peppers, cumin, oregano, bay leaf, salt, and pepper and stir to combine. Add the chicken broth and bring to a boil. Once at a boil, move the Dutch oven to the edge of the grate so it is over lower heat and reduce to a simmer.

3. Add the Great Northern beans (these are heartier and will hold together) and cannellini beans (these will break down a little, and the starch will thicken the chili perfectly) and simmer for 30 minutes. Serve garnished with a squeeze of fresh lime, shredded cheese, cilantro, scallions, tomato, and sour cream.

There's a fire in there somewhere!

2 tablespoons olive oil

4 garlic cloves, minced

2 pounds lean ground turkey

1 large sweet onion, diced

3 celery stalks, diced

1 jalapeño pepper, seeded and minced

4 poblano peppers, roasted, peeled, seeded, and diced

1 tablespoon ground cumin

1 teaspoon dried oregano

1 bay leaf

Kosher salt and freshly ground black pepper

6 cups low-sodium chicken broth

Two 15½-ounce cans Great Northern beans, drained and rinsed

One 15½-ounce can cannellini beans, drained and rinsed

Lime wedges, for garnish

Shredded Jack cheese, for garnish

Chopped fresh cilantro, for garnish

Chopped scallions, for garnish

Diced Roma (plum) tomato, for garnish

Sour cream, for garnish

Forget Proust, I'll take my nostalgia with cheese, toasted over the fire.

Camping Sandwiches

Hands down, one of my favorite childhood memories is of making camping sandwiches. Get ready for greatness.

CONVENTIONAL COOKING METHOD

To make these at home, cook them over a gas burner. Hold the press directly over a medium-high flame and cook for 2 minutes, turning multiple times. The heat is more concentrated, so they cook faster than over a campfire.

MAKES: Each recipe is for 1 pressed sandwich

TIME: 8 to 10 minutes

YOU'LL NEED: Campfire, sandwich presses, foil-wrapped bricks

PREP-AHEAD TIP: Set the sandwich presses over the fire to heat up as you prepare the sandwiches so they're nice and hot when you're ready for some toasting action.

Camping Sandwich Combos

Make other pressed sandwiches by stuffing a variety of camping leftovers into the sandwich, such as pulled pork with BBQ sauce; shredded smoked chicken and sliced green chiles; steak and peppers from fajitas; or ground turkey with Jack cheese, fire-roasted tomato salsa, and black beans.

For a breakfast sandwich, try diced roasted potatoes and crumbled chorizo with shredded Cheddar and scrambled eggs.

You can make dessert camping sandwiches as well. Slice them or serve whole: sautéed peaches and sweetened ricotta; peanut butter and strawberries; sliced apples and caramel sauce; roasted pineapple, bananas, and honey; chocolate chunks, marshmallows, and graham cracker crumbs; sliced ripe banana, brown sugar, and Nutella.

Chili sandwich

2 slices Pullman bread

3 tablespoons chili (see the recipe for Smoky Bean Chili, page 40 or use your favorite), room temp

2 tablespoons shredded sharp Cheddar cheese

1 teaspoon diced sweet pickles

1 teaspoon diced sweet onion

Nonstick cooking spray

Berry cream cheese

2 slices Pullman bread

2 tablespoons softened cream cheese

2 tablespoons berry preserves (such as blueberry, strawberry, raspberry)

Nonstick cooking spray

Pepperoni pizza

2 slices Pullman bread

2 tablespoons marinara sauce

1 tablespoon shredded mozzarella

3 thin slices of pepperoni, julienned

1 pinch of dried oregano

Nonstick cooking spray

Mac-n-Cheese

2 slices Pullman bread

3 tablespoons leftover mac-n-cheese

1 tablespoon shredded Fontina or cheddar cheese

1 teaspoon crumbled cooked bacon, optional

Nonstick cooking spray

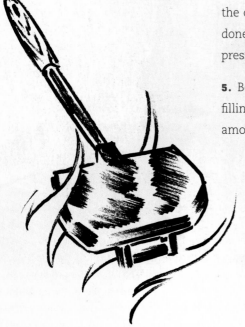

1. Camping sandwiches can be prepared ahead of time and made in either square or circular presses—both work fine. Depending on your make and model, adjust the filling amounts so the sandwiches are full but not too full (or they'll ooze while being toasted). The fillings can vary, and it's a good way to utilize leftover chili, mac-n-cheese, and other ingredients when camping.

2. For circular sandwiches, punch out the bread into 4¼-inch circles or the size of your sandwich press.

3. Prepare a campfire with wood and wait until the flames die down and the coals glow red with white ash. Place a grilling rack so that it sits just above the coals. Place the presses on the grill so they heat up.

4. Assemble each sandwich with the desired fillings, leaving a ½-inch border around the edges. Remove the presses from the hot grill, open, and spray with nonstick cooking spray. Place a sandwich in each press (it will sizzle—this preheating helps it form a nice crispy crust) and close tightly. Place on the grill and cook for 1 or 2 minutes per side. You can check the sandwich as it cooks by opening the press and checking the color—it should be golden brown and crispy on both sides when done. (Depending on how hot your coals are, you can also place the press directly on coals to make it cook faster—just keep an eye on it!)

5. Be sure to use room temperature (versus cold) ingredients in the filling—otherwise lower the flame and toast the sandwich for a longer amount of time to sufficiently warm the filling.

Toasties

When I went camping as a kid I can't say we had a lot of snacks. We didn't have multiple boxes of crackers; yes, maybe there were some adult-style crackers, such as Triscuits (which I loved even as a kid) or tortilla chips from Bien Padre, the local chip maker in Northern California, but that was about it. So if I wanted a tasty snack between major meals, the camping sandwich press always came in handy. Now, I prided myself in having a pretty eclectic mix of toasty sandwiches: grilled cheese, of course; roast beef and Cheddar; I think there was even a hot dog and nacho cheese combo one time. Regardless of the filling, I believe the time, effort, and creativity (along with anticipation) made every one of those a culinary masterpiece when I opened them up.

And however many times I scoped out the area, did my reconnaissance, and tried to hide, when I would finish cooking that camping sandwich, my dad would inevitably show up and take a huge adult bite, just the way he would when I had a perfect scoop of ice cream on a cone. And now I do the same thing to Hunter and Ryder.

Cooking toasties with a crowd.

Waldorf Chicken Salad Panini

No ascot or formal dinner reservations necessary to enjoy my version of the famous 1893 Waldorf Astoria salad. Heck, this one even travels well, 'cause it comes in a panini.

CONVENTIONAL COOKING METHOD

Use the same method with a stovetop.

Poached chicken

3 skin-on, bone-in chicken breasts

Low-sodium chicken stock, as needed to cover

½ cup white wine

2 bay leaves

2 fresh parsley sprigs

2 fresh thyme sprigs

1 tablespoon kosher salt

1 teaspoon black peppercorns

Salad

¾ cup mayonnaise

½ cup whipped cream cheese

2 tablespoons fresh lemon juice

½ cup halved red seedless grapes

½ cup finely sliced green apple (skin on)

⅓ cup chopped toasted walnuts

½ cup finely diced celery

4 ciabatta rolls

4 thin slices pepper Jack cheese

2 cups lightly packed watercress

MAKES: 4 sandwiches

TIME: 35 minutes

YOU'LL NEED: Campfire with grill grate, instant-read thermometer, 2 cast-iron skillets, heavy pot

PREP-AHEAD TIP: Poach the chicken ahead of time and bring it with you in the cooler, or if you're camping and have leftover roasted or grilled chicken from previous meals, use that.

1. Start a wood campfire and wait until the flames die down and the coals glow red with white ash. Place a grilling grate so that it sits above the coals and you have nice, even, medium heat.

2. To poach the chicken, place the chicken breasts in a large, heavy-bottomed pot. Cover the chicken with stock and add the wine, bay leaves, parsley, thyme, salt, and peppercorns. Place the pot on the grate over the coals and bring to a boil, then move the pot to the edge of the grate. Cover and simmer for about 25 minutes, until an instant-read thermometer reads 160°F. Remove and rest under foil until the meat is cool enough to handle. Remove the skin and use a large knife to cut under the breast to detach the meat from the bone. Dice the chicken into 1-inch cubes.

3. Whisk together the mayonnaise, cream cheese, and lemon juice. Fold in the grapes, apple, nuts, celery, and cubed chicken. Taste for seasoning. Toast the inside of the ciabatta rolls over a hot grill until crispy and charred around the edges. Pile the chicken salad onto the ciabatta rolls and top with a slice of cheese and a handful of fresh watercress. Press the rolls closed, then place the sandwiches in a large cast-iron skillet over medium heat. Top with another heated skillet and press gently on the sandwiches until the bread is toasted and the cheese has melted.

Pork Katsu Sandwich with Bacon Mayonnaise

Pork freezes well, thaws well, and is super versatile, so it's perfect for camping. Buy yourself a pack of pork chops, and they can do anything from Cajun to Asian and everything in between. Here's a great breakfast, lunch, or dinner recipe. Just pound it out, give it a good breading of what you have available, and season.

CONVENTIONAL COOKING METHOD

Use the same method on your stovetop at home.

Two 8-ounce boneless pork chops, trimmed

¾ cup all-purpose flour

2 cups "Whatever You Have" Breading (page 145)

Kosher salt and freshly ground black pepper

2 large eggs, lightly beaten

Canola oil, as needed

1 lemon

¼ cup finely grated Parmesan cheese

1 sourdough baguette

Bacon Mayo (recipe follows)

8 slices crisped applewood-smoked bacon (reserved from mayo recipe)

2 roasted red bell peppers, thinly sliced

4 slices provolone cheese

1½ cups baby arugula

MAKES: 2 to 4 servings

TIME: 30 minutes

YOU'LL NEED: Campfire with grill grate, cast-iron skillet, toothpicks

PREP-AHEAD TIP: Pound the pork before you head out camping; store, wrapped tightly in plastic, in the refrigerator or cooler. Make the bacon mayo 1 or 2 days in advance; keep refrigerated or chilled in a cooler.

1. Start a wood campfire and wait until the flames die down and the coals glow red with white ash. Place a grilling grate so that it sits above the coals and you have nice, even, medium heat.

2. Slice the pork chops in half lengthwise so you have 2 long pieces, then cut those in half; place each piece between two sheets of plastic wrap and use the smooth side of a meat mallet to pound ¼ inch thick. They should be long, thin rectangular strips (like wide chicken tenders).

3. Put the flour and breadcrumbs in two separate shallow dishes and season each with salt and pepper. Pour the eggs into a third shallow dish. Season the pork with salt and pepper, then dredge first in the flour, shaking off any excess; next the egg; and finally the breadcrumbs.

4. In a large, cast-iron skillet over the high-heat campfire (lower the grate to be closer to the coals if need be), heat ¼ cup canola oil. Shallow-fry the cutlets until golden brown, 2 to 3 minutes per side. While still warm, squeeze fresh lemon juice over the cutlets and sprinkle with grated Parmesan. Season with salt and pepper.

5. Cut the baguette in half lengthwise and toast both sides over an open grill until golden and crusty, about 1 minute. While still warm, spread both sides liberally with bacon mayo. Evenly spread the pork cutlets across the bottom half and top with slices of crisped bacon, roasted red pepper, provolone, and the arugula. Add the top baguette half and secure with toothpicks in 4 places. Using a serrated knife, cut the baguette into 4 portions and serve.

Bacon Mayo

1. Cook the bacon in a large skillet over medium heat for 6 to 7 minutes per side, until it's crispy and the fat has rendered. Transfer the bacon to a paper towel–lined plate to drain. Carefully pour the accumulated bacon fat into a heatproof measuring cup; measure ⅔ cup and allow to cool. Use canola oil if you need to supplement the yield. When the bacon is cool enough to handle, finely dice 4 pieces for the mayo; the rest goes in the sandwich!

2. Place the egg yolks, vinegar, and mustard in a large bowl (or a blender). Whisk until the ingredients are well combined, then slowly pour in the bacon fat in a steady, thin stream until the mixture is thick and creamy. Finish with the lemon juice, sour cream, fresh ground black pepper, and salt. Pour the mayonnaise into a clean bowl and fold in the diced bacon. Cover and keep chilled until ready to use. The bacon mayo will keep for 3 to 4 days in an airtight container, chilled.

MAKES: 1 cup

TIME: 30 minutes

12 slices applewood-smoked bacon

4 large egg yolks

2 teaspoons apple cider vinegar

1 teaspoon Dijon mustard

1 tablespoon fresh lemon juice

¼ cup sour cream

¼ teaspoon freshly ground black pepper

½ teaspoon kosher salt

Funky Mash

This is a dish that will stick to your ribs, fuel you up, and warm you from the inside. Make extra and keep it properly stored in a cooler. It can be easily reheated in an aluminum foil pouch.

CONVENTIONAL COOKING METHOD

Make it on a stovetop; the chiles can be charred over a gas burner.

MAKES: 8 to 10 servings

TIME: 30 to 35 minutes

YOU'LL NEED: Campfire with grilling grate or propane burner, large pot, skillet

PREP-AHEAD TIP: Scrub and wash the potatoes before you head out camping.

1 large red bell pepper

1 large orange bell pepper

2 poblano peppers

5 pounds medium Yukon gold potatoes

Kosher salt

2 tablespoons olive oil

1 large sweet onion, thinly sliced

3 garlic cloves, minced

Freshly ground black pepper

2 tablespoons unsalted butter

½ cup half-and-half

1 cup grated Parmesan cheese

Paprika, for garnish

Chopped scallions, for garnish

1. Start a wood campfire and wait until the flames die down and the coals glow red with white ash. Place a grilling grate so that it sits above the coals and you have nice, even, medium heat.

2. Place the bell and poblano peppers on the grate and allow the open flame of the campfire to char them all over, 3 to 4 minutes per side. Place the peppers in a large bowl, cover with plastic wrap, and leave to sweat for 5 minutes. Remove from the bowl; carefully peel the outer skin and discard. Remove the seeds and stems, then finely chop the peppers.

3. Scrub the potatoes and wash them under cold water (leave the skins on). Put in a large pot with cold water to cover by about 1 inch. Season generously with salt, then place the pot on the grate directly over the coals, so that the heat is high. Bring to a boil and simmer for 25 to 30 minutes, until the potatoes are fork tender.

4. Meanwhile, in a skillet over medium-high heat, heat the olive oil. Add the onion and cook until translucent, about 3 to 4 minutes. Add the garlic and cook until softened and lightly browned, about 2 minutes. Fold in the chopped peppers and season lightly with salt and pepper.

5. Drain the the potatoes and return to the pot off the heat. Add the butter and half-and-half. Use a potato masher to mash the potatoes until fairly smooth but still textured. Fold in the vegetable mixture and the Parmesan and stir until well combined. Season with salt and pepper. Garnish with a sprinkle of paprika and chopped scallions.

Camping Baked Potatoes with Herbed Sour Cream

This has got to be the oldest recipe, straight out of the first edition of Caveman Can Cook. These go great with Stout-Braised Short Ribs with Pearl Barley (page 216).

CONVENTIONAL COOKING METHOD

Bake the potatoes directly on the center rack of a preheated 350°F oven for 45 to 50 minutes.

1. Start a wood campfire and wait until the flames die down and the coals glow red with white ash. Place a grilling grate so that it sits above the coals and you have nice, even, medium heat.

2. Wash the potatoes well in cold water, prick them all over with the tip of a knife, rub them all over with olive oil, and season with salt. Rub salt all over the potatoes; this will help crisp the skin. Tightly wrap each potato in aluminum foil. Place the potatoes on a grill grate over red coals (medium heat) and cook for 1 hour, turning halfway through. When done, the tip of a paring knife will go straight through the potato without resistance (you can do this through the foil).

3. In a small bowl, combine the scallions, chopped herbs, and sour cream. Set aside.

4. Cut the potatoes open through the foil and peel back the foil to expose the potato. Squeeze the potato gently from the bottom to expose the soft, fluffy inside. Season with salt and pepper, top with butter, and finish with a big spoonful of herbed sour cream.

MAKES: 4 servings

TIME: 1 hour

YOU'LL NEED: Campfire with grill grate, heavy-duty aluminum foil

PREP-AHEAD TIP: Prepare the potatoes and wrap each in foil before you head out camping so they're ready to cook as soon as you get your fire going. Make the herbed sour cream the day before as well and keep it chilled in an airtight container.

4 medium baking potatoes (Idaho or Russet)

¼ cup olive oil

Kosher salt

¼ cup finely sliced scallions

¼ cup mixed chopped fresh herbs, such as chives, dill, and parsley

1½ cups sour cream (or plain Greek yogurt)

Freshly ground black pepper

½ stick (¼ cup) unsalted butter, at room temperature

Roasted Vegetable Camping Pouches

One of your go-to tools for camping is heavy-duty aluminum foil. You're going to love the anticipation and surprise of your friends and family when you slice open these foil pouches of perfection, wafting aromas of roasted vegetables.

MAKES: each packet is an individual serving

TIME: 25 to 30 minutes

YOU'LL NEED: Campfire with grill grate, heavy-duty aluminum foil

PREP-AHEAD TIP: Assemble pouches the night before and store in the fridge. These are great to put together before you head out camping. No cleanup and no dishes! Just throw 'em on the fire to cook. The recipes below are for individual servings, but you can make larger packets for more servings.

Brussels Sprouts with Thyme and Garlic

6 to 8 Brussels sprouts, trimmed and cut in half

¼ teaspoon picked fresh thyme leaves

1 garlic clove, smashed

1 tablespoon extra-virgin olive oil

1 teaspoon apple cider vinegar

Kosher salt and freshly ground black pepper

Heavy-Duty Aluminum Foil

If someone were to ask me, "Guy, what three things would you want with you if you were lost in the forest?," my first answer would be heavy-duty aluminum foil. It's like culinary duct tape. You can use it to wrap, cover, and seal. And, believe it or not, if you have enough of it, you can make a pot to heat water.

There are many creative ways to utilize heavy-duty aluminum foil, and one of my favorites is to roast potatoes and vegetables. It means one less pan you have to carry when you're backpacking and one less pot you have to clean when water is limited. But most important are the cooking properties and principles foil enables. It can lock in flavor and moisture and, if executed correctly, the steam created inside expedites the cooking process.

1. Start a wood campfire and wait until flames die down and coals glow red with white ash. Place a grilling rack so it sits about 4 to 5 inches above the coals.

2. Choose the combination of your choice and toss the ingredients together in a large mixing bowl, mixing to coat the vegetables evenly. Season well with salt and pepper.

3. Tear off a large sheet of foil and fold it in half to double up the layers. Place the mixture in an even layer in the center of the foil. Place another single sheet of foil on top and fold up the edges to form a rectangular pouch about 9 by 6 inches. Crimp the edges tightly so the pouches are well sealed.

4. Place on the grill over medium heat and cook for 15 to 18 minutes. To serve, slice open the top of the pouch.

Potatoes with Parmesan, Garlic, and Rosemary

4 Yukon creamer potatoes

2 tablespoons minced sweet onion

1 garlic clove, minced

¼ teaspoon chopped fresh rosemary

1 tablespoon unsalted butter, cut into small cubes

2 tablespoons heavy cream

1 tablespoon grated Parmesan

Kosher salt and freshly ground black pepper

Carrots with Cumin, Ginger, and Honey

4 or 5 organic carrots, trimmed

¼ teaspoon ground cumin

¼ teaspoon ground ginger

1 tablespoon unsalted butter, cut into small cubes

1 teaspoon honey

1 garlic clove, smashed

½ teaspoon extra-virgin olive oil

Kosher salt and freshly ground black pepper

Roasted Vegetable Camping Pouches, shining in all their foiled glory.

Basmati Rice Pilaf

Pilaf is the kitchen-sink cousin to chili, breakfast hash, and salads—you can add just about anything you want. Just make sure you have the rice.

CONVENTIONAL COOKING METHOD

Cook on a stovetop using the same method. Monitor the cooking time, as it may be slightly less on your home burner.

2 cups basmati rice

1 teaspoon unsalted butter

1 teaspoon olive oil

¼ cup finely diced yellow onion

¼ cup diced mixed green and red bell pepper

3 cups low-sodium chicken or vegetable broth

1½ teaspoons kosher salt

¼ teaspoon freshly ground black pepper

¼ teaspoon turmeric

1 bay leaf

2 tablespoons chopped fresh cilantro

2 tablespoons finely sliced scallions

MAKES: 4 to 6 servings

TIME: 35 minutes

YOU'LL NEED: Propane burner, saucepan with lid

PREP-AHEAD TIP: Not a lot to prep ahead here, but you could get your vegetable dicing out of the way.

1. Start a wood campfire and wait until the flames die down and the coals glow red with white ash. Place a grilling grate so that it sits above the coals and you have nice, even, medium heat.

2. Wash the rice in a colander under cold running water until the water runs clear. This removes any excess starch and makes the pilaf light and fluffy.

3. Set a pot at the edge of the grill where the heat is low and melt the butter; add the olive oil, then sauté the diced onion and peppers until translucent and softened, 5 to 7 minutes. Add the rice and stir to completely coat the grains. Move the pot to a hotter part of the grate (right over the coals) and toast the grains, stirring often, for about 5 minutes, until fragrant and slightly golden.

4. Stir in the broth and add the salt, pepper, turmeric, and bay leaf. Bring to a boil, then move the pot back to a lower heat zone and simmer, covered for 18 to 20 minutes, until all of the liquid has been absorbed and the rice is tender. Remove from the heat, gently fluff the rice with a fork (discard the bay leaf), then fold in the chopped cilantro and scallions to finish.

Rice Rules

Listen, the great thing about rice is it's a fantastic medium to stretch any and all odds and ends into a meal. If you're stuck out there camping with only a package of raisin and nut trail mix, a can of tuna fish, a cup of rice, and a chicken bouillon cube, that cup of rice means you've got some funky version of a poor man's paella!

Old-School Baked Beans with Molasses

When was the last time you had baked beans that didn't come out of a can? Well, now is your turn to make 'em from scratch. They're worth the wait.

To the table, fresh off the fire, see them come runnin'.

1. In a large pot, cover the beans with water and soak overnight. The next day, start a wood campfire and wait until flames die down and coals glow red with white ash. Place a grilling rack so it sits just above the coals. Add the bay leaves to the pot and bring to a boil by setting it directly over the hot coals on the grate. Boil for 30 minutes, then drain the beans, reserving the liquid.

2. Set a large Dutch oven over the grate adjacent to the coals so you have medium-high heat. Heat the canola oil, add the bacon, and render it until crispy and golden brown. Using a slotted spoon, transfer the bacon to a paper towel–lined plate to drain. Reduce the heat by moving the Dutch oven to the edge of the grate (or by increasing the height of the grill). Add the onion and pepper to the leftover bacon fat and sauté until translucent, 7 to 8 minutes. Add the beans and bacon back to the pot and stir in the remaining ingredients. Season with salt and pepper. Pour in just enough of the reserved soaking water to cover the beans.

3. Cover with a tight-fitting lid and simmer over low heat for 50 minutes, stirring occasionally so the beans cook evenly. Check occasionally and add more water if the liquid has reduced too much. Increase the heat and cook for 30 minutes more to reduce the sauce. Cook until the beans are tender and the sauce has reduced to a thick consistency that clings to the beans. It's also nice to mash a few beans into the sauce to naturally thicken the braising liquid.

MAKES: 8 to 10 servings

TIME: 3 to 3½ hours (plus overnight soaking)

YOU'LL NEED: Campfire with grill grate, Dutch oven

PREP-AHEAD TIP: Soak the beans before you head out camping or place them in an airtight container with water to cover so they soak as you travel or you can use canned, your call. Me, I love the texture of dried beans especially when they are the star of the dish. You could also combine all the flavorings in a resealable container for easy addition to the beans.

1 pound dried pinto, navy, or red kidney beans

2 bay leaves

1 tablespoon canola oil

6 slices bacon, cut into ½-inch pieces

1 medium yellow onion, diced

½ green bell pepper, finely diced

¼ cup molasses

¼ cup dark brown sugar

½ cup bourbon

½ cup BBQ sauce

2 tablespoons apple cider vinegar

1 teaspoon mustard powder

1 tablespoon Worcestershire sauce

Kosher salt and freshly ground black pepper

Campfire Baking in a Cast-iron Dutch Oven

Do not confuse a cast-iron skillet with a cast-iron Dutch oven. A cast-iron skillet is made the same way as a Dutch oven, but it's thinner, lighter, and doesn't typically have a lid. Cast-iron skillets are great for camping because they don't develop hot spots like the typical household sauté pan. They're thick enough that they develop equal, radiant heat throughout the pan, plus they're very durable, and as I've said many times, they're the original nonstick. A cast-iron skillet's great for sautéing, cooking bacon, and so forth, but to do baking and any type of steaming you need to have the tight-fitting lid that you find on a Dutch oven. The majority of Dutch oven lids are designed to also be utilized almost like a sauté pan. You place the lid upside down on hot coals and use the interior of the lid as a cooking surface or a miniature sauté pan or flat top. (You can cook pancakes on that surface!) But the genius of the Dutch oven is the ability to bake something, to use steam, and have consistent heat. The basic technique is to heat up the Dutch oven while it's empty, much like you'd preheat your oven. Then you put in what needs to be cooked, whether it's Pineapple Upside-Down Cake or water and vegetables to steam and seal it with the top. As the fire burns down, take the Dutch oven and place it next to but not in the heat source, with about a 1-inch layer of coals on top, then spin the Dutch oven a quarter turn every 15 minutes. The key is not to set it up on top of your grilling grate, because then you're only getting heat from below and above (with the coals you've placed on top) but nothing on the sides. At no point in time should the Dutch oven be over hot direct heat, or it would be like cooking a birthday cake in a sauté pan on the stovetop—all you're going to get is burned cake. Use the radiant heat of the cast-iron to cook your food through in almost a low and slow manner.

Hunter keeping an experienced eye on the baked beans.

Griddle Hominy Cakes with Guacamole

~~Camping Tip 101~~ No . . . Life Tip 101: Never throw away your bacon grease. You might think hominy cakes are a little boring and lacking in flavor until you try these bad boys crisped up in some bacon fat. To me, hominy is one of the most unappreciated and underutilized ingredients in the United States. Eat it whole or grind it—it takes on every flavor you can throw at it, and more.

CONVENTIONAL COOKING METHOD

These cook well at home in a nonstick sauté pan.

Solo cups, the crystal glasses for camping.

MAKES: 5 servings (10 cakes)

TIME: 40 minutes

YOU'LL NEED: Campfire with grill grate, cast-iron skillet or griddle

PREP-AHEAD TIP: Pickle the onions before you head out camping. You can also prep and make the guacamole and bring it with you; just press a piece of plastic wrap directly onto the surface to keep it from turning, and store chilled.

Hominy cakes

10 slices bacon

½ cup corn kernels

½ cup canned hominy, drained, rinsed, and finely chopped

2 large eggs

½ cup buttermilk

1 cup masa harina (yellow corn flour)

1 teaspoon baking powder

¼ cup finely minced yellow onion

1 jalapeño pepper, seeded and minced

¼ cup chopped scallions

1 to 2 tablespoons canola oil

1 cup coarse cornmeal

Accompaniments

¾ cup Guacamole (recipe follows)

Sour cream

Crumbled Cotija cheese

Chopped fresh cilantro

Pickled Red Onion (recipe follows)

1. Start a wood campfire and wait until the flames die down and the coals glow red with white ash. Place a grilling grate so that it sits above the coals and you have nice, even, medium heat.

2. In a large cast-iron skillet on a grate over the medium heat of the campfire render the bacon until crispy. Transfer with a slotted spoon to a paper towel–lined plate; reserve the drippings. When the bacon is cool enough to handle, chop into small pieces and place in a medium bowl. Fold in the corn kernels and hominy.

3. Combine the eggs and buttermilk in a small bowl and whisk. In a large bowl, mix the corn flour and baking powder, then pour in the wet ingredients and mix until just combined. Fold in the hominy mixture, onion, jalapeño, and scallions.

4. Heat a griddle or large skillet on the grate over the fire so it has a nice medium heat. Coat with an even mix of bacon grease and canola oil. Form golf ball–size balls of dough, flatten them into discs about 2 inches wide by ½ inch thick, and lightly sprinkle each side with coarse cornmeal. Working in batches as needed, place the cakes on the pan and cook slowly, allowing the first side to develop a crust, 3 to 4 minutes. Turn and cook the other side, another 2 to 3 minutes. Transfer to a paper towel–lined plate to drain.

5. Serve each hominy cake topped with 1 tablespoon of guacamole, a drizzle of sour cream, crumbled Cotija cheese, cilantro, and a few strips of pickled red onion.

Guacamole

MAKES: About 2 cups

TIME: 5 minutes

Combine all the ingredients in a large bowl. Using a fork, gently mash the avocado and incorporate with the other ingredients. Taste for seasoning.

2 ripe avocados

2 tablespoons chopped fresh cilantro

1 tablespoon fresh lime juice

½ teaspoon kosher salt

¼ teaspoon freshly ground black pepper

1 garlic clove, minced

Pickled Red Onion

MAKES: 1 to 2 cups

TIME: 1 hour

Bring 2 tablespoons water, the vinegar, sugar, and salt to a boil over medium heat. Place the onion in a heatproof bowl and pour the mixture on top. Let the onion sit at room temperature for 1 hour. Pickled onions keep for 3 or 4 days in an airtight container in the fridge.

½ cup red wine vinegar

2 tablespoons sugar

1 teaspoon kosher salt

1 red onion, thinly sliced

Camping S'more Madness

To my kids, these are about as important as having gas in the boat. Things just aren't going to work unless we're going to have s'mores. But the reality is that sometimes you have to improvise, because the store is closed, the marina is closed, and there are no Hershey's bars available. Oh boy, have we become creative. . . . The only downside is, now it's never as simple as grabbing a bag of chocolate bars, marshmallows, and a graham cracker box. Here are some of my ideas for different variations. Just use what's on hand and pair ingredients together that make sense.

Campfire S'more Cones

MAKES: 4 servings

TIME: 30 minutes

YOU'LL NEED: Campfire with grill rack, long hardwood sticks or skewers, Dutch oven, squeeze bottle, heavy-duty aluminum foil

PREP-AHEAD TIP: Assemble the s'more cones ahead of time and hold in the refrigerator or cooler until ready to warm and toast over fire. Melt the chocolate up to an hour ahead of time.

4 ounces semi-sweet chocolate, 1 ounce reserved for drizzle

¾ cup crushed graham crackers

1½ tablespoons butter, melted

½ tablespoon sugar

¼ teaspoon ground cinnamon

4 sugar cones

4 heaping tablespoons Marshmallow Fluff

1. To make the chocolate, place a Dutch oven filled halfway with water on the grill rack over the fire. Place a heat-resistant bowl with the chocolate on top of the Dutch oven to melt the chocolate. Stir constantly until glossy and smooth. Remove from the heat and place in a squeeze bottle. Keep warm until ready for use.

2. To make the graham cracker filling, in a large bowl, mix the crushed graham crackers with the melted butter, sugar, and cinnamon. Reserve.

3. To assemble the cones, drizzle 2 teaspoons of melted chocolate into the bottom of each sugar cone. Spoon 2 teaspoons of graham cracker mixture on top of the chocolate. Next, layer 2 teaspoons of Marshmallow Fluff. Repeat the layers until you reach the top of the cone. Using a spatula or the back of a knife, level the top of the cone by pressing down gently and running the spatula across the top to remove any excess.

4. Wrap the cones in aluminum foil, leaving a little space at the top so the Fluff doesn't touch the foil. Place the cones on the rack over medium indirect heat (so they don't burn) and cook for 3 minutes, until warmed through.

5. To serve, unwrap the top of the cones to expose the marshmallow on top. Hold the tops near fire to brown the top of the Marshmallow Fluff, about 30 to 40 seconds. Drizzle with a little chocolate and serve.

Snickers Apple Pie S'more

1. Cut the Snickers bars in half crosswise, then cut each half lengthwise into three ⅓-inch planks. You'll have 12 planks that will match the dimensions of the graham crackers.

2. Roughly chop the apples in the apple pie filling so the pieces are finely diced.

3. To roast the marshmallows, skewer them on a hardwood or metal stick that's long enough to reach the fire without burning yourself. Turning frequently, roast the marshmallows until they're done to your preference.

4. To assemble, break each graham cracker in half so that you have 12 cracker squares. Place the roasted marshmallow on the bottom of the cracker. Top with a teaspoon of the apple filling. Place two of the Snickers planks on top of that and follow with the remaining cracker. Allow the heat from the marshmallow to slowly melt the Snickers before eating.

MAKES: 6 servings

TIME: 20 minutes

YOU'LL NEED: Campfire with grill rack, long hardwood sticks or skewers

PREP-AHEAD TIP: Slice the Snickers and chop the apple filling up to a few hours ahead of time.

6 large graham crackers

Two 3.3-ounce Snickers bars

6 teaspoons apple pie filling (canned)

6 large marshmallows

PB&J S'mores

MAKES: 6 servings

TIME: 20 minutes

YOU'LL NEED: Campfire, long hardwood sticks or skewers

PREP-AHEAD TIP: These are best assembled right before roasting.

6 large marshmallows

6 large graham crackers

4 tablespoons peanut butter

One 1.55-ounce Hershey's Chocolate Bar

2 tablespoons grape jelly

1. To roast the marshmallows, skewer them on a hardwood or metal stick that's long enough to reach the fire without burning yourself. Turning frequently, roast the marshmallows until they're done to your preference.

2. To assemble, break each graham cracker in half so that you have 12 cracker squares. Smear peanut butter on one side of all 12 squares. Place a square of Hershey's chocolate on top of the peanut butter on only 6 of the squares, followed by the roasted marshmallow and a teaspoon of grape jelly. Top with the remaining cracker and allow the heat from the marshmallow to slowly melt the chocolate.

Oatmeal Chocolate Raisin S'mores

MAKES: 4 servings

TIME: 10 minutes

YOU'LL NEED: Campfire with grill rack, heavy-duty aluminum foil

PREP-AHEAD TIP: Fold the chocolate raisins into the Fluff and zest the orange up to a few hours ahead of time.

½ cup chocolate-covered raisins, roughly chopped

1 teaspoon orange zest

4 heaping tablespoons Marshmallow Fluff

8 packaged iced oatmeal cookies

1. Preheat the grill or set up the campfire.

2. To assemble, mix together the chopped raisins and orange zest with the Marshmallow Fluff till just combined; do not overmix. Spread the Fluff on the bottom of 4 cookies. Top with another cookie to form a sandwich. Double-wrap each sandwich in foil and place on the grill over medium heat, turning frequently to prevent burning. Bake until warmed through, about 1 to 2 minutes.

Lemon Meringue S'mores

1. Preheat a grill or set up a campfire.

2. In a small bowl, swirl the lemon curd into the Marshmallow Fluff. Be careful not to overstir.

3. To assemble, break each graham cracker in half so that you have 8 cracker squares. Place a square of the Hershey's bar on top of each of 4 crackers followed a tablespoon of the lemon curd Marshmallow Fluff. Top with the remaining cracker. Double-wrap each sandwich in foil and place on the grill, turning frequently to prevent burning, about 1 minute.

MAKES: 4 servings

TIME: 15 minutes

YOU'LL NEED: Campfire with grill rack or grill, heavy-duty aluminum foil

PREP-AHEAD TIP: These are best assembled right before grilling.

2 teaspoons lemon curd

4 heaping tablespoons Marshmallow Fluff

4 large graham crackers

One 1.55-ounce Hershey's Cookies 'n' Creme Bar

HOLIDAY COOKOUT

CREAM CIT
AN
"WE DON'T NEED NO
LICENS

My house has always been the epicenter of holiday gatherings. Even when I was a kid, I remember my parents saying that they wanted to have the kind of house where my friends and I could always be comfortable, because then they knew where I was. I've strived for the same atmosphere at my house, and I have a big backyard, so Hunter, Ryder, and Jules can have a variety of things to do and places to play. That has translated to now having the majority of holidays at our house.

So, whether it's the activities that draw me outside, or the type of food for the event, like a pig roast at Christmas or Huli Huli chicken on the Fourth of July, I'm often cooking outdoors. Of course, yet another reason might be that Lori makes me cook outside because running two ovens with big turkeys in them makes the house too hot. But the main reason is that I love being outdoors and cooking outdoors, and after all, you don't have to clean up a spill that lands on the ground. The other key to staying in the sun and avoiding the kitchen during your holiday is the prep-ahead, so pay attention to those tips, get your meal battle plan together a week in advance, and execute it. (And pull a propane burner out of your camping supplies if need be!)

Holidays in Ferndale

Ferndale is my original hometown, located in Northern California, about twenty minutes south of Eureka, California. It's an incredible place, with Victorian homes and a beautiful Main Street with no stoplights. And it has one of the best high school football teams in the country (go Wildcats!). Ferndale is where I grew up, learned to cook, and started the pretzel cart business (see *Guy Fieri Food* for that story). We still own the home that I grew up in, right there on Rose Avenue. So, it's become a tradition on Thanksgiving that a bunch of the Krew will load up the trailers and RVs and make the four-hour pilgrimage to Ferndale from Santa Rosa. We remove part of the fence on one of the fields surrounding the house and open up the "Cream City RV Park" for a couple of days. I bring up my twenty-six-foot-long barbecue trailer, fitted with an eight-foot horizon smoker and a six-foot charcoal grill. On this culinary vessel my buddies and I prepare the weekend's menu and a Thanksgiving feast for around sixty people.

My friends have become accustomed to the unique styles of food and offerings, so each year I feel I have to outdo myself. Last year I did six turkeys, two hams, mashed potatoes, sage stuffing, sweet potatoes, green beans in porcini mushroom sauce, garlic bread, and pappardelle with Italian sausage and plum tomato. What a feast.

The Ryder original.

Caramel Apple French Toast

This is a Ryder original. Both of my boys have very high expectations about what they're going to eat. They ponder their choices carefully, and I swear Ryder likes to ask for things knowing that I don't have all the ingredients at the house. So one day Lori was out and he wanted French toast. But we were out of syrup, and I wasn't up for going to the store. So . . . I made caramel applesauce to put on top instead.

Now, getting Ryder to move off of something he particularly likes is very, very tough. And he likes his French toast and syrup a particular way, down to what color it is—and here I was messing with it. I was thinking, oh, I've failed for sure. So he takes a bite and . . . wait for it . . . wait for it . . . he says, "Dad, why don't you always make it like this?"

MAKES: 4 to 6 servings

TIME: 20 minutes

YOU'LL NEED: Stovetop or propane burner, cast-iron skillet or griddle

PREP-AHEAD TIP: Make the French toast batter the night before and store in an airtight container in the fridge.

1. To make the caramel apple sauce, in a large cast-iron skillet, melt the butter over medium heat; add the sugar, cinnamon, nutmeg, salt, and orange zest. Add the apples and toss to coat. Off the heat, add the brandy; tip the edge of the skillet toward the flame to ignite and cook until the liquor has burned out. Cook for 5 to 7 minutes, stirring occasionally. When the apples are tender, remove them from the skillet and set aside.

2. In a shallow dish, whisk the eggs, milk, vanilla, and cinnamon until well combined. Lay the challah slices in the mixture to coat, 1 to 2 minutes per side.

3. To make the French toast, in the same skillet, melt the 2 tablespoons butter. Cook each slice of challah until golden brown, 2 to 3 minutes per side. Immediately garnish with toasted walnuts and warm caramel apples. Dust with powdered sugar and lemon zest.

Caramel apple sauce

½ stick (¼ cup) unsalted butter

¾ cup dark brown sugar

1 teaspoon ground cinnamon

¼ teaspoon ground nutmeg

¼ teaspoon kosher salt

1 teaspoon grated orange zest

4 Granny Smith apples, peeled, cored, and diced

¼ cup Calvados (apple brandy)

French toast

4 large eggs

1 cup whole milk

1 teaspoon vanilla extract

¼ teaspoon ground cinnamon

1 loaf challah bread, cut into 1-inch-thick slices

2 tablespoons unsalted butter

½ cup chopped toasted walnuts

¼ cup powdered sugar, for garnish

1 teaspoon grated lemon zest, for garnish

Crab Cakes with Southwestern Relish

When I go home to Ferndale during the holidays, one of my buddies, usually Sotomyer or Sisemore, shows up with some fresh Dungeness crab. On the West Coast, Dungeness crab during the holidays is a staple—and it's one of my favorite things.

Canola oil, as needed

1 small red bell pepper, finely diced

1 small green bell pepper, finely diced

1 medium sweet onion, finely diced

1 celery stalk, finely diced

2 garlic cloves, minced

Kosher salt and freshly ground black pepper

Tabasco sauce, optional

Juice of 2 limes, plus 2 limes, cut into wedges, for garnish

3 tablespoons chopped fresh cilantro

3 tablespoons mayonnaise

1 large egg

1 cup panko (Japanese breadcrumbs), plus additional for breading

1½ pounds fresh jumbo lump crabmeat, drained and patted dry

One of my favorite places on earth—
my hometown, Ferndale.

MAKES: 4 servings

TIME: 1 hour

YOU'LL NEED: Stovetop or propane burner, grill, cast-iron skillet, nonstick skillet

PREP-AHEAD TIP: Southwestern relish can be made ahead of time.

1. Heat 1 tablespoon canola oil in a cast-iron skillet over medium heat. Add the peppers, onion, celery, and garlic and sweat until the vegetables begin to soften, 7 to 8 minutes. Season with salt, pepper, and a dash or two of Tabasco sauce, if desired. Set mixture aside to cool.

2. In a large bowl, whisk the lime juice, cilantro, mayonnaise, and egg until well combined. Fold in the panko and cooled vegetables. Gently fold in the crabmeat until just combined, then season with salt and pepper. Using a half-cup measure, scoop out the mixture and form into 3-inch cakes. Lightly press each cake into a shallow plate of panko, or use your hands to press the breadcrumbs into both sides. Refrigerate the crab cakes for 20 to 30 minutes to set.

3. MEANWHILE, MAKE THE RELISH: In the cast-iron skillet over medium-high heat, heat the canola oil. Add the corn kernels and sauté until charred, 8 to 10 minutes; cool slightly. In a large bowl, combine the corn with the rest of the relish ingredients, season with salt and pepper, and refrigerate until ready to use.

4. Heat 2 to 3 tablespoons canola oil in a large nonstick skillet. Sear the crab cakes on each side for 3 to 4 minutes, until golden brown and crisp. Top each crab cake with a spoonful of relish and a squeeze of fresh lime.

Southwestern relish

1 teaspoon canola oil

2 cups corn kernels

½ red bell pepper, finely diced

½ red onion, finely diced

1 scallion, chopped

1 cup canned black beans, drained and rinsed

½ jalapeño pepper, seeded and finely diced

1 mango, finely diced

2 tablespoons chopped fresh cilantro

Juice of 1 lime

Kosher salt and freshly ground black pepper

Fire-Roasted Tomato Salsa

If you want to take your salsa to the next level and really round out those flavors, fire-roasting the jalapeños, garlic, tomatoes, and onions will do the trick.

2½ pounds vine-ripe tomatoes, cored and sliced in half

1 red onion, cut into large chunks

2 jalapeño peppers

3 tablespoons olive oil

1 teaspoon kosher salt

½ teaspoon freshly ground black pepper

1 garlic clove, smashed

1 chipotle chile in adobo, plus 1 tablespoon adobo sauce

½ teaspoon sugar

1 tablespoon fresh lime juice

¼ cup chopped fresh cilantro

MAKES: About 4 cups

TIME: 30 minutes

YOU'LL NEED: Grill, food processor

PREP-AHEAD TIP: The salsa can be made 2 or 3 days ahead of time and stored in the fridge.

1. Preheat a grill to high heat.

2. In a large bowl, toss the tomatoes, onion, and jalapeños with 2 tablespoons of the olive oil, the salt, and the pepper. Grill the vegetables for 10 to 12 minutes, turning occasionally, until they start to soften, blister, and char around the edges. Remove the tomatoes and onions from the grill and set aside. Place the jalapeños in a bowl and cover tightly with plastic wrap. After 10 minutes, remove the skins, then scrape out and discard the seeds and stem.

3. Combine the jalapeños, onions, tomatoes, garlic, chipotles and adobo, and sugar in a food processor. Pulse until blended. Add the lime juice, remaining 1 tablespoon olive oil, and chopped cilantro; taste for seasoning. Store covered in the refrigerator.

Black Bean Avocado Salsa with Corn

This is a salsa that eats like a meal. If you're making tacos, you don't even need to throw a protein in. This has enough big flavor and texture to do the trick.

MAKES: 4 servings

TIME: 20 minutes

YOU'LL NEED: Stovetop or propane burner

PREP-AHEAD TIP: This salad can be made the night before and held covered in the refrigerator until ready to serve.

1. Heat a skillet over medium-high heat. Pour in the canola oil and corn kernels. Cook until the corn is nicely charred, 8 to 10 minutes. Set aside to cool in a large bowl.

2. Add the cherry tomatoes, avocados, black beans, and onion to the corn kernels.

3. In a small bowl, whisk together the dressing ingredients. Pour the dressing over the corn mixture and mix gently to coat well. Fold in the cilantro and scallions and serve.

Salsa

1 teaspoon extra-virgin olive oil

Kernels from 1 ear of corn

1 cup quartered cherry tomatoes

2 ripe avocados, diced

One 15½-ounce can black beans, drained and rinsed

½ medium red onion, diced

3 tablespoons chopped fresh cilantro

3 scallions, finely chopped

Dressing

2 tablespoons extra-virgin olive oil

1 teaspoon agave syrup

½ teaspoon ground cumin

¼ teaspoon minced garlic

Juice of 1 to 2 limes

1 serrano chile, seeded and finely diced

Pinch of cayenne pepper

Kosher salt and freshly ground black pepper, to taste

Crunch Crazy Asparagus Spears

I love Asparagus, by Guy

I love asparagus any way you can think to make it, except overcooked. In salads? I'll take it. Soups? You got it. Grilled, sautéed, or fried? I'll take it. This recipe is a great way to make asparagus spears so rich and hearty that they can take over the center of the plate.

MAKES: 4 servings

TIME: 35 minutes

YOU'LL NEED: Oven, wire rack, baking sheet

PREP-AHEAD TIP: Combine the breading ingredients a day ahead.

2 large egg whites

1 tablespoon mayonnaise

Kosher salt and freshly cracked black pepper

2 cups panko (Japanese breadcrumbs)

½ cup grated Parmesan cheese

1 teaspoon Italian seasoning

1 teaspoon paprika

1 pound medium asparagus (about 20 spears), woody stems trimmed

Extra-virgin olive oil

1. Preheat the oven to 425°F.

2. Set up a breading station. First, whip the egg whites and mayonnaise together in a shallow dish (the mayonnaise helps the whites stick to the asparagus). Sprinkle with some salt and pepper. In a separate dish, combine the panko, Parmesan, Italian seasoning, and paprika. Sprinkle with salt and pepper and mix.

3. Dip each asparagus spear in the egg whites, then coat evenly in the seasoned panko. Place the spears on a wire rack set over a baking sheet and lightly drizzle with some olive oil (this will help them crisp up).

4. Bake until golden and crispy, 15 to 17 minutes. Serve immediately.

Fire-Roasted Margherita Pizza

Kids expect a lot of unique food during the holidays, but one thing they'll never expect? Exactly . . . a little California-style Margherita pizza.

MAKES: 1 pizza (1 or 2 servings)

TIME: 2 hours

YOU'LL NEED: Oven (with pizza stone) or pizza oven, pizza peel, instant-read thermometer

PREP-AHEAD TIP: The pizza dough can be made ahead of time, wrapped in plastic, and frozen if not being used immediately. The tomato sauce can be made 2 days in advance and stored in an airtight container in the fridge.

1. Place a pizza stone on the middle rack of the oven and preheat the oven to 500°F for 1 hour.

2. To make the tomato sauce, in a saucepan over medium heat, combine the olive oil, garlic, thyme, and oregano. Cook until fragrant, about 1 minute (don't burn the garlic). Add the crushed tomatoes and tomato paste and season with salt and pepper. Lower the heat and simmer for 10 minutes, or until slightly thickened. Remove from the heat and set aside.

3. Carefully stretch the pizza dough into a 6 by 12-inch rectangle and lay it on a flour-dusted pizza peel. Spread a thin layer of tomato sauce over the dough and evenly place the slices of mozzarella on top. Tear half the basil leaves and sprinkle them on top. Drizzle with olive oil, transfer to the preheated pizza stone, and bake for 10 to 12 minutes, or until the pizza is hot and bubbly. Garnish with grated parmesan and remaining torn fresh basil leaves. Sprinkle with red pepper flakes as desired.

2 tablespoons extra-virgin olive oil, plus more for drizzling

2 garlic cloves, thinly sliced

1 tablespoon fresh thyme

1 teaspoon dried oregano

One 28-ounce can fire-roasted crushed tomatoes (such as Muir Glen)

1 teaspoon tomato paste

Kosher salt and freshly ground black pepper

1 ball Pizza Dough (recipe follows)

All-purpose flour or cornmeal, for dusting the peel

8 ounces fresh buffalo mozzarella, cut into ¼-inch slices

6 fresh basil leaves

2 tablespoons grated Parmesan cheese

Dried red pepper flakes, optional

Pizza Dough

1 teaspoon sugar

1 cup warm water (113°F)

1 tablespoon active dry yeast
(2 packets)

2 tablespoons olive oil, plus more
to grease the bowl

1 teaspoon fine sea salt

2½ cups all-purpose flour, plus
more for dusting

MAKES: 1 large or 2 small pizzas

TIME: 1 hour 30 minutes

YOU'LL NEED: Stand mixer with dough hook

1. In the bowl of a stand mixer fitted with a dough hook, dissolve the sugar in the warm water. Sprinkle the yeast on top. Let stand until foamy, about 10 minutes.

2. Add the olive oil and salt to the yeast mixture and mix in the flour on low speed until the dough comes together. Add more flour if dough sticks to edges and allow the machine to knead the dough until it has come together and is smooth, about 10 minutes. Oil a large bowl and turn the dough in the bowl to coat the surface. Cover the bowl with a towel and let stand in a warm place until the dough has doubled in size, about 1 hour.

3. Turn out the dough onto a floured surface and divide it into 2 pieces. Form the pieces into smooth, tight balls. Cover them loosely with plastic wrap and set in a warm place to rise again for 30 minutes, or in the refrigerator overnight.

4. Once risen, use immediately or wrap and freeze until ready for use, up to 2 weeks.

My First Wood-Fired Oven

I'd always thought I wanted a wood-fired pizza oven, and after my experiences on Triple D with wood-fired ovens, really spending a lot of time with them, I was sure I had to have one. So I called a good friend of mine, Rob Myers, owner of Myers' Restaurant Supply (www.myersrestaurantsupply.com), and said, "Please have your team do the research to find out who makes the best wood-fired Italian oven and let me know."

He responded, "I don't even have to investigate—it's a company called Mugnaini [www.mugnaini.com], and you've got to meet the owner, Andrea."

I said, "Whatever it takes—get me an oven and have it delivered immediately."

So the oven was made and delivered, and Andrea wanted to come over and show me how to use it. My schedule was busy, and for the most part I'm pretty confident in my ability to work a pizza oven. We were going to have a large party in two weeks, and there was a lot to do to get the oven working. The fires are made inside this ceramic Italian oven that's imported in pieces, assembled in California, built on a metal base, and put in place. Then you have to make 24 fires in the oven to cure it. We had the right kindling, the right fire starters, and the right type of hardwood (my choice is oak), and there was a schedule to follow. So I did the burns, because I take things like this very seriously, writing them down on the chart, listing how much wood I used, and so on. Finally I was finished with the preliminary burns, and I lit a fire inside the pizza oven. I brought out my pizza dough and made the most outrageous, delicious, incredible, phenomenal pizza I've ever made in my life.

Two days later Ryder wanted pizza again. We invited some friends over, I made the fire, we got the oven ready, I brought out my pizza dough, I put the pizza in, and it *burned on the bottom*. How could it burn on the bottom? I heated the oven up some more, tried again, and it didn't burn on the bottom, it burned on the top. I was devastated. I was almost ready to go to one of my restaurants to have dinner.

Mind you, all the time this was going on, my dad was speaking with Andrea, the owner of the company, and she continued to insist that she needed to come over to show me how to use my oven. I continued to say to my dad, my schedule is too busy—what is she going to show me about lighting a fire?

So, the next day I fired up the pizza oven, built my fire again, put in the pizza, and got pretty good results. It didn't make any sense. I was lighting the fire the same way, using the same wood. Why one day good and the next terrible? Finally, realizing that I was just not achieving the success that I had that first day, I decided to call and get instruction.

Andrea laughed when she walked in. She said, "I wondered how long it was going to take you."

"Why?"

"These ovens are incredible and very simple, but you have to follow certain instructions." And she proceeded to teach me the process: the center burn, the side burn, and the finish. The fire took one hour to make the pizza oven hot, and the pizza was phenomenal, once again. And it has been now for years. Just goes to show that you never know it all, even with something as simple as a pizza oven.

I love my wood-fired oven so much that I had to be able to take it with me, so I put another one on the back of a trailer. Thank you, Andrea, for teaching an old dog new tricks.

Spicy Ahi Tuna Flatbread? Yep, this one just might redefine your food definition boundaries.

Spicy Ahi Tuna Flatbread

I've said it once, I'll say it again: I love ahi tuna any way I can find it . . . with the exception of in a vending chine. But if you want to taste killer ahi tuna, try serving it on some hot, crispy, fresh-baked flatbread. Okay, that I'd eat out of a vending machine.

MAKES: 4 servings

TIME: 3 hours

YOU'LL NEED: Oven (with pizza stone) or pizza oven, pizza peel, instant-read thermometer

PREP-AHEAD TIP: The pizza dough can be made ahead of time, wrapped in plastic, and frozen if not being used immediately. The spicy mayonnaise can be made a day in advance. Tuna should be cut just before serving to ensure that it maintains its bright ruby-red color and doesn't oxidize.

1. To make the flatbread, place a pizza stone on the middle rack of the oven and preheat the oven to to 500°F for 1 hour. (If you don't have a pizza stone, use a sheet pan turned upside down in the oven.)

2. Divide one recipe of pizza dough into 2 pieces of dough. Stretch each piece of pizza dough very thinly, dusting with flour. Roll out each piece wafer thin. Drizzle the dough with the olive oil, smearing evenly. Top with the shaved garlic, rosemary, sea salt, and pepper. Transfer to a flour-dusted pizza peel. Bake until crispy, golden, and bubbled up around the edges, 2 to 4 minutes for each piece. Break the crisp flatbread into pieces.

3. To make the spicy mayo, in a medium bowl, combine the mayonnaise, sour cream, lemon juice, Sriracha, sesame oil, and some kosher salt and pepper.

4. To serve, mound the tuna in a bowl and drizzle with spicy mayo. Season with a little aged balsamic vinegar. Garnish with toasted sesame seeds and greens and serve with the pieces of flatbread.

Flatbread

1 recipe Pizza Dough (page 276)

All-purpose flour, for dusting

1 tablespoon extra-virgin olive oil

2 garlic cloves, finely shaved

1 tablespoon fresh rosemary leaves

Flaked sea salt and freshly cracked black pepper

Tuna

2 teaspoons mayonnaise

2 teaspoons sour cream

½ teaspoon fresh lemon juice

1 teaspoon Sriracha (Asian hot sauce)

2 or 3 dashes toasted sesame oil, to taste

Kosher salt and freshly cracked black pepper

⅓ pound maguro (sushi-grade tuna), cut into ¼- to ½-inch dice

Good-quality aged balsamic vinegar, to taste

Toasted black and white sesame seeds, for garninsh

Micro greens or radish sprouts, for garnish

Asian BBQ Pork Belly Flatbread

Pork belly . . . no matter how you serve it, it's awesome. How could it get any more incredible? I don't know. Oh wait a second, hold on: Put it on flatbread and hit it with some Asian attitude.

CONVENTIONAL COOKING METHOD

If not baking in a pizza oven, use a pizza stone and heat it in the oven for 1 hour, so it is extremely hot. This helps the pizza crust bubble and ensures it is light and crusty when baked.

Marinade

1 cup orange juice

½ cup soy sauce

2 tablespoons hoisin sauce

2 tablespoons oyster sauce

2 tablespoons honey

2 tablespoons dark brown sugar

2 garlic cloves, minced

½-inch piece fresh ginger root, minced

1½ cups low-sodium chicken stock

MAKES: 1 flatbread (1 or 2 servings)

TIME: 2 hours

YOU'LL NEED: Pizza oven or pizza stone, instant-read thermometer, roasting pan

PREP-AHEAD TIP: The pork belly can be roasted and shredded 2 to 3 days in advance. The dough should be made the morning of and proofed.

1. Combine the marinade ingredients except the chicken stock in a large freezer bag and add the pork belly. Seal and refrigerate overnight.

2. The morning of, make the pork. Bring the pork to room temperature and preheat the oven to 325°F. Place the pork belly, skin side down, in a glass baking dish or roasting pan. Pour the marinade and chicken stock over the pork. Roast for 1 hour, flip the pork belly, and roast for another 1½ hours. Remove from the oven and allow to cool. Using a fork, shred the meat into small pieces.

3. Place a pizza stone on the middle rack of your oven. Preheat the oven to 500°F for 1 hour.

4. Meanwhile, in a skillet over high heat, heat the canola oil. Add the mushrooms and sauté for 8 to 10 minutes, until lightly browned. Season with salt and pepper.

5. Carefully stretch the pizza dough to about a 12 by 6-inch rectangle and lay it on a flour-dusted pizza peel. Brush a thin layer of olive oil over the dough. Scatter the pork belly, mozzarella, and mushrooms across the flatbread. Transfer the dough to the preheated pizza stone and bake for 10 to 12 minutes, until hot and bubbly. Remove the pizza and immediately garnish with arugula, sesame seeds, and scallions.

Cooking for 300 of my mother's "closest friends" at a barn dance for her fiftieth birthday . . . me, Uncle Bill, and cousin Paul.

Pizza

1½-pound slab pork belly

1 ball Pizza Dough (page 276)

1 tablespoon canola oil

½ pound oyster mushrooms

Kosher salt and freshly ground black pepper

All-purpose flour or cornmeal, for the pizza peel

Extra-virgin olive oil, for brushing the dough

4 ounces fresh buffalo mozzarella, cut into thin matchsticks

Arugula, for garnish

Black sesame seeds, for garnish

Thinly sliced scallions, for garnish

Shaved Brussels Sprout and Bacon Pizza

Once I was converted to the awesome world of Brussels sprouts, I've wanted to do everything with them—fried Brussels sprout chips, Brussels sprout gratin (see page 320)—so why not? Brussels sprout and bacon pizza.

1 ball Pizza Dough (page 276)

All-purpose flour or cornmeal, for the pizza peel

2 tablespoons extra-virgin olive oil

3 ounces fresh buffalo mozzarella, cut into ¼-inch slices

⅔ cup grated Pecorino Romano cheese

3 slices applewood smoked bacon, finely diced

2 garlic cloves, thinly sliced

3 cups Brussels sprouts, shaved thin on a mandoline

Sea salt and freshly ground black pepper

¼ teaspoon dried red pepper flakes

½ lemon

MAKES: 1 flatbread (1 or 2 servings)

TIME: 2 hours

YOU'LL NEED: Oven (with pizza stone) or pizza oven, pizza peel, stock pot

PREP-AHEAD TIP: The pizza dough can be made ahead of time and wrapped and frozen if not being used immediately.

1. Place a pizza stone on the middle rack of the oven. Preheat the oven to 500°F for 1 hour.

2. Carefully stretch the pizza dough to about a 12 by 6-inch rectangle and lay it on a flour-dusted pizza peel. Brush a thin layer of olive oil over the dough and top with the mozzarella and Pecorino. Scatter with bacon and garlic and loosely pile Brussels sprouts on top. Season with sea salt, black pepper, and red pepper flakes. Drizzle with more olive oil, transfer to the preheated pizza stone, and bake for 10 to 12 minutes, until hot and bubbly. Remove the pizza and finish with a squeeze of fresh lemon juice.

Grilled Corn Chowder with Chipotle Cream and Spicy Saltines

Just because a recipe is called "chowder" doesn't mean it's heavy on the cream. Let the corn cob do the work for you!

Don't ask . . . I have no clue why I'm laughing.

MAKES: 6 to 8 servings

TIME: 2 hours 15 minutes

YOU'LL NEED: Grill, stovetop or propane burner, stockpot or other large pot, blender, electric mixer

PREP-AHEAD TIP: Make the grilled corn stock 2 or 3 days ahead and keep it in the fridge. The chipotle cream can be made 1 to 2 days early. The spicy saltines can be made a day ahead if cooled and stored in an airtight container.

Grilled corn stock

8 ears of corn, husks and silks removed

1 quart low-sodium chicken stock

1 teaspoon kosher salt

1 teaspoon freshly cracked black pepper

¼ cup roughly chopped garlic cloves

1 Anaheim pepper, seeded and roughly chopped

1 cup roughly chopped fresh cilantro stems

2 shallots, roughly chopped

3 celery stalks, roughly chopped

Chowder

2 cups red potatoes, peeled and cut into ½-inch dice

5 tablespoons unsalted butter

1 sweet onion, diced

1 Anaheim pepper, seeded and cut into small dice

¼ cup diced poblano pepper

1 tablespoon minced garlic

¾ cup diced bacon

½ teaspoon kosher salt

½ teaspoon freshly cracked black pepper

½ cup heavy cream

½ cup minced fresh cilantro leaves, for garnish

Chipotle Cream (recipe follows)

Spicy Saltines (recipes follows)

1. Preheat a grill to medium-high heat. Set the corn directly on the grate and grill for 5 to 6 minutes, turning as needed, until evenly browned. When the corn is cool enough to handle, cut the kernels from the cob with a sharp knife. Reserve the kernels in a bowl.

2. To make the stock, put the corncobs in a large stockpot and add 2 quarts water, the chicken stock, salt, pepper, garlic, Anaheim pepper, cilantro stems, shallots, and celery. Bring the mixture to a rolling boil over high heat, reduce heat to a simmer, and cook for 45 minutes. Strain out the solids and set the stock aside to cool. Wipe stockpot clean.

3. In a medium saucepan, cover the diced potatoes with 3 cups of the cooled stock and bring to a boil over medium heat. Cook until fork tender, about 15 minutes. Remove from heat and set aside.

4. In the stockpot over medium-high heat, melt 4 tablespoons of the butter. Add the onion, half of the reserved corn kernels, and the peppers. Sauté until a golden froth starts to form on the bottom of the pan, 6 to 8 minutes. Add the garlic and cook for 1 minute more, stirring frequently. Stir in 3 cups of the stock and simmer for 30 minutes. Cool the mixture for about 5 minutes, then carefully pour it into a blender and puree until smooth.

5. Wipe the stockpot clean, set over medium-high heat, and add the bacon. Cook until crisp, then drain on a paper towel–lined plate. Add the remaining 1 tablespoon butter to the bacon fat, along with the remaining corn. Season with the salt and pepper and sauté for 4 to 5 minutes. Add the stock and potatoes and combine well. Stir in the heavy cream and add the pureed corn mixture. Heat through and adjust the seasoning, if necessary.

6. Serve garnished with the cilantro and a dollop of the chipotle cream, with spicy saltines crumbled on top.

Chipotle Cream

MAKES: About ⅔ cup

In a medium glass bowl, beat the cream with an electric mixer until stiff, 3 to 4 minutes. Add the chipotle paste, salt and pepper to taste, and lime zest and juice and beat until incorporated. Mix in the cilantro and reseason with salt, if necessary. Refrigerate, covered, until ready to use.

½ cup heavy cream

2 teaspoons chipotle paste

Kosher salt and freshly ground black pepper

Grated zest of 1 lime

Juice of ½ lime

¼ cup minced fresh cilantro leaves

Spicy Saltines

MAKES: 30 saltines

1. Preheat the oven to 325°F. Set a wire rack inside a baking sheet.

2. Combine all the spices in a small bowl and mix well. In a separate small bowl, beat the butter with an electric mixer until fluffy. Add the spices and beat until incorporated.

3. Gently spread about ½ teaspoon of the mixture onto each cracker and set on the rack in the baking sheet. Bake the saltines for 7 to 10 minutes, until crisp and golden. Remove and cool completely. Store in an airtight container.

1 tablespoon granulated garlic

¼ teaspoon mustard powder

¼ teaspoon cayenne pepper

¼ teaspoon fine sea salt

⅛ teaspoon ancho chile powder

⅛ teaspoon hot paprika

⅛ teaspoon ground white pepper

1 stick (½ cup) unsalted butter, at room temperature

1 sleeve unsalted saltine crackers (about 30)

Holiday Minestrone with Chicken Meatballs

If I didn't know better I'd think *minestrone* translated to "the kitchen sink" in Italian, 'cause it contains just about everything: beans, veggies, chicken, macaroni, and of course big flavor.

Meatballs

2 garlic cloves, grated

1 tablespoon whole milk

½ cup grated Parmesan cheese

¼ cup Italian seasoned breadcrumbs

¼ cup chopped fresh parsley

1 teaspoon dried oregano

¾ teaspoon kosher salt

½ teaspoon freshly ground black pepper

1 large egg, beaten

1 pound ground chicken

2 tablespoons olive oil

MAKES: 6 servings

TIME: 1 hour 15 minutes

YOU'LL NEED: Stovetop or propane burner, Dutch oven or large pot

PREP-AHEAD TIP: Pesto can be made 2 or 3 days ahead of time and refrigerated. The meatballs can be browned a day ahead and refrigerated.

1. In a large mixing bowl, combine the garlic, milk, Parmesan, bread-crumbs, parsley, oregano, salt, pepper, and egg. Stir well, then add the ground chicken and mix until just bound together. Using a small ice cream scoop, form ¾-inch meatballs (about 40 mini meatballs). In a heavy pot or Dutch oven over medium heat, heat 2 tablespoons olive oil and brown the meatballs in batches, about 2 minutes per side. Using a slotted spoon, remove the meatballs and set aside.

2. In the same Dutch oven, heat 1 tablespoon olive oil over medium-high heat. Add the garlic and sauté for 1 to 2 minutes, until golden. Add the leeks and sauté for 5 to 6 minutes, until softened. Add the carrots, celery, and tomato paste and sauté for 1 to 2 minutes, until all vegetables are soft; season with salt and pepper.

3. Add the chicken broth and bay leaf, bring to a boil, then reduce to a simmer. Add the kidney beans and zucchini and simmer for 25 to 30 minutes, or until vegetables and beans are soft. Taste for seasoning and adjust if necessary.

4. Meanwhile, cook the elbow macaroni according to package instructions until al dente. Drain and add to the pot of minestrone.

5. To finish, add the meatballs and macaroni to the soup and stir to combine. Bring to a simmer, then add the spinach and wilt, about 2 minutes. Serve in bowls, garnished with grated Parmesan and a drizzle of olive oil, with pesto bruschetta on the side.

Soup

1 tablespoon olive oil, plus more for drizzling

2 garlic cloves, minced

2 leeks, white parts, thoroughly rinsed and chopped

3 carrots, diced

3 celery stalks, diced

2 tablespoons tomato paste

Kosher salt and freshly ground black pepper

3 cups low-sodium chicken broth

1 bay leaf

¾ cup canned white kidney beans, drained

2 small zucchini, diced

¾ cup elbow macaroni

1½ cups baby spinach

Grated Parmesan cheese, for garnish

Pesto Bruschetta, for serving (recipe follows)

Pesto Bruschetta

MAKES: 6 servings

½ cup pine nuts, toasted

3 tablespoons chopped garlic

4 cups fresh basil leaves

1 cup fresh flat-leaf parsley leaves

1 teaspoon kosher salt

1 teaspoon freshly ground black pepper

1½ cups extra-virgin olive oil

1 cup grated Parmesan cheese

½ French baguette, cut on the bias into ½-inch slices

1. Place the nuts and garlic in the bowl of a food processor. Pulse for 10 seconds. Add the basil, parsley, salt, and pepper. With the processor running, slowly add the olive oil in a thin, steady stream until the pesto is thoroughly pureed. Add the Parmesan cheese and pulse 2 or 3 more times to incorporate.

2. Preheat the broiler. Place the bread on a sheet pan and broil until golden brown, 1 to 2 minutes per side. Spread a thin layer of pesto on each slice of hot bread and serve.

The Kulinary Krew at Thanksgiving.

The Greatest Food Fight France Has Ever Seen!

In France, Mardi Gras—or Fat Tuesday—is a really big deal. It's like Halloween is for us—everybody comes to school dressed up and there's a very festive feeling. We went to the dining hall that day and everything *seemed* normal. There was the usual laundry basket of bread being filled from a large bin the size of a Dumpster. (Yes, literally—a laundry basket was filled with bread for each table.) The kids got their bread and we started to have the usual civilized meal. But on this particular Fat Tuesday, somebody decided to lob a single piece of French bread soaked in water across the dining room at the assistant vice principal . . . and the biggest food fight ever was *on*. All of a sudden, people were jumping under their tables, and, others were flipping tables on their sides to use as barricades. You had to get positioned in the north, south, east or west of the room. Most of the girls scurried out as the guys were getting into this, full-tilt boogie. They were holding up the chafing pans to guard their faces with one hand and throwing with their other hand. The West had conquered the bread bin, so they had the best supply of bread, but we had the faucet that supplied the water. So they were throwing limp pieces of bread at us and we were taking them, soaking them, and firing them back. By the time it got busted up, after 15 or 20 minutes, there were probably three hundred kids involved and all the food and dishes were destroyed. It went on so long and created such destruction that the kids on the second lunch shift had to eat outside. I've never seen a food fight like this in my whole life. It was the *Animal House* meets *Gladiator* of food fights times one hundred.

Chicken Posole

My dad and I are posole junkies. Posole is kinda like étouffée—when it's good, it's really good, and when it's bad, it's still good. The great thing about this dish is that you can make it ahead of time and the flavor just gets deeper. This one's in honor of my dad.

8 bone-in, skin-on chicken thighs

Kosher salt and freshly ground black pepper

2 tablespoons canola oil

1 large yellow onion, diced

2 jalapeño peppers, seeded and minced

4 garlic cloves, minced

1½ tablespoons smoked paprika

1 tablespoon dried oregano

1½ tablespoons ground cumin

1 teaspoon chopped fresh thyme

6 cups low-sodium chicken stock

One 28-ounce can white hominy, drained

2 cups yellow corn kernels

Flour tortillas, for serving

2 cups finely shredded green cabbage

2 Roma (plum) tomatoes, diced, for garnish

1 ripe avocado, diced, for garnish

¼ cup fresh cilantro leaves, for garnish

Lime wedges, for garnish

MAKES: 4 to 6 servings

TIME: 1 hour 15 minutes

YOU'LL NEED: Stovetop or propane burner, Dutch oven, food processor

PREP-AHEAD TIP: You can make this up to one day ahead. Prepare through step two—this is right before you add the shredded chicken, then reheat with the chicken and proceed with the rest of the recipe.

1. Season the chicken with salt and pepper. In a large Dutch oven over medium-high heat, heat the canola oil. Add the chicken and brown it on all sides, about 7 to 8 minutes. Remove and set aside. When the chicken is cool enough to handle, remove the skin and shred the meat from the bones with a fork. Set the meat aside.

2. Pour off all but 2 tablespoons of the fat in the Dutch oven. Add the onion, jalapeños, and garlic and sweat until translucent, 6 to 7 minutes. Add the paprika, oregano, cumin, and thyme and season with salt and pepper. Pour the mixture into a food processor and process until smooth; return to the Dutch oven and allow the mixture to thicken over medium-low heat for 5 to 10 minutes. Add the chicken stock, hominy, and corn. Bring to a boil, then simmer for 30 minutes.

3. Add the shredded chicken and simmer for 10 minutes more. Season with salt and pepper.

4. In a dry pan, over high heat, warm tortillas, turning frequently, about 2 or 3 times until hot and malleable. To serve, place ¼ cup cabbage in each bowl. Top with soup and garnish with tomatoes, avocado, cilantro, and lime wedges. Serve with the warm tortillas.

You'll have to fight me and my dad off for this bowl of Chicken Posole goodness.

Bouillabaisse with Seared Halibut and Garlicky Rouille

In *Guy Fieri Food* you loved the crab cioppino. In *Guy on Fire* you're going to have your second honeymoon, right here.

¼ cup extra-virgin olive oil

1 small fennel bulb, bulb sliced and fronds reserved, for garnish

1 small yellow onion, diced

1 tablespoon minced garlic

1 teaspoon saffron threads

1¾ cups dry white wine

2 tablespoons licorice liqueur, such as Pernod

1¾ cups chopped fire-roasted tomatoes, with liquid

1¾ cups fish stock

1 teaspoon dried thyme leaves

1 bay leaf

⅔ pound gold creamer potatoes

⅔ pound littleneck clams, in the shell

⅔ pound mussels, in the shell

⅓ pound 21/25 shrimp, peeled and deveined, tail on

Four 6-ounce boneless and skinless halibut fillets

Kosher salt and freshly cracked black pepper

¼ cup chopped fresh parsley, for garnish

3 scallions, chopped, for garnish

1 lemon, cut into wedges

Garlicky Rouille, for serving (recipe follows)

MAKES: 4 servings

TIME: 2 hours 30 minutes

YOU'LL NEED: Stovetop or propane burner, Dutch oven; nonstick sauté pan, food processor

PREP-AHEAD TIP: The rouille can be made 1 to 2 days ahead of time.

1. Set a large Dutch oven over medium-high heat and heat 2 tablespoons of the olive oil until shimmering. Add the fennel and onion and sauté until the vegetables are softened, about 3 minutes. Stir in the garlic and saffron and cook until fragrant, about 1 minute. Deglaze with the white wine and licorice liqueur, scraping up any browned bits. Reduce the liquid until almost completely evaporated. Add the tomatoes, fish stock, thyme, and bay leaf. Add the potatoes, bring to a boil, and cook until just tender, about 10 minutes. Add the clams and mussels and simmer for 3 minutes to give them a head start. Add the shrimp, simmering until the shellfish open, a final 2 minutes. Discard any unopened shellfish.

2. Bring a large nonstick sauté pan to medium-high heat and add the remaining 2 tablespoons oil. Pat the halibut fillets dry with a paper towel and sprinkle both sides generously with salt and pepper. Once the oil begins to smoke lightly, sear the halibut. Cook until the bottom is golden and crispy, 4 to 5 minutes on the first side. Flip and finish cooking for 1 to 2 minutes on the second side. Remove pan from heat and set aside. Fish will stay warm in pan.

3. To serve, place a halibut fillet in the bottom of a shallow serving bowl. Arrange a few potatoes, shrimp, clams, and mussels around the fish. Ladle broth into the bowl. Garnish with parsley, scallions, a few fennel fronds, and lemon wedges. Serve immediately with Garlicky Rouille.

Garlicky Rouille

MAKES: About 1½ cups

⅓ pound fingerling potatoes, boiled

¼ cup jarred fire-roasted red peppers

3 garlic cloves

1 cup mayonnaise

1 teaspoon fresh lemon juice

½ teaspoon sweet paprika

Pinch of cayenne, or to taste

Kosher salt

Peel and roughly chop the potato. Place the potato, red pepper, and garlic in the bowl of a food processor and pulse until just coarsely chopped. Add the mayonnaise, lemon juice, and paprika. Process until smooth and creamy; season with cayenne and salt to taste. Refrigerate, covered, for 10 to 15 minutes to chill and allow the flavors to come together.

Santa Maria Tri-Tip with Achiote Oil

Tri-tip is one of the most preferred cuts of meat west of the Mississippi, and is made for the grill. It has incredible texture, is marbled with fat, and only gets better with a little dry rub and smoke. Man cannot survive the holidays on turkey and stuffing alone.

MAKES: 6 servings

TIME: 8 hours

YOU'LL NEED: Grill, instant-read thermometer

PREP-AHEAD TIP: Achiote oil can be made weeks in advance. Marinate and wrap the tri-tip at least 1 day before.

2 tablespoons granulated garlic

⅓ cup freshly cracked black pepper

½ cup garlic cloves

3 tablespoons kosher salt

2 tablespoons sugar

2 tablespoons Achiote Oil (recipe follows)

One 3- to 4-pound prime tri-tip roast

1. Combine the granulated garlic and pepper in a small bowl and set aside. Mince the garlic and slowly incorporate the salt and sugar, alternating, to create a paste. Add the Achiote Oil and mix well. Be careful; this oil will stain.

2. Rinse the roast under cold water and pat it dry. Rub with the garlic-achiote paste, evenly coating the meat. Sprinkle evenly with the granulated garlic and pepper mixture and wrap tightly in plastic. Refrigerate for at least 24 hours and up to 48 hours.

3. Remove the wrap and allow the roast to come up in temperature while you preheat a well-oiled grill to medium-high heat. (If available, cook on grills over an open pit of red oak, which is traditional Santa Maria style).

4. Place the tri-tip on the grill and cook for 9 minutes, flip, cook for 9 minutes more on second side, and check the temperature with an instant-read thermometer. Once it reaches 90°F, increase the grill heat to high and sear all sides of the roast, making sure to get a nice crust on it about 3 to 4 minutes each side. Set it aside to rest for 10 to 15 minutes, loosely covered with aluminum foil.

5. Slice the tri-tip across the grain into thin (⅛-inch) pieces, drizzle any juices that have accumulated back onto the sliced meat, and serve immediately.

Achiote Oil

In a small saucepan over medium-high heat, toast the seeds for 2 to 3 minutes. Add the oil, reduce the heat to low, and cook for 5 to 6 minutes. The oil will become bright orange. Immediately remove from the heat, cool, and strain. Store the oil in a glass container in the refrigerator. The oil will keep for several months.

MAKES: ½ cup

1½ tablespoons achiote seeds

½ cup canola oil

Brandied Green Peppercorn Hanger Steak

The hanger steak, also known as the butcher's cut, is probably one of the most underappreciated pieces of meat. If you can get your hands on one, this recipe is going to wow the crowd. (Skirt steak is a reasonable substitute.)

MAKES: 4 servings

TIME: 50 minutes

YOU'LL NEED: Oven, stovetop, cast-iron grill pan, cast-iron skillet

PREP-AHEAD TIP: Remove the steak from the fridge 20 to 30 minutes ahead of time to allow it to come to room temperature before cooking.

2 pounds hanger steak (or skirt steak), trimmed

Kosher salt and freshly cracked black pepper

4 tablespoons canola–olive oil blend

2 shallots, finely diced

1 teaspoon fresh thyme leaves

¼ cup brandy

½ cup heavy cream

2 tablespoons rinsed and chopped brined green peppercorns

3 tablespoons cold unsalted butter

1. Preheat the oven to 250°F. Bring a large cast-iron grill pan to medium-high heat on the stovetop.

2. Pat the steak dry and sprinkle liberally with salt and pepper. Drizzle with one tablespoon of the oil. Place the steak in the pan and sear until browned on the bottom (without moving the steak), 3 to 4 minutes. Turn the steak and cook for 3 to 4 minutes on the second side for medium-rare. Put the pan in the oven for 5 minutes to finish cooking. Set the steak on a plate to rest while you prepare the sauce.

3. Place a cast-iron pan over medium heat and heat the remaining 3 tablespoons oil. When the oil is hot, add the shallots to the pan. Sauté until translucent, 3 to 4 minutes. Add the thyme leaves, then remove the pan from flame (for safety purposes) and add the brandy. Ignite the brandy by returning to the stovetop and tilting the pan toward the open flame, or by carefully lighting with a lighter or match. Once the flames subside, add the cream and swirl to incorporate. Add the peppercorns and simmer the sauce until it has reduced by two-thirds to a smooth, slightly thick consistency, 3 to 5 minutes. Season with salt, if needed. To finish, remove the pan from the heat and swirl in the butter.

4. To serve, slice the steak into ½-inch strips, against the grain, and serve with a drizzle of brandied green peppercorn sauce over the top.

A Tale of Survival, No Snacks Allowed

Living in France as an exchange student I had something like a culinary awakening. For some reason, everything tasted better there. I lived in Chantilly and Senlis, about a half hour north of Paris. Let me explain what was so interesting to me about this place. Food was the center of the universe, but in a very different way from the United States. There were no fast-food restaurants, and store hours were very peculiar to me, coming from the United States where everything was open 9 to 5 or even all night—none of that. The stores would open from 7 a.m. to 2 p.m. and then 5 to 7 p.m. So when I got out of school at four o'clock, I could maybe buy a bag of potato chips or a soda at a place I wouldn't even call a convenience store, or I could go to a bar and get a crocque monsieur and a coffee, but there was nothing in between, like a hot dog or taco stand. There were no snack machines at school or gas stations where you could buy sunflower seeds or corn chips. American-style snacking simply did not exist. It killed me. So I had to plan my meals very diligently.

There was a routine for breakfast every morning, and that routine involved getting my ass down to the boulangerie by 7 a.m. You had to get down there and in line at a particular boulangerie, and if you didn't you had to go to the less favorable bakery for the bread. If you came back with the second choice, you were not greeted with open arms at my hosts' house. Breakfast usually consisted of bread, butter, some type of really good jam, and coffee. That was it, and there was no taking snacks in your school backpack, either, so when I got to school I was already so looking forward to eating lunch. All I could think about was food.

My high school was called the Lycee de Chantilly, and there were 2,500 kids in attendance. My best friend was a guy named Vincent Oisel, and we'd wait in line with great anticipation for the doors to open to the lunchroom. There were two meal periods and you wanted to be at the first one, because we were convinced there was not as much food in the trays at the second seating. Imagine this—a thousand kids in line, going through four double doors into a huge room the size of a gymnasium with slick, tiled floors. There were forty tables of four-tops and the rest were eight-tops. When the doors opened it was like the running of the bulls. You wanted a four-top near where the food came out—our rationale was that with fewer people at the table, there would be more food to go around. It was strategic. The lunch lady would come around with a cart, with food served in large chafing pans. Everybody would serve each other as the food was passed around, and no one would eat until everyone was served. For a bunch of high school students to behave this way was the most civilized thing I'd ever seen, and the food was awesome. We would have this great meal of haricots verts and rice and, oh yes, they did serve crazy things like lamb's tongue and blood sausage. But then we'd get out of school at four, snackless, and be famished again by dinner at six.

Thankfully, the second family I lived with, the Heirs, were fantastic home cooks, serving an abundance of amazing food, and that was the first time I had brandied peppercorn sauce. I remember sopping it up with my bread like there was no tomorrow.

Mac-n-Cheese with Roasted Chicken and Bacon

When you're preparing for the big holiday, you don't always have time to make a bunch of extra dishes outside of the main event. So, my advice is to make one dish that really counts—and keeps them from bothering you with, "Can I have something else to eat?" This is it.

Cookin' on my big trailer in my backyard . . . doesn't get any better.

1. Preheat the oven to 350°F. Bring a large pot of salted water to a boil over high heat. Add the pasta and cook al dente according to the package instructions. Drain, drizzle with olive oil, and set aside.

2. In a large cast-iron skillet over medium heat, cook the bacon until crispy. Transfer to a paper towel–lined dish to cool, then chop into bite-size pieces.

3. Next, make a roux. Pour off all but 1 tablespoon of the bacon grease in the skillet and add the butter (you need 3 tablespoons of fat). Gradually whisk in the flour until smooth. Cook over medium heat until the mixture turns a light golden color and is the consistency of wet sand, 1 to 2 minutes. Slowly pour in the milk, whisking continuously until very smooth. Bring to a boil over medium-high heat, add the thyme and bay leaf, and cook for 5 minutes, whisking frequently.

4. Add the cheeses, one at a time, and whisk until each is fully incorporated into the sauce. Add the nutmeg, mustard, cooked pasta, bacon, and chicken and stir well to combine. Season with salt and pepper. (If desired, add more milk to achieve a looser consistency.)

5. Sprinkle the panko across the mac-n-cheese and bake, uncovered, for 20 minutes, until bubbling and lightly browned. Garnish with fresh parsley.

MAKES: 8 to 10 servings

TIME: 45 to 50 minutes

YOU'LL NEED: Oven, stovetop, cast-iron skillet

PREP-AHEAD TIP: The mac-n-cheese can be assembled in the skillet and baked a day early.

1 pound elbow macaroni or small shell pasta

Olive oil, for drizzling

4 slices bacon

2 tablespoons unsalted butter

3 tablespoons all-purpose flour

1 quart whole milk, plus more as needed

2 leaves from fresh thyme sprigs

1 bay leaf

2 cups shredded sharp white Cheddar cheese

2 cups shredded Gouda cheese

½ cup shredded Gruyère cheese

Pinch of grated nutmeg

1½ tablespoons Dijon mustard

1 to 2 cups leftover shredded or cubed roasted chicken*

Kosher salt and freshly ground black pepper

½ cup panko (Japanese breadcrumbs)

2 tablespoons chopped fresh parsley, for garnish

* This is a great opportunity to use any leftover proteins you have from previous meals. Toss in chicken, turkey, lump crabmeat, crumbled sausage, diced ham, or shredded pork or steak . . . even grilled vegetables for this mac-n-cheese. (Well, maybe not at the same time.)

Grilled Lamb with Mint Mojo Sauce and Homemade Herbed Pita

For me, Thanksgiving is not all about turkey and stuffing. This rich lamb, complemented by the fresh, vibrant mojo, is a real change-up to the traditional holiday fare. Cooking a leg of lamb on the bone makes for great flavor, but the task of slicing it off the bone can be a little difficult. So we make it simple here, with a butterflied leg of lamb that will cook evenly and cut easily.

lamb

One 5- to 6-pound boneless leg of lamb, butterflied (ask your butcher if you like)

Kosher salt and freshly ground black pepper

2 teaspoons ground cumin

2 teaspoons onion powder

1½ tablespoons dried oregano

Olive oil, for drizzling

Mint Mojo Sauce (recipe follows)

Lemon Greek Yogurt (recipe follows)

Homemade Herbed Pita (recipe follows)

MAKES: 8 to 10 servings

TIME: 2 hours 45 minutes

YOU'LL NEED: Grill

PREP-AHEAD TIP: To lighten your load on the big day, make the mojo and yogurt sauces the day before and refrigerate, covered. The flatbreads can also be made ahead of time and reheated in the oven.

1. Place the lamb in a large freezer bag. Add the marinade ingredients, seal, and refrigerate for at least 2 hours, or overnight.

2. Preheat the grill to medium-high heat.

3. Remove the lamb from the marinade and wipe off any excess with paper towels. Combine all the dry spices. Unfold the lamb, drizzle with a little olive oil, and sprinkle well with the mixed spices. Grill for about 15 minutes, then flip and cook until the lamb is medium rare, and charred on outside, 12 to 15 minutes more. The internal temperature should be 145°F. Remove the lamb from the grill, tent with foil, and let rest for 10 to 12 minutes, then carve it across the grain into thin slices.

4. Serve with Mint Mojo Sauce, Lemon Greek Yogurt, and Homemade Herbed Pita.

This is your lamb in a cilantro, garlic, and jalapeño camoflage.

Marinade

8 garlic cloves, smashed

1 jalapeño pepper, seeded and minced

1 quart fresh orange juice

2½ cups fresh lime juice (about 15 limes)

¼ cup white wine vinegar

1 cup extra-virgin olive oil

1 yellow onion, thinly sliced

2 cups fresh cilantro leaves

Mint Mojo Sauce

This sauce is great with roasted potatoes or any type of grilled vegetable.

MAKES: 1 cup

Combine the ingredients in a blender and process until smooth. Refrigerate and allow to meld for 20 minutes before serving.

1 cup fresh mint leaves

½ cup fresh cilantro leaves

½ cup fresh flat-leaf parsley leaves

1 garlic clove, peeled and smashed

1 tablespoon minced sweet onion

Juice of 1 lemon

2 teaspoons sugar

1 cup extra-virgin olive oil

½ teaspoon kosher salt

Pinch of freshly ground black pepper

How to feed a crowd . . .
Grilled lamb with Mojo and
Homemade Herbed Pita.

Lemon Greek Yogurt

This is great on fresh fruit, shrimp, or a Greek salad.

MAKES: About 1½ cups

Combine all the ingredients except the olive oil in a small mixing bowl and whisk together. For serving, pour into a bowl or individual ramekins and drizzle with olive oil.

1½ cups plain Greek yogurt

Grated zest and juice of 1 lemon

½ teaspoon kosher salt

Pinch of ground cumin

½ teaspoon honey

Extra-virgin olive oil, for drizzling

Homemade Herbed Pita

MAKES: 6 servings

TIME: 40 minutes

1. Smash the garlic into a paste with a fork and combine it with the yogurt in a small bowl. In a medium mixing bowl, combine the flour, baking powder, salt, and herbs. Mix in the yogurt mixture, ¼ cup at a time, until the dough is smooth. Wrap the dough in plastic and refrigerate for 30 minutes.

2. Divide the dough into 6 equal portions. On a floured surface, use your hands or a rolling pin to flatten each dough ball into a large oval about 6 inches long.

3. Set a large skillet over medium-high heat and heat 1 tablespoon canola oil. Add a single flatbread oval and cook it for 1 to 2 minutes per side, or until cooked and warmed through. Brush each side with melted butter, if desired. Repeat to make the rest of the pitas.

4. Serve immediately or let cook, then wrap in plastic and store in the refrigerator. Reheat in a low oven.

2 garlic cloves

¾ cup plain Greek yogurt

1 cup whole wheat flour, plus more for dusting

1½ teaspoons baking powder

1 teaspoon kosher salt

2 tablespoons chopped fresh parsley

2 tablespoons chopped fresh thyme

2 tablespoons chopped fresh oregano

Canola oil, as needed

Melted butter, optional

Jimbo's Hambo with Fruit Salsa

The two family holiday food traditions that stand out in my memory are leg of lamb studded with garlic and my dad's ham, or as I affectionately call it, Jimbo's Hambo. This was a staple when I was a kid, and continues today for my kids. It goes low and slow, has tons of flavor, and the only disappointment you'll have is that by the time you're done cooking it, cutting it, and eating it, you'll wish you'd made two so you have one just for leftovers. Hey—it's not too late—make two now! No regrets!

Ham

One 8- to 10-pound smoked, unglazed ham

20 whole cloves

Glaze

2 tablespoons olive oil

½ cup minced yellow onion

5 garlic cloves, minced

3 tablespoons cognac

¼ cup yellow mustard

¼ cup Dijon mustard

½ cup pineapple juice

⅓ cup apple juice

1½ tablespoons brown sugar

¼ cup honey

Kosher salt and freshly ground black pepper

MAKES: 8 servings

TIME: About 3 hours

YOU'LL NEED: Oven, stovetop, grill pan, large roasting pan with rack

PREP-AHEAD TIP: The glaze can be made 2 to 3 days in advance, and you can score and glaze the ham the night before and refrigerate until ready to cook.

1. Preheat the oven to 350°F.

2. Make diagonal cuts in the ham 1½ to 2 inches deep, then make cuts across the first ones to form the classic "diamond" pattern. Press a whole clove into the center of each diamond. Place the ham on a rack in a large roasting pan. Add 1 cup of water to the pan to keep the drippings from burning. Bake for 1½ hours.

3. Meanwhile, to make the glaze, heat the olive oil in a large sauté pan over medium heat. Add the onion and garlic and sauté until the onion is translucent, about 2 to 3 minutes. Remove the pan from the heat and carefully add the cognac (the alcohol can flame up). Return the pan to the heat and cook to reduce for 2 minutes. Stir in the mustards, pineapple juice, apple juice, brown sugar, and honey and season to taste with salt and pepper. Turn the heat to low and cook for 15 to 20 minutes, or until the mixture has reduced by a third, stirring occasionally. Set aside.

Let me introduce you to Jimbo's Hambo, you'll be great friends.

Fruit salsa

1 pineapple, peeled, cored, and quartered

2 mangos, sliced

1 jalapeño pepper, seeded and finely diced

1 red onion, minced

2 tablespoons olive oil

Juice of ½ lemon

Kosher salt and freshly ground black pepper

4. To make the salsa, heat an oiled grill pan over medium-high heat. Grill the pineapple and mango slices until they're grill-marked and caramelized, 2 to 3 minutes per side. Remove and let cool, then cut the fruit into ½-inch dice. Toss in a large bowl with the jalapeño, onion, olive oil, and lemon juice. Season with salt and pepper to taste. Set aside.

5. Liberally apply the mustard glaze to the ham and bake for 30 minutes, or until the glaze begins to turn brown and caramelize. Remove the ham from the oven, cover with foil, and let rest for 10 minutes. Slice and serve with the salsa.

The ham moon of Flavortown.

Prosciutto, Provolone, and Pepper—Stuffed Pork Chops (AKA "Triple P" Pork Chops)

Pork chops are typically underrated and overcooked. This recipe will help solve both issues. Brining keeps them from drying out, and there's no way you can be underrated with prosciutto, sweet Italian peppers, and provolone in the mix.

Triple P Pork Chops are lined up, stuffed, and ready for the fire.

MAKES: 4 servings

TIME: 1 hour 55 minutes

YOU'LL NEED: Oven, stovetop, cast-iron skillet, large saucepan

PREP-AHEAD TIP: Brine the chops the night before. Make the stuffing the night before and keep it refrigerated.

Brine

½ cup light brown sugar

¼ cup white vinegar

1 tablespoon granulated garlic

1 tablespoon black peppercorns

1 tablespoon dried thyme

1 teaspoon mustard powder

Pinch of dried red pepper flakes

2 cups ice cubes

Pork chops

4 boneless pork loin chops, about 1½ inches thick

Extra-virgin olive oil

1 shallot, diced

2 Italian sweet peppers, seeded and finely diced

2 poblano peppers, seeded and diced

Kosher salt and freshly ground black pepper

1 cup grated provolone

6 thin prosciutto slices, roughly chopped

1 tablespoon chopped fresh rosemary

½ cup dry white wine

2 teaspoons whole-grain mustard

¾ cup chicken stock

1 teaspoon unsalted butter

1. To make the brine, combine 2 cups water and all the brine ingredients except the ice cubes in a large saucepan over high heat. Bring to a simmer and stir until the sugar has dissolved. Remove the pan from the heat and add the ice cubes to bring down the temperature. Once cooled, pour the brine into a large resealable plastic bag.

2. With the tip of a paring knife, make an incision in the side of each pork chop. Carefully work the tip of the knife into the chop to make a small pocket that goes almost to the edges. Add the pork chops to the brine and refrigerate for 1 hour.

3. Preheat the oven to 350°F.

4. Meanwhile, set a large cast-iron skillet over high heat. Add a drizzle of olive oil and sauté the shallot and peppers for 3 to 4 minutes, until the shallot is translucent. Season with salt and pepper, transfer to a large mixing bowl, and set aside to cool. Add the provolone and prosciutto to the bowl.

5. Remove the chops from the brine and pat dry with paper towels (removing the excess moisture on the surface allows the pork to sear and caramelize). Stuff each chop with a heaping tablespoon of the filling, packing it tightly into the pocket. Squeeze at the ends to seal the pork chops. Sprinkle lightly with salt and pepper.

6. Return the skillet to high heat and add a drizzle of oil. Add the pork chops to the pan and cook until well browned on the bottom, 7 to 8 minutes. Turn the chops over, then place the whole pan in the oven to cook the chops through, 10 to 12 minutes. Set the pork chops aside to rest.

7. To make the pan sauce, return the pan to the stove over medium heat. Remove all but 2 tablespoons of fat from the skillet. Add the rosemary and cook for 30 to 40 seconds to infuse the fat. Add the wine and deglaze, scraping up any brown bits from the bottom of the pan. Simmer until reduced by half, about 3 to 4 minutes. Stir in the mustard and stock and simmer until slightly thickened, 3 to 4 minutes. Finish with butter and taste for seasoning. Pour the sauce over the pork chops to serve.

Triple P Pork Chops fresh off the grill . . . ahhh, the power of pork.

Turkey Cordon Bleu

Everyone likes Turkey Cordon Bleu, but in my family everyone has an opinion. Lori likes it traditional, I like it spicy, and of course the boys like anything with pepperoni—you be the judge.

MAKES: 4 to 6 servings

TIME: 40 to 50 minutes

YOU'LL NEED: Grill, oven, twine, baking dish

PREP-AHEAD TIP: Make the filling a day in advance. You can even prep the turkey breast, stuff it, and tie it the day before so it's ready to simply sear and cook on the day you want to serve it.

4 poblano peppers

Kosher salt and freshly ground black pepper

1½ cups grated Monterey Jack cheese

½ cup cream cheese

2 scallions, finely chopped

One 4- to 5-pound boneless, skinless turkey breast

4 thin slices cooked deli ham

Extra-virgin olive oil

1. To make the filling, preheat a grill to high heat (you can use a broiler if you don't have a grill). Place the poblanos on the grill and cook until well charred and blistered, turning every 2 to 3 minutes. Transfer to a heatproof bowl and cover with plastic wrap so the peppers "sweat," making them easier to peel. Let the poblanos stand for 5 minutes, then rub off and discard the skins. Remove the cores and seeds and finely chop the peppers. Transfer to a medium mixing bowl and season with salt and pepper. Add the cheeses and scallions and stir until smooth. Set aside until ready to use.

2. To butterfly the turkey breast: make a horizontal cut down the length of the turkey breast, cutting almost all the way through but leaving the breast intact down one side. Open the breast like a book so it lies flat. Cover with plastic wrap and gently pound the breast with the flat side of a meat tenderizer until it's flattened and of even thickness of about 1½-inches. Remove the plastic and season with salt and pepper.

3. Lay the deli ham slices on the flattened breast so they cover it from one side to the other. Smear the poblano-cheese stuffing on the ham in a tight log shape, leaving a small border of ham around the edge. Roll the turkey breast up and around the ham and filling. Secure the stuffed breast with kitchen twine. Season the outside with salt and pepper.

4. Preheat the oven to 350°F.

1. After the poblanos are prepared, stir together the filling.

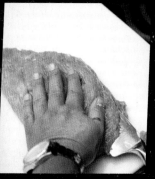

2. Make a horizontal cut down the length of the turkey breast, leaving halves attached.

3. Open up like a book, cover in plastic wrap and pound until flat and of even thickness.

4. Season with salt and pepper.

5. Lay the ham on the breast from one side to the other.

6. Smear the cheese stuffing onto the ham in a tight log.

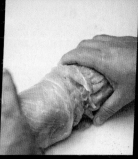

7. Roll the turkey breast up around the filling.

8. Secure the stuffed breast with kitchen twine.

9. Season the outside with salt and pepper.

10. Drizzle a little olive oil in a heavy pan, add the turkey and then a little water into the pan.

11. Cover tightly with foil before placing in the oven.

12. After it's rested for ten minutes, cut into thick slices, drizzle with pan juices and . . . ready, steady . . . go.

5. Drizzle a little olive oil in a heavy baking dish and add the turkey. Add 1 cup water to the pan, cover tightly with foil, and place in the center of the oven. Roast for 20 minutes, then remove the foil and increase the oven temperature to 400°F. Cook until the outside of the turkey is golden brown, 8 to 10 minutes.

6. Transfer the turkey to a platter and let it rest for 10 minutes. Remove the kitchen twine and cut the turkey into thick slices. Drizzle with the pan juices.

Skirt Steak Fajitas

So you have a lot of people coming over, and some like a little, some like a lot, some like it mild, some like it hot. One of my favorite go-to foods for large parties and outdoor grilling is skirt steak fajitas. If we're making tacos or fajitas or anything Mexican, we've got to have beans for Ryder. So serve these with Smoky Black Beans and Chorizo (page 319).

MAKES: 6 servings

TIME: 2 hours 30 minutes

YOU'LL NEED: Stovetop or propane burner, cast-iron grill pan, cast-iron skillet

PREP-AHEAD TIP: You can make the mojo marinade a day before dropping the skirt steak into it.

1. Combine all the marinade ingredients and the steak in a large freezer bag. Refrigerate for at least 2 hours up to 4 hours.

2. For the fajitas, in a large cast-iron skillet, sauté the peppers and onions in the canola oil over medium-high heat. Cook until the vegetables are tender, but still crisp, and slightly charred, about 3 to 4 minutes; season with salt and pepper.

3. Meanwhile, on a hot cast-iron grill pan, pat the steak dry and cook for 4 to 5 minutes per side for medium rare. Rest under foil for 10 minutes. Place limes on the grill 1 to 2 minutes and set aside. Slice the steak against the grain into thin strips and serve with the peppers and onions, tortillas, lime wedges, cilantro, and avocado.

Mojo marinade

½ cup olive oil

3 tablespoons Worcestershire sauce

Juice of 4 limes

3 garlic cloves, minced

1 jalapeño pepper, seeded and minced

1 tablespoon ground cumin

1 tablespoon ancho chile powder

1 teaspoon kosher salt

½ teaspoon freshly ground black pepper

1 tablespoon smoked paprika

Fajita fixings

2 pounds skirt steak

2 red bell peppers, thinly sliced

1 yellow bell pepper, thinly sliced

2 large yellow onions, thinly sliced

2 tablespoons canola oil

Kosher salt and freshly ground black pepper

Flour tortillas, for serving

Grilled lime wedges, for garnish

Chopped fresh cilantro, for garnish

Avocado, sliced, for garnish

Thanksgiving Panini

There's something about the combination of turkey, stuffing, and cranberries that transports you to Thanksgiving any time of year. And when you eat it, you go, oh, why don't I eat this every day? It's so surprising to me that we don't eat this combination more often. Cranberries just don't get enough love and respect throughout the year.

8 slices walnut-raisin bread, sliced ½ inch thick

½ cup Cranberry Mayonnaise (recipe follows)

1 cup leftover Turkey Sausage and Sage Stuffing (recipe follows)

1 pound leftover turkey, white and dark meat mix, finely sliced

1 cup shaved Brussels Sprout and Apple Slaw (recipe follows)

1 cup shredded Italian Fontina cheese

MAKES: 4 sandwiches

TIME: 10 minutes

YOU'LL NEED: Panini press or stovetop and cast-iron pan, oven

PREP-AHEAD TIP: If you're not using leftovers for all the components below, the mayo, stuffing, and slaw can all be made 2 to 3 days in advance. If you really want to get ahead of the game, assemble the sandwiches the morning of, wrap 'em in plastic or wax paper, and store them in the fridge. Then all you have to do is toast the sandwiches when you're ready to cook.

For each sandwich, smear 1 tablespoon cranberry mayonnaise on a slice of bread. Spread ¼ cup stuffing in a thin layer over the bread and top with 1 slice of turkey, ¼ cup slaw, and ¼ cup shredded cheese. Spread cranberry mayo on a second piece of bread, close the sandwich, and flatten using a cast-iron pan over medium heat with a second pan pressing on top or a panini press, until the cheese has melted and bread is toasted.

Cranberry Mayonnaise

½ cup mayonnaise

½ cup whole-berry cranberry sauce

2 teaspoons Dijon mustard

Kosher salt and freshly ground black pepper

MAKES: About 1 cup

TIME: 5 minutes

Whisk together all ingredients until well combined. Refrigerate until ready to use.

Turkey Sausage and Sage Stuffing

MAKES: 5 or 6 servings

TIME: 1 hour 20 minutes

1. Preheat the oven to 350°F and butter a square ceramic baking dish.

2. Heat the canola oil in a large skillet. Add the sausage and cook until browned, breaking it up with a large wooden spoon as it cooks. Use a slotted spoon to transfer the sausage to a large bowl. To the same skillet, add the onion, celery, garlic, and sage; cook until the vegetables are just softened, 5 to 7 minutes. Add the vegetable mixture to the bowl, along with the bread cubes, salt, pepper, parsley, chicken stock, egg, and raisins. Gently toss to combine all the ingredients.

3. Spread the mixture in the prepared baking dish and dot with the butter cubes. Bake for 50 to 60 minutes, until the stuffing is golden brown.

3 tablespoons unsalted butter, cubed, plus more for the dish

1 teaspoon canola oil

½ pound turkey sausage

1 small yellow onion, diced

2½ celery stalks, diced

2 garlic cloves, minced

¼ cup chopped fresh sage leaves

1 sourdough baguette, cut into 1-inch cubes (preferably somewhat stale)

½ teaspoon kosher salt

¼ teaspoon freshly ground black pepper

2 tablespoons chopped fresh parsley

1½ cups low-sodium chicken stock

1 large egg, lightly beaten

½ cup golden raisins

Brussels Sprout and Apple Slaw

MAKES: About 3 cups

TIME: 30 minutes

Using a sharp knife or mandoline, shave the Brussels sprouts into very thin slices. Toss in a large bowl to separate the layers. Add the apple, cabbage, olive oil, lemon juice, and honey and toss to combine; season with salt and pepper. Refrigerate until ready to use.

1½ pounds Brussels sprouts, trimmed

1 large tart apple, cored and cut into thin matchsticks

1 cup thinly shredded red cabbage

½ cup extra-virgin olive oil

3 tablespoons fresh lemon juice

1 tablespoon honey

Kosher salt and freshly ground black pepper

Green Bean Casserole with Homemade Mushroom Gravy and Fried Shallots

This dish is an inspiration from the years of cream of mushroom green bean casserole we all had as kids. The beans were overcooked and mushy and the gravy was gelatinous, but we all somehow woulda missed it if it weren't on the table. Well, you'll find none of the bad here, but all of the good. It's comfort food, redefined.

1½ pounds green beans, trimmed

2 tablespoons unsalted butter

1 tablespoon vegetable oil, plus more for frying

1 pound mixed gourmet mushrooms, such as shiitake, cremini, and oyster, cleaned and quartered

½ teaspoon fresh thyme leaves

2 garlic cloves, minced

Kosher salt and freshly ground black pepper

¼ teaspoon cayenne pepper

¼ teaspoon ground nutmeg

1 cup plus 2 tablespoons all-purpose flour

1 cup low-sodium chicken broth

1 cup sour cream

½ cup heavy cream

¼ cup grated Parmesan cheese

4 medium shallots, sliced and separated into thin rounds

MAKES: 6 to 8 servings

TIME: 45 minutes

YOU'LL NEED: Oven, stovetop, deep skillet, cast-iron skillet, roasting tray, frying thermometer

PREP-AHEAD TIP: The shallots can be fried a day ahead, cooled, and stored in an airtight container. The green beans can be blanched, dried, and stored in the fridge the night before.

1. Preheat the oven to 450°F.

2. Bring a large pot of salted water to a boil and set up a large bowl of ice water. Add the green beans to the boiling water and cook until they just turn bright green, 2 to 3 minutes. (You don't want to cook the green beans through, as they'll cook in the oven as well.) Strain and plunge the beans immediately in the ice water to stop the cooking process. When cool, drain and set out to dry on paper towels.

3. Set a 12-inch cast-iron skillet over medium-high heat. Add the butter and the 1 tablespoon vegetable oil. When the butter is melted and the pan is hot, add the mushrooms. Cook undisturbed so the mushrooms sear nicely, about 1 minute. Add the thyme and garlic and continue cooking until the mushrooms achieve some nice color, about 7 to 8 minutes. Season with the salt, pepper, cayenne, and nutmeg.

Green Bean Casserole . . . minus any grandma ingredients.

Cook 2 to 3 more minutes, dusting the mushrooms with the 2 table-spoons flour as they release moisture. Stir with a whisk to incorporate the flour until flour is golden (just like making a roux) and gradually add the chicken broth. Bring to a simmer, then reduce the heat and add the sour cream and heavy cream. Stir gently and cook over low heat until the gravy thickens, 5 to 6 minutes. Add the blanched green beans and fold together to mix well.

4. Spread the green bean mixture evenly in the cast-iron skillet and sprinkle with the grated Parmesan. Place the pan on a roasting tray or rimmed baking sheet to catch any spill-over. Bake until the casserole is bubbly and the top is melted and golden, 15 minutes.

5. To fry the shallots, pour 2 inches of vegetable oil into a deep skillet and heat to 350°F. Pour the 1 cup flour into a large mixing bowl and sprinkle generously with salt and pepper. Toss the shallot rounds in the seasoned flour, then place in a strainer and shake off any excess. Fry the shallots in the hot oil in small batches until golden brown, 3 to 5 minutes. Remove with a slotted spoon, drain on paper towels, and season with salt while still hot.

6. Top the green bean casserole with the fried shallots and serve.

Smoky Black Beans and Chorizo

Basic canned black beans can be boring, but they're incredibly versatile and should be stocked in your pantry. If you want to bring them to life, nothing does it better than a little chorizo.

MAKES: 4 to 6 servings

TIME: 25 minutes

YOU'LL NEED: Stovetop, saucepan

PREP-AHEAD TIP: Use a potato masher to mash a small amount of the cooked beans to thicken the sauce.

4 ounces Mexican chorizo (about 2 links)

Canola oil, for greasing the pan

1 garlic clove, minced

½ jalapeño pepper, minced

½ cup diced yellow onion

½ cup diced red bell pepper

1 tablespoon ground cumin

Two 15½-ounce cans black beans, drained and rinsed

Juice of ½ lime

Kosher salt and freshly ground black pepper

½ cup water (or beer, if you dare)

½ cup crumbled Cotija cheese

1 cup grated green cabbage

2 tablespoons chopped fresh cilantro

1. Remove the chorizo links from their casings. Set a medium saucepan over medium heat and coat with a little canola oil. Add the chorizo and use a wooden spoon to break the links into smaller chunks. Add the garlic, onion, and jalapeño and bell pepper and cook until the chorizo is lightly brown and fat is rendered, about 5 to 6 minutes. When the oil is fragrant and red from the chorizo spices, add the cumin and black beans (including the liquid from one of the cans). Add the water or beer, bring to a simmer, and cook for 15 minutes to allow the flavors to come together. Add the lime juice and season with salt and pepper.

2. Serve the beans in a large bowl garnished with crumbled Cotija cheese, cabbage, and chopped cilantro.

Creamy Cheddar Brussels Sprout Gratin

At one point, during *The Next Food Network Star,* Season 2, we were down to four people—Reggie, Carissa, Nate, and me—and we had to do the culinary challenge. Everybody had picked a favorite ingredient and piled it on their cutting boards. But as we got ready to cook, Mark Summers said, "Everybody move to the cutting board on your left." I ended up getting Nate's cutting board, and at that point in my life I was not a big fan of Brussels sprouts. I'd only eaten them boiled to death to the point where they had no texture, and the bitterness probably didn't appeal to me when I was a kid. But I took the Brussels sprouts, cut them down, made a gratin, and it was off the hook. I am now a certifiable Brussels sprouts junkie.

Any time you want to get rid of something your kids don't like, bury it in a creamy gratin. But all kidding aside, you mix the bitterness of the Brussels sprouts with the salty sweetness of the gratin and you're going to ask yourself, "Can I do this to everything I don't enjoy? Can I do a gratin of liver?" No, liver is not allowed.

2 pounds Brussels sprouts, cleaned and trimmed

1 cup whole milk

1 cup heavy cream

1 teaspoon picked fresh thyme leaves

2 garlic cloves, peeled and minced

Pinch ground nutmeg

2 tablespoons unsalted butter, melted

1½ cups grated sharp white Cheddar cheese

Kosher salt and freshly cracked black pepper

½ cup grated Parmesan cheese

1 cup panko breadcrumbs (or "Whatever You Have" Breading, page 145)

2 to 3 tablespoons extra-virgin olive oil

2 tablespoons chopped flat-leaf parsley

MAKES: 4 servings

TIME: 30 to 35 minutes

YOU'LL NEED: Oven, baking dish, sharp knife or mandolin

PREP-AHEAD TIP: Make the milk and cream mixture the night before, but don't shave the Brussels sprouts until the morning of or they'll turn brown.

1. Preheat the oven to 375°F.

2. Shave the Brussels sprouts horizontally into ⅛-inch slices with a sharp knife or mandolin. Set aside.

3. Whisk the milk and cream together in a large mixing bowl. Add the thyme, garlic, nutmeg, melted butter, and Cheddar, whisking briskly to combine for about 30 seconds. Add the Brussels sprouts, season lightly with salt and black pepper, and mix.

4. Transfer the mixture to a gratin/baking dish and pat down lightly. Sprinkle the top with the Parmesan cheese and breadcrumbs. Drizzle with a little olive oil (this will help it crisp up and get nice and golden).

Cover the dish with foil and bake for 15 to 20 minutes, or until the Brussels sprouts are tender and sauce is bubbling. Remove the foil and finish under the broiler for 2 to 3 minutes, until the top is golden and crispy.

5. Garnish with chopped parsley and serve.

Cheesy Twice-Baked Potatoes

During the holidays it's all about utilizing the leftovers, and nothing works better than a leftover baked potato. Hollow it out, mix it up, stuff it, and bake it. And that's all she wrote.

2 large Idaho potatoes, scrubbed

¾ cup heavy cream

½ stick (¼ cup) unsalted butter, cut into small pieces and softened

1 tablespoon roasted garlic puree

¼ cup shredded sharp white Cheddar, plus 1 cup for topping

¼ cup grated Parmesan cheese, plus 2 tablespoons for topping

½ teaspoon kosher salt

½ teaspoon cayenne pepper

2 slices applewood smoked bacon, cooked until crisp, crumbled

Sour cream, for serving

Chopped scallions, for garnish

MAKES: 2 servings

TIME: 1 hour 20 minutes

YOU'LL NEED: Oven, baking sheet

PREP-AHEAD TIP: Bake the potatoes a day in advance. Make the stuffing and prep the potatoes a day in advance, then wrap and store in the fridge.

1. Preheat the oven to 375°F. Pierce each potato with a fork and place on a foil-lined baking sheet or in a cast-iron skillet. Bake for 45 to 50 minutes, until soft. Set the potatoes aside until cool enough to handle.

2. Split the potatoes in half lengthwise and scoop the flesh into a large mixing bowl, leaving ¼- to ½-inch shell of skin. Add the cream, butter, roasted garlic, Cheddar, Parmesan, salt, and cayenne and mix until well incorporated. Gently spoon the filling back into the skins and top each with a bit of Parmesan and Cheddar. Bake until golden brown, 15 to 20 minutes.

3. If available, turn on the broiler, or a propane torch, the "true" camping broiler. Top with the crumbled bacon and broil for 30 to 40 seconds to finish and brown. Serve with a dollop of sour cream on top and garnish with chopped scallions.

Peas and Prosciutto

One of my favorite Italian restaurants up in Harlem is a place where you gotta know somebody who knows some-body to get a table: Rao's. It was there that I had peas and prosciutto for the first time. It was simple and delicious.

MAKES: 6 servings

TIME: 20 minutes

YOU'LL NEED: Stovetop or propane burner, large skillet

PREP-AHEAD TIP: This is a simple recipe with no need for advance prep.

Kosher salt

1 pound frozen peas

4 ounces prosciutto
(⅛-inch-thick slices)

2 shallots, minced

2 garlic cloves, minced

¼ cup white wine

Pinch of dried red pepper flakes

1 teaspoon grated lemon zest

1 tablespoon grated Parmesan

1. Prepare a large pot of boiling salted water and a large bowl of ice water. Blanch the frozen peas for 30 seconds; immediately shock them in the ice bath, drain, and transfer to a paper towel–lined plate.

2. Meanwhile, in a large skillet over medium-high heat, cook the pro-sciutto slices until crisp and golden brown. Transfer to a paper towel–lined plate to drain.

3. Put the shallots and garlic in the same skillet, and cook for 2 to 3 minutes in the accumulated pork fat. Deglaze the pan with the wine. Add the peas, red pepper flakes, and lemon zest and sauté until heated through. Crumble the prosciutto and fold it into the mixture right be-fore serving. Garnish with the Parmesan.

Peas, prosciutto, and peace.

Roasted Spiced Cauliflower and Chickpeas

I have a thing about conquering foods I don't like. So over the last twenty years of my life, if I recognize that I don't like a certain food, I try to find a way to like it. I ask chef friends to cook it, or I order it when I see it on a menu in a different style and give it a chance. But I'll be damned if I'm going to be a chef with barriers about food. (Aside: No, I will never like over-easy eggs or beef liver. End of story.)

Chickpeas and cauliflower used to be two of my unappreciated foods as a kid. Chickpeas were hard and chalky, and cauliflower was the bleached-blond broccoli—and I used to not be a broccoli fan. But they both roast well and have great texture, so I've realized that—done right—there's nothing not to like here.

MAKES: 4 servings

TIME: 55 minutes

YOU'LL NEED: Oven, sheet pan

PREP-AHEAD TIP: This dish can be roasted in advance and reheated when ready to eat. Both the cauliflower and chickpeas maintain their texture and flavor well.

1 tablespoon ground coriander

1 tablespoon turmeric

1 teaspoon cumin seeds

1 teaspoon fennel seeds

¼ teaspoon cayenne pepper

¼ cup vegetable oil

1 tablespoon grated fresh ginger root

1 cauliflower head, cored and cut into florets

One 19-ounce can chickpeas, drained

½ sweet onion, sliced

Kosher salt and freshly cracked black pepper

Fresh cilantro sprigs, for garnish

½ lime

1. Preheat the oven to 400°F.

2. Toast the coriander, turmeric, cumin seeds, fennel seeds, and cayenne in a dry skillet over high heat until fragrant, 2 to 3 minutes. Pour the oil into a large mixing bowl, then add the toasted spices. Add the ginger, cauliflower, chickpeas, and onion and toss to coat everything evenly. Spread the mixture on a sheet pan and season with salt and pepper. Roast until the cauliflower is browned and tender, 30 to 35 minutes. Serve finished with a squeeze of fresh lime juice.

Spicy Red Lentil Salad with Pickled Vegetables

I get mental with my lentil. Lentils play a substantial role in most of the world's cuisine, but sadly they're barely recognized in American cooking. After you taste this you'll wonder why. This makes an unexpected holiday side dish.

Lentils

1 pound red lentils

½ teaspoon ground cumin

¼ teaspoon dried red pepper flakes

1 bay leaf

Kosher salt and freshly ground black pepper

Salad

12 ounces giardiniera (pickled vegetables)

6 cups lightly packed baby arugula

Vinaigrette

1 tablespoon red wine vinegar

1 teaspoon Dijon mustard

1 tablespoon sugar

Kosher salt and freshly ground black pepper

¼ cup extra-virgin olive oil

MAKES: 4 to 6 servings

TIME: 25 minutes

YOU'LL NEED: Stovetop, large saucepan

PREP-AHEAD TIP: Lentils can be made 2 to 3 days in advance as long as they are drained well, chilled, and kept in an airtight container. The vinaigrette can be made 1 or 2 days in advance and stored in the fridge.

1. To make the lentils, set a large saucepan over high heat. Add the lentils and toast in the dry pan until they just turn color a little (this will give the finished lentils a little texture), 20 to 30 seconds. Add 3½ cups water, the cumin, red pepper flakes, bay leaf, and some salt and pepper. Bring to a boil, then reduce the heat and simmer, uncovered, until the lentils are tender and all the liquid has been absorbed, about 12 minutes. Pour the lentils out onto a sheet pan in a thin layer so they cool faster and don't get too soft. Cool in the refrigerator for 5 minutes.

2. Meanwhile, drain the giardiniera, reserving 1 tablespoon of the pickling juice, and roughly chop. Wash the arugula and dry well.

3. In a large mixing bowl, make a quick vinaigrette by combining the reserved pickling juice with the red wine vinegar, Dijon mustard, sugar, and some salt and pepper. While whisking, add the olive oil to emulsify. To the bowl, add the lentils, giardiniera, and arugula. Toss and serve.

Holdin' holiday court!

Roasted Roots and Radiatore Pasta Salad

Caramelizing root vegetables is a great way to bring out their rich flavors. You need to choose pasta that can stand up to all that browned goodness, and one of the heartiest pastas I know is the "little radiators," radiatore.

MAKES: 4 servings

TIME: 1 hour 15 minutes

YOU'LL NEED: Oven, large roasting pan, pasta pot

PREP-AHEAD TIP: Roast the root vegetables a day ahead. The vinaigrette can be made 1 to 2 days in advance and stored in an airtight container in the fridge.

1. To make the roasted root vegetables, preheat the oven to 375°F. Place a large roasting pan in the oven (preheating the pan will ensure that the vegetables don't stick and get a nice initial sear on the bottom). In a large mixing bowl, combine the vegetables, olive oil, thyme, garlic, and salt and pepper to taste. Toss to coat the vegetables evenly. Pour the vegetables onto the preheated pan and spread them out evenly. Roast until the vegetables are tender and nicely caramelized on the outside, 35 to 45 minutes. Let cool slightly, then transfer to a large bowl.

2. Meanwhile, bring a large pot of lightly salted water to a boil. Add the pasta and cook until al dente, 8 to 10 minutes. Drain and toss together with the warm roasted root vegetables.

3. To make the vinaigrette, combine the vinegar, honey, mustard, and garlic in a small bowl. Whisking constantly, add the olive oil until it's emulsified. Stir in the parsley, scallions, and thyme and season with salt and pepper. Mix the vinaigrette into the pasta, top with the crumbled goat cheese and extra parsley, and serve.

Roasted root vegetables

1 pound small or medium carrots, cut into bite-size pieces

1 pound parsnips, peeled and split, woody core removed, cut into bite-size pieces

1 pound turnips, cut into bite-size pieces

1 large onion, cut into medium dice

¼ cup extra-virgin olive oil

2 teaspoons fresh thyme leaves

1 garlic clove, minced

Kosher salt and freshly ground black pepper

Pasta

One 12-ounce package radiatore pasta

½ cup crumbled goat cheese

Kosher salt and freshly ground black pepper

Vinaigrette

2 tablespoons red wine vinegar

1 tablespoon honey

1 teaspoon Dijon mustard

1 garlic clove, minced and mashed into a paste

⅓ cup olive oil

2 tablespoons chopped fresh flat-leaf parsley, plus more for garnish

2 tablespoons sliced scallions

½ teaspoon fresh thyme leaves

Kosher salt and freshly ground black pepper

Shaved Fennel and Arugula Salad with Grapefruit

This is a nice light, refreshing dish, and the fennel goes great with a lamb main course.

Beyond breakfast, grapefruits are not used enough, and I think one of the reasons is the tough skin on the outside. The key to getting more grapefruit into your life is supreming. Keeping the fruit whole, use a knife to cut off the skin as well as the white pith—then it's easy to identify and slice out each segment.

Grapefruit vinaigrette

½ cup fresh grapefruit juice

4 teaspoons fresh lime juice

½ teaspoon Dijon mustard

1 teaspoon honey, or to taste

2 tablespoons olive oil

Kosher salt

Freshly ground black pepper

1 tablespoon chopped fennel fronds

Salad

1 fennel bulb, shaved thin on a mandoline (use the fronds in the vinaigrette)

½ small red onion, shaved thin on a mandoline

4 cups lightly packed baby arugula

1 avocado, sliced

1 cup walnuts, toasted

2 grapefruits, segmented, juice reserved

MAKES: 4 to 6 servings

TIME: 15 minutes

YOU'LL NEED: Mandoline

PREP-AHEAD TIP: The fennel can be cleaned and cut the night before; store it in an airtight container with a wet paper towel over it to keep fresh. The grapefruit can be segmented and held in its own juice in the fridge until ready to serve. The vinaigrette can be made a day in advance and stored in the fridge.

1. Whisk together the vinaigrette ingredients; taste for sweetness, adding more honey as desired, and adjust the salt and pepper.

2. Gently toss the fennel, red onion, arugula, and avocado with enough dressing to lightly coat the ingredients. Garnish with toasted walnuts and grapefruit segments; serve immediately.

May Shaved
Fennel and
Arugula Salad
with Grapefruit
be your holiday
palate cleanser
forevermore.

Recipes by Category

Poultry

Fish and Seafood

Soups, Stews, Chili, and Risotto

Guy Thanks

LORI, HUNTER, JULES, RYDER, JIM, PENNY, MORGAN, AND ALL OF MY FAMILY.

The Knuckle Sandwich team, Anthony Hoy Fong, Ann Volkwein, John Lee, Joe Leonard, the Krew, WME, William Morrow, Sunshine Sachs, Ron Wargo, Tom Howard, Food Network, the *Guy's Big Bite* crew, the *DDD* crew, the *GGG* crew, the *RvG* crews, the Johnny Garlic's and Tex Wasabi's teams, Carnival Cruise Lines, the Guy's Burger Joint teams, Sodexo and the GFOC teams, Caesars Entertainment and the Vegas and Baltimore teams, SSP, Motley Que Crew, Rolaids, Miller Lite, Davis Family Vineyards, Golden West Meats/Completely Fresh Foods, Lifetime Brands, Gia Brands, Single Cup Coffee, Myers Restaurant Supply, Chefworks, Cartronics, Bogosse, Chevrolet, Polaris, Room 101, NYCWFF, SBWFF, PBFW, Jimmy John's, and Cooking with Kids.

Index

MAY -- 2014 M

BW Nov/15